James F. Grebey
Moving On

James F. Grebey
Moving On

─────

Getting the Most from the Sale of Your Small Business

DE
G
PRESS

This publication is sold with the understanding that neither the author nor the publisher is engaged in rendering legal, accounting, securities trading, or other professional services. If legal or accounting advice or other expert assistance is required, the services of a competent professional should be sought.

ISBN 978-1-5474-1637-0
e-ISBN (PDF) 978-1-5474-0024-9
e-ISBN (EPUB) 978-1-5474-0026-3

Library of Congress Control Number: 2018946348

Bibliographic information published by the Deutsche Nationalbibliothek
The Deutsche Nationalbibliothek lists this publication in the Deutsche Nationalbibliografie; detailed bibliographic data are available on the Internet at http://dnb.dnb.de.

© 2018 James F. Grebey
Published by Walter de Gruyter Inc., Boston/Berlin
Printing and binding: CPI books GmbH, Leck
Typesetting: MacPS, LLC, Carmel
Cover image: Liu Nian/E+/Getty Images

www.degruyter.com

To Winnie... above everything else

DOI 10.1515/9781547400249-201

About De|G PRESS

Five Stars as a Rule

De|G PRESS, the startup born out of one of the world's most venerable publishers, De Gruyter, promises to bring you an unbiased, valuable, and meticulously edited work on important topics in the fields of business, information technology, computing, engineering, and mathematics. By selecting the finest authors to present, without bias, information necessary for their chosen topic *for professionals*, in the depth you would hope for, we wish to satisfy your needs and earn our five-star ranking.

In keeping with these principles, the books you read from De|G PRESS will be practical, efficient and, if we have done our job right, yield many returns on their price.

We invite businesses to order our books in bulk in print or electronic form as a best solution to meeting the learning needs of your organization, or parts of your organization, in a most cost-effective manner.

There is no better way to learn about a subject in depth than from a book that is efficient, clear, well organized, and information rich. A great book can provide life-changing knowledge. We hope that with De|G PRESS books you will find that to be the case.

DOI 10.1515/9781547400249-202

Acknowledgments

I would like to acknowledge the following people for making this book a reality:
- Winnie, James, Jesse, Sean, Dan, Denise, Dale, Tanner, Chase, Aaron, Myah, Bud, Carol, and Marie for their constant love and encouragement
- Bud Strang, Ingram Leedy, and Jon Molayem for their contributions and support for this project
- Mike and Diane Phillips, Paul McMahon, and Nancy Tupper for their friendship and for allowing me to use them as a sounding board

David Repetto, Jeffrey Pepper, Jaya Dalal, and the good people at De Gruyter who helped bring this book to life.

DOI 10.1515/9781547400249-203

Contents

DOI 10.1515/9781547400249-204

Preface

I took a break. It was a week away from my consulting business where I hoped to get some much-needed rest. I was sitting on the fishing pier in Cocoa Beach, watching the locals cast their lines out into the channel and waving to the sport fishing boats headed off-shore. There was an older man next to me on the pier who had laid his rod down on the ground. It just looked like he wasn't having a good day.

"Nothing biting today?" I asked.

"Not unless you've got one of those hundred-thousand-dollar fishing rigs," he answered, pointing to one of the fishing boats headed out of the channel towards the blue water. I could feel his pain and offered, *"Yeah, but the difference is, when you catch a fish it only costs you for the bait."* *"He has to catch a lot of fish just to pay for his gas let alone the cost of the boat."* We talked a little bit and he asked about my job and told me he had recently retired after selling the business he had started thirty years earlier.

The fisherman looked at me and said, *"Nope, the difference between them and me is, when he retired he sold his business for enough to pay for the boat, and when I retired I settled for what I could get... and what I got was taken!"* I told him I had seen that happen too many times in my work. He continued to talk for quite a while, but his message was, *"When I sold my business and retired I had no idea what I was doing... and everyone I dealt with knew how to play the game."* *"Now I fish from the pier because I can't afford the boat."* And then he showed his true level of seller's remorse.

"I don't know why I ever sold my business."

We have all heard stories about entrepreneurs who have taken their chances and, one way or another, made building a business their life's work. They are the entrepreneurs who become the envy of their friends, family, and employees, none of which seem to understand the effort that went into growing that business. What you don't always hear however is how that story ends.

Growing a business from the ground up takes courage and skill and the determination to achieve your goals. The life-long goal of most determined entrepreneurs[1] is singularly to grow their business. They put all their energy into the day-to-day operation of the business and only pay lip service to the day they may decide to sell that business and move on to something else. They may think about

---

[1] "The Determined Entrepreneur" by James F Grebey: Published by Authorhouse

DOI 10.1515/9781547400249-205

the value of the business they're building but never actually set a goal to sell their business and cash in on that value. Their story becomes a story without an end. These entrepreneurs are like runners who run the race and are almost to the finish line when they suddenly seem to run out of energy.

"I'll think about selling my business when I'm ready to retire... I guess."

Moving on from their business becomes an afterthought many entrepreneurs never really take time to consider... until, for some reason, something brings them to the point where they suddenly decide, now is the time. Now I'm ready to move on.

If you don't set a goal to maximize the return from the sale of your business and establish a plan that sets aside the time to make that happen, then you may well be deciding to be the guy watching from the pier and not the guy with the boat. The same energy and strategic planning that goes into building your business needs to go into your eventual exit from that business. I recognize a common symptom that an owner is running out of steam. It is when I hear them ask,

"Can we get this sale done in the next six months?"

It's the wrong question. It says they haven't been thinking about moving on as a goal to be achieved in the same way they planned the other accomplishments they made in their business. They haven't taken the time to plan for this event in advance of that day.

Selling a business takes planning and patience. These are the exact opposite of what most small business owners are feeling when they finally decide to move on. Instead they are anxious to get on with life and are now finding themselves blindsided by reality. When you own and rely on a small business, moving on isn't easy... it's exhausting, it can be expensive, and it can be frightening because, while a lot depends on the outcome, you're heading down a path you may not have been down before... or if you have, it may not have been your best experience.

"There is just so much riding on my decision to move on..."

The problem many business owners face is... exiting a business is not what they do. It's not in their skill set or life experience. Suddenly, after a lifetime of work, they find they are not prepared for one of the most important events of their life. The sale of the business they took so much time to build. So... they find themselves operating without a net (that's a tightrope parody, not another fish story). If that's where you are (or are trying to avoid being) it's time to look around and find a way to make up for your lack of experience selling a business. This book is a good start.

Not all small business owners will find themselves sitting on the pier... some will own the boat and then buy the pier and plan to sell both at a profit. There are small business owners who seem to have the Midas touch and by luck, skill or sheer determination manage to turn their projects into gold. If you're one of those and you've already sold three or four businesses this book may not be for you. Of course, as you read it, you might find yourself having an "Ah-Ha" moment where you find yourself saying "so that's what was going on." You might not even have realized at the time that you were being negotiated by a prospective buyer. You made money... but you could have made more. Well now you will know, and hopefully you won't make the same mistake again. Small business owners tend to learn a lot from trial and error. Unfortunately, failing to maximize the return from the sale of your small business may not be a lesson you can afford to learn the hard way. You need to get this right the first time.

There are also small business owners who started a business for something other than money. Or at least money wasn't their primary focus. Their goal was to grow a business to support some altruistic purpose. Many businesses fall into this category. The owners' primary concern isn't to maximize their return when they sell. Their greater concern may be to preserve their legacy (*"I'm not interested in selling if they're going to change the name"*), or to support a religious or political cause (*"I only want to sell to someone who believes as I do"*), or even to support some method or technology (*"I want to sell my business to someone who will continue manufacturing parts for steam engines"*).

These are the small business owners who started a business and managed to make a living doing what they loved to do while they were advancing some greater cause, and that cause became their true motivation. My assumption in writing this book is, even if you're only seeking to find a buyer who is motivated to further advance the same cause you built your business on and maximizing the monetary return from the sale is only your secondary goal, the information provided in this book will assist you in achieving both goals. It really doesn't matter how you measure your success. Your future now depends on a successful sale.

> "We opened our pet shop to help shelter lost dogs and, while we hope to get the most we can from the sale of our business, we want to find a buyer who will continue to support that cause."

And finally, the reader should recognize that the process used for selling a small business is somewhat fluid and varies over time and under different circumstances. Buyers and sellers adopt and change the activities described here to suit their own needs. Don't be surprised if you come across someone who does something different than that described here by adding or deleting steps in the process. Be glad you took the time to educate yourself on the process before you entered into it. If someone modifies the sales process, it may be for their own advantage and not yours. And now you will be prepared to defend your own position and needs. Best of luck.

—Jim Grebey

Chapter 1
Let's Have a Conversation

Early in my career I worked for several large corporations—huge monolithic businesses that employed tens of thousands of people who mostly worked on large projects. Even though my job was secure, I found myself constantly drawn toward small businesses. While we had the safety net of my corporate day job, my wife and I launched a couple of small businesses—one successful and one a painful failure. It wasn't always fun, and the work was hard, but we loved "doing our own thing" and the feeling that we were creating something of our own. Our small businesses were something we could grow and do with as we wanted, but our businesses were more like hobbies than serious ventures. With a large family and bills to pay, it was hard to walk away from my corporate safety net.

Then the economy changed, and the big corporations changed along with it. It was like having a picnic in the middle of an elephant herd, only now the elephants were starting to move and the safety net I thought I had was beginning to disappear. Corporate buyouts, corporate moves, corporate closings. I felt I had no control over my life—I only had the ability to react. At one point I worked for a corporation that was bought out, and bought out again, and bought out yet again. I had the same job—even the same desk—but my employer, who I depended on, continued to change. It was a tremendously insecure feeling. People got laid off. I was lucky and was not laid off, but my livelihood and my family were dependent on factors over which I had little control. It was the luck of the draw.

I had an opportunity to go to work for a small business and I decided it was a good time to make a change and move out of the large corporate world. I loved my new job and the feeling that every employee was making a contribution. I felt I had gained some control over my life. I learned a lot and was working at a level I never would have attained in a large corporation. Unfortunately, the owners of that small business proved to have questionable ethics, and I simply could not tolerate that. I went to work for another small business whose owners were highly ethical and who went out of their way to take care of their employees. I loved working for them, and I continued to learn. In the meantime, my wife and I continued to operate one of the side businesses we had started. My wife, whose energy seems unbounded, had also returned to corporate life after taking time out of her career to stay home while our four sons were young. She became the director of a non-profit company providing workforce training for small manufacturers. She liked working with small businesses but didn't like the government bureaucracy that came with her job.

DOI 10.1515/9781547400249-001

Our side business, Diligent, Inc., started to grow. Diligent allowed us to do what we loved. My wife and I used our combined experience to work with small businesses to improve their operations. We also worked with investors who saw value in these small businesses. Some of these businesses were growing, some were struggling, and some were trying to position themselves to attract investors. Diligent put us in control of our own destiny. At one point we had the opportunity to work in Asia, helping Asian investors looking to invest in US businesses and helping US businesses look for offshore manufacturing partners. We decided to take the opportunity and moved to Asia. We also decided when we were ready to return home. It wasn't always easy, but at least we were making our own choices. The ability to make your own choices is one advantage of owning a small business. We know that at some point we will also decide it's time to move on from our business.

Over twenty plus years, we have had the opportunity to meet and work with many small business owners. The entrepreneurs who built these businesses generally felt like we did. They had taken their destiny into their own hands. They had created a business and nurtured it. Some had gotten wealthy, and some had put everything they had earned back into the business. Some were serial entrepreneurs—people who grew a business only to sell it and then invest the money they gained into their next adventure. Still others were staying in their business and had made it their life's work, and couldn't imagine doing anything else. All these people had one thing in common—at some point, their current business, their current adventure, would come to an end, and they would be ready to move on.

When you work for a corporation, you are a cog in the machine. When you move on, for whatever reason, the corporate machine is designed to keep running without you. You are a replaceable part. It's not the same when owning your own business—small business owners are not a cog in someone else's machine.

To cash in on the value the owner has built, a small business must be able to continue operating after the current owner leaves. Unlike larger corporations, though, the ability of a small business to sustain its operations after the owner decides to move on isn't necessarily built in. There's no guarantee the owner will get the true value from the sale of the business, unless it has been intentionally positioned for a change in ownership. When a small business owner decides to move on, the owner makes the commitment to prepare the business for sale. The owner must prepare the business, so it will continue to operate after the cog (themselves) is removed. What we have seen many times, while working with small business owners, is that the owners have focused only on growing their business and have never properly prepared their business to be sold. They know how to run their business, but not how to *position* the business to earn the maximum return when it is sold. As a result, they don't get the full value of their business from the sale—value they are depending on once they move on.

These small business owners enter the sales process with little or no experience with selling a business at a time when they can't afford to make a mistake. There are things the owners can do to improve their return, but they don't start planning for this event soon enough. They allow others to lead them through the sales process, and they forget some of the lessons they learned early as an entrepreneur. Take control of your own destiny! If you want things to go your way, you need to drive them. And if *you* don't put in the work, no one else is going to do it for you. In our business we remind other small business owners of those lessons. Now is not the time for owners to relax. There is still a lot work to do after a business owner decides to sell.

One of the first things most small business owners realize as they think about selling their business is that many people will want a piece of the pie. The government wants to collect taxes on the sale. Your employees, vendors, and the professionals you hire to help with the sale will all have their hands out. It quickly becomes clear—it's not how much your business will sell for, but how much of that you will be able to retain that will determine your return from the sale.

What most small business owners can use the most is a trusted friend or advisor they can talk to who has no skin in the game and nothing to gain from the sale of their business.

At this point, what most small business owners can use the most is a trusted friend or advisor they can talk to who has no skin in the game and nothing to gain from the sale of their business. Someone who they can have a conversation and ask, "What is this going to take? Where do I go from here?"

That's what this book attempts to do. This is not a textbook. It is a conversation with a professional who has worked in the trenches and is offering practical advice and a glimpse into the sales process to help you avoid common mistakes owners often make.

Shadow of the Missing Owner

Have you considered what your business will be like without you? What will happen to it when you leave? You will need to prepare your business and yourself for these changes. The obvious question you may be asking is, *"Once I sell it, why will I care?"* The answer is you shouldn't—but that is not the reaction all former owners have.

When you started your business, you, no doubt, created a corporate culture and an operations infrastructure that worked the way you wanted them to work. You built your business operation around the way *you* were comfortable working. Creating a working environment you enjoy is a common reason for starting a business.

Your personality has had an impact and become part of your business's culture. If you are formal, wear a jacket and tie to work, and tend to hold structured meetings, your business, more likely, has a formal work environment. If you prefer to wear jeans to work and your meetings tend to be held in the kitchen over a cup of coffee, your business probably is a casual place to work. If you treat your employees honestly and show respect to the people around you, your employees are probably honest and show respect for each other. If you express value for your customers, your employees probably treat your customers fairly. These are things *you* put in place. You have cast your shadow over the business through the example you set. Now you will need to consider what happens when it's time for someone else's shadow to be cast over the business.

> "When he was here we would never have been able to do that, but the new guys expect it."

If maintaining the "status quo" after you leave is important to you, then you may not be ready to go. Changes to the business are not necessarily a critique about you. Another person will likely want to do things their way and not yours. It's not about right or wrong—it's about preference. You will need to adjust to these changes. If you are seriously considering selling your business and maintaining your legacy is a big consideration, then finding a qualified buyer is going to be a difficult—if not impossible—task. No matter how hard you try to find someone similar to you, a new owner will cast their own shadow on the business. You may find that selling is not the right option for you at this time.

Staying In or Getting Out

In the next chapter we will discuss the common reasons people cite for selling their business. But before we do that, let's talk about some reasons *not* to sell your business. As you consider whether to stay in or get out, take some time to consider your motives for selling. Let's make sure that leaving is the right answer for you. Deciding to sell your business should never be an impulse decision. If your decision is made almost as a reaction—"OMG I'm going to need to sell my business"—stop whatever you're doing and go to your favorite thinking place. The decision to sell your business should never be compelled or made on impulse in response to external life events.

Frequently the decision to sell a business has more to do with an owner's personal compulsion than it does with any true desire to leave the business. Take the time to consider your actions. Are you really ready to completely break ties with your business, or is there something else compelling your actions?

> "I created my business and the last thing I wanted to do was get out—until this happened, and I didn't think I had any choice. I guess I didn't think it through."

Try looking for answers other than getting out. Maybe it doesn't make sense for you to continue as the chief executive officer any longer, but is selling your business really your only choice?

Health issues are a common reason a small business owner may feel compelled to sell. If you are experiencing health issues, staying in may not be an option. Before deciding which path is best for you, be sure to have a conversation with your doctor. Depending on the nature of your illness and your ability to continue working, there may be other alternatives to selling your business.

Consider finding another way to do your job that requires less direct physical involvement and allows you to continue to participate in the business in some manner. You may be at the point where you are no longer able to load the truck, so maybe it's time to hire someone younger to do the lifting while you take on the role of supervisor. Promote yourself to supervisor (and stay on the company health insurance plan). Maybe it's possible to hire an assistant that can drive you to appointments or help you with your other physical needs. Leaving may be the easier decision but letting a health condition force you into a lifestyle change you're not ready for might have a further negative impact on your health! Be creative finding a solution. Accommodation may be easier to live with than selling.

Leaving may be the easier decision but letting a health condition force you to into a lifestyle change you're not ready for might have a further negative impact on your health!

Work-induced stress is another reason that compels owners to sell. Stress can cause both physical and mental issues, and stress symptoms have a habit of showing up in different ways for different people. The connection between high-stress jobs and health issues is also well documented. Leaving may help reduce your current stress, but it may also cause your stress to take on a different form. Consider hiring a chief operating officer (COO) to handle the day-to-day problems and find more free time to relax.

"I couldn't take the stress of my job anymore, but after I sold my business and retired I found the stress of not being able to continue my former lifestyle was even more stressful."

Some business owners are trapped by their own success. If your business has grown far beyond anything you ever imagined, you may find yourself suffering from boiling frog syndrome. The boiling frog fable says that, if you boil water and put a frog in it, the frog will jump out. But if you put the frog in the water while the water is still cold and slowly raise the heat, the frog will eventually be boiled.

If you're at a point where your business has grown beyond your experience or ability, getting out while you are at this peak in your career may not be your best decision. You grew your business to this point. Now you recognize that you're in over your head, and the future growth of your business is being constrained by your personal inability to keep up with its growth. You feel compelled to sell because you think the *only* solution is to get out. It can be tough to admit weakness, but many times, not admitting a weakness can cause a business to eventually fail . You're looking around and suddenly realize the water is boiling! Jumping out may not be your only answer. Maybe you can find a way to turn down the heat.

Acknowledging your weakness is the first step. Why not try to preserve your income while you're still at the top of your career? Certainly, you can hire a consultant to advise you or hire a person to operate the business for you—if you can get used to the idea of letting someone else direct your business. The best solution may be to hire people who can cover your weaknesses and advise you in those areas. You may not be ready to leave, and, as you will see later in the book, selling your business could put constraints on your future activities—constraints you may not be willing to accept. Consider alternatives such as promoting yourself to chairman of the board and hiring a CEO who has the experience you lack. Make your new CEO responsible for future growth strategies.

Selling your business could put constraints on your future activities that you may not be willing to accept.

There are also owners who, for no apparent reason, feel like getting out immediately because they are no longer happy doing what they are doing (for what I'll simply describe as emotional reasons). Time changes people, and the things that challenged you at one point in your life may not seem as important later. Important decisions, made for emotional reasons, can easily end up in seller's remorse. Selling a business, without preparing it or yourself for that event well in advance, can be a costly error both in the loss of value in the business and the owner's loss of income. If you truly are unhappy and want to get out, take the time to develop an exit strategy and plan your next move carefully.

> "I was 55 and in the middle of a full-blown case of midlife crisis when I decided I was tired of what I was doing and wanted to sell my business."

Maybe you are a true entrepreneur who started out with one business that has now grown into multiple businesses. You began one business and sometime later bought another . . . and another . . . and another. You have grown faster than your business. Now you find you don't have the time to make the day-to-day decisions needed to operate all of your interests and wonder if it's time to sell one business to give you time to focus on another. Instead of divesting, remember there is security in diversification and consider other options such as changing the model you use to manage your holdings. The solution may be to hire someone to manage each of your businesses in your place. Each business is an asset you want to continue growing, but now your job is running your holdings corporation. Choosing to stay in can be a strategic decision.

Choosing to stay in can be a strategic decision.

There is a common thread running through each of these scenarios. In each case the business owner is not ready to sever themselves from their business. Selling their business would not have been their first choice, but they have not considered other alternatives. Each owner has a reason to stay in rather than getting out. Don't jump to sell. Jump to think.

Ask for help identifying an alternate answer. Make sure you are considering selling your business for the right reasons. In the next chapter we will explore some of those reasons. When asked why you are selling your business, what will you say?

Who Will This Book Help?

Small businesses range in size from single proprietor home offices, to small retail stores and restaurants, to much larger manufacturing and service businesses and high-tech software-as-a-service (SaaS) software development companies. They include everything from early stage start-ups and franchises to well-established online web businesses with nationally recognized brands. My intent is to be as inclusive as possible, but this is a difficult task with such a varied audience. When working with small businesses, it is rarely a case of "one size fits all." I am regularly told by clients that some of my recommended actions seem like overkill for their small business. Some of the recommendations that follow may seem like overkill to you. As you go through this book, you will have to determine which items are appropriate or make sense for your situation. My suggestion is: even if you think some of these suggestions are overdone and don't apply to your business, don't just write them off. Accept each one as a challenge.

Challenge yourself by converting each suggestion into an opportunity to demonstrate your business's value. For example, if your business only has two employees, you probably don't need to take the time to create an organization chart.

"That's silly—we're just not big enough to need that."

Buyers will still want to know what responsibility each person on your team has, how many hours each employee works, and what jobs they perform every day. Maybe detailed job descriptions that explain the division of responsibilities and separation of skills between the two employees would be a better answer for your business, because it explains the type of skills a buyer's staff will need to operate your business. This may be the only opportunity you have to inform a buyer that your business possesses these skills. Don't just blow an action off and assume you don't need to do anything.

Don't just blow an action off and assume you don't need to do anything.

Take the challenge. See how many of my recommendations you can apply or adapt to your business, knowing that each time you do, you will be conveying value to a potential buyer and helping to maximize your return.

Chapter 2
Avoiding Seller's Remorse

If you're like every other small business owner, you know your business is going to have good days and bad days. Days when you love your business and can't imagine doing anything else, and days when you're ready to throw up your hands and say,

"I'm done. . ... It's time to move on."

It's easy to understand why you would think about selling your business on those bad days—days when you have to deal with angry customers; days when you're struggling to make payroll; days when, for whatever reason, things are just not going the way you want them to. But most times, selling your business is just a passing thought. You grit your teeth and wait for things to get better. The desire to move on, on a bad day, is a natural reaction to stress; but what do you do when you find yourself thinking about selling your business on a good day? Selling your business when things are going well would be a logical decision. Deciding that it's time to move on while you're at the top of your game might make a lot of sense. However, you enjoy what you're doing, and (let's face it) most days selling your business is just an impulsive idea. If you think about it logically, the times when your business is running smoothly and it's making money are the times when you can expect the greatest return. Even though you know selling your business is the smart thing to do, you're not really ready to make the move. Not today—not just yet. You love your business, your job. Why would you want to leave it now? Good or bad, you've built this business. You've put your mark on it and maybe even (literally) your name. When the thought passes you realize you're just not ready to walk away. Not yet.

The idea of selling your business and moving on can be disturbing. It can gnaw at you, keeping you awake at night and keep you from making that logical, rational decision that it is time to move on. It becomes a distraction the Temptations once called a "Ball of Confusion."[1] If you're seriously considering moving on, the first thing you need to do is examine the motives behind your decision. You don't want to wake up the day after you sell your business with seller's remorse. Sitting by the pool with a rum punch in your hand and wondering what

---

1 "Ball of Confusion (That's What the World Is Today)," written by Norman Whitfield and Barrett Strong, side A, track 3, on The Temptations, *Greatest Hits II*, Motown, 1970, 33 1/3 rpm.

DOI 10.1515/9781547400249-002

to do today can get boring quickly. The decision to sell your business and move on to your next adventure should be made without regrets. There should be no looking back.

The decision to sell your business and move on to your next adventure should be made without regrets.

Most small business owners have a thousand reasons, good and bad, why they would consider selling their business, but then they check their emotions, get over it and get back to work. That is, until that one day that is different from all the rest. Something finally brings them to the point where they are ready to make a rational decision rather than an emotional one. Maybe it won't be next month, or even next year, but they'll know. And that's where you are at now—wondering where to begin.

Why Are You Selling Your Business?

Selling your business is a big decision, and knowing where, when, and how to start that process presents immediate obstacles for most small business owners. It raises a lot of questions that can cause even more sleepless nights. You're not selling your business because you feel coerced into doing it. You're selling your business because you made a decision. It's time to move on. But selling a business is not your business; at least, it's not what you do on a regular basis. You may be familiar with the sales process, maybe you even went through it if you bought your business. But this is an important milestone in your life, and you don't want and probably can't afford to make a mistake. Your day has come. It's time to get answers to some of your questions. It's time to get busy.

The good news is you are taking measures to ensure you do it right. You're not going to sell today, but you've made the decision. You're ready. Now your goal is to get the most from the sale of your business and maximize your return.

Your goal is to get the most from the sale of your business and maximize your return.

You're not alone. Small business owners make the decision to sell for lots of reasons and those are as diverse as their reasons were to start a business. According to *Forbes* magazine, there are close to 28 million U.S. small businesses; and, according to the Small Business Administration, roughly 750,000 new small businesses are started every year in the United States.[2] Determining the exact number of businesses sold each year is difficult, because many times the assets are sold, and the original business closes. Here are some of the common reasons owners decide to sell. Do they sound familiar to you?

Retirement

Some small business owners work for years to build a great business that has long-term resiliency. These businesses represent a lifetime accomplishment that the owners are proud of and which they have even become emotionally attached to. Now they've decided it's time to sell the business and relocate to the beach (or some similar venue). The owners may feel like they're losing a long-time friend, but they've decided it's time to cash out. Now they're looking to exit the business (hopefully with some solid transition planning) in a way that will support their retirement. The problem with this scenario (and some of the others that follow) is that they have little or no experience selling a business.

Selling a high-value business, one you've built from the ground up, is a major event that most small business owners hope to experience at some point in their lives. But let's be honest—many small business owners never see that kind of success. Most small business owners don't expect to have the opportunity to make a sale like this in their lifetime, and that means they can't afford the risk of making the mistake of not getting the maximum return on this sale. Getting the most from the sale of their business will help determine the standard of their retired lifestyle.

Stepping Up

These business owners are somewhere in the middle of their career. They're not ready to retire, and they hope to use the equity they've built in their current business as a platform to launch them into their next adventure. They own a business

2 Jason Nazar, "16 Surprising Statistics About Small Businesses," *Forbes*, September 9, 2013. According to the Small Business Administration, "from 2007 to 2010, employer establishment births dropped 12 percent from 844,000 to 742,000. Of the total number of new businesses, about 85 percent are small business startups, while the remaining 15 percent tend to be new locations for existing businesses that are expanding their operations." U.S. Small Business Administration, Office of Advocacy, "Startup Rates," *Small Business Facts*, March 2012, https://www.sba.gov/sites/default/files/Startup%20Rates.pdf.

that provides them with a decent income and regularly pays the bills and payroll, and even though they do all right, they know their current business isn't going to break any records. They could continue trying to grow their current business, but their decision to sell is based on an expectation that the sale will provide the stepping stone they need to help launch them into their next venture as well as accelerate their wealth (or the wealth of the investors in their current business who may be pushing for the sale). This business is one stop on their entrepreneurial strategic plan. They've gained some experience and are ready to move on to what they hope will be a more lucrative opportunity. In their case, moving on must be done with great care. They need to optimize the value of their current business to get the greatest return so that they have the resources to help launch their next opportunity.

Getting Out from Under

Then there are the small business owners who are just trying to get out from under a business without losing their shirt or their home. The business is failing because the partnership with their brother-in-law (insert your own family member name here) didn't work out, or the technology became obsolete, or the market has passed them by and no one wants eight-track tapes (or cassettes, CDs, VHS tapes, or any other obsolete product) anymore, or their business plan didn't work for a thousand different reasons. Bummer!

The sad truth is that not all businesses are salable. You can lock the door, pay off your creditors, and walk away, but most businesses have some value (assets, client lists, even customer goodwill) and it may be possible to sell the assets. In some cases, the parts may turn out to be worth more than the whole (particularly when a bad business reputation or bad market decisions have been holding the business back). That surf shop you opened in a ski area, which you thought would attract athletes with similar skills, may find out that the store's inventory of 200 surfboards is of interest and salable to someone else who is located at the beach. It may be time to get creative or to seek some expert advice. What seems like a great "out of the box" idea at the beginning of a business often turns out to be a big mistake in judgment in the end and leaves the owner trapped.

The sad truth is that not all businesses are salable.

Many would-be entrepreneurs learn the hard way how hard it is to start a business and are now ready to move on with the next phase of their lives by getting out from under their current problem. They're searching to find any path that helps them move on, short of closing the doors and walking away. If you do decide to close the door and dissolve the business, you still have work to do. A business dissolution form must be filed with the IRS and any other contracts or agreements will also need to be addressed. The business is not over until the paperwork is done! If you find yourself in this category, don't be disheartened. Many successful entrepreneurs have had similar experiences. They have learned some valuable and maybe hard lessons and have gone on to apply those lessons in new ventures, where they eventually found the success they were looking for. Maybe they now realize that opening a surf shop in the mountains wasn't a good idea! Their goal in selling is to minimize their out-of-pocket expenses or even to avoid a bankruptcy or foreclosure. These business owners wish move on to a venture with more opportunity. Or, maybe they've decided they're not cut out to be an entrepreneur and want to find a job working for someone else.

Many of these businesses have value and will find buyers in the form of other entrepreneurs who feel that they can make changes that will allow your business to become successful. Sometimes it's easier to see the problems with a business when you're considering it from the outside with clear hindsight of the prior owner's mistakes. I know this from my own consulting experience in improving small business operations as I help owners who were too close to the issues to see them clearly! Getting the most from a business's sale may require resolving the existing problems before putting up the "For Sale" sign.

Partial Exits

Some owners are more interested in continuing to grow their business and aren't looking for an exit strategy at all (at least not at this time). They are the determined entrepreneurs who are seeking to sell part of their business to an equity partner who will invest the additional capital needed to help the business move on to its next level of growth.

Selling part of your business brings on new opportunities along with new challenges. It requires careful thought. One of the possible challenges to the owner is the loss of control. Even if you retain more than 50 percent of the business, you are allowing someone else to share in your ownership. They *will* want to have an input on the future of the business. Accept this and be prepared for it. As long as the benefits of adding a financial partner outweigh the challenges, your goal should be to make the partnership work before proceeding.

Bringing on an investment partner, rather than continuing to bootstrap the business, is an acknowledgment that "a small slice of a big pie may be better than a big slice of a small pie." If this describes your current situation, then your goal is to optimize your return by getting the greatest possible valuation for your business, even if you only sell part of it. The information provided in this book will also be important to you. Read on!

Your Goal Is to Maximize the Value of Your Business

No matter why you're considering the sale of all or part of your business, you're making a critical decision about your future. You've decided that it's time to put your current business behind you and move on to something else. Maybe your business was or wasn't performing well. Whether your business was or was not successful. It doesn't matter. Everyone has the same goal when they sell a business. It is to optimize the value of their business and get the greatest possible return from the sale, so they can afford to move on to the next stage of their lives. Everything we will discuss from this point on is intended to help you get the most from the sale of your business and to maximize the value it returns.

Everyone has the same goal when they sell a business. It is to optimize the value of their business and get the greatest possible return from the sale.

Now that you have made the decision to move on with the sale, you will need to understand the process you are about to begin. It's time to become proactive. You must be prepared to be the one who drives the sale. You can get advisors, but you can't delegate this job to others—you must be prepared to take it on yourself if you're going to have a successful sale.

Not Every Business Can Be Sold

The simple fact is that not every business can be sold. Take the time to gain some situational awareness by examining the environment you're trying to sell your business into. Is the industry growing or shrinking? Is the location still conducive to this kind of business? Is the economy encouraging investors or are people being conservative about beginning a new venture? These environmental factors are beyond your control but can be factors in the sale of your business. Ask yourself the following question--sometimes the answer is hard to hear.

"Is this the right time to sell a business or would I benefit from waiting a year?"

The simple fact is that not all businesses can be sold.

There are many reasons why even profitable businesses can't be sold. Okay, so now you're confused . . . or maybe it's me. Just a couple of paragraphs ago I said, "most businesses have some value." Some businesses may have value to the owner but not for a buyer. Identifying something of value for a potential buyer is the goal in a sale. In my previous comments I was making the point that even a business that is not profitable may have value for some buyers. In the example of the surf shop, I pointed to the potential asset value of a business (its inventory of surfboards). The value could be in the real estate, equipment, intellectual property (IP), or even a popular business name (its brand) can have market value. These things have potential value to a buyer; even if the business itself isn't profitable, there may be a buyer out there who sees some value in it and is interested in purchasing some part of the business. Profitability is not the sole measure of a business's value (although profitability doesn't hurt, either). The projected or future value of a business is also transferrable value if a buyer believes in that future. There are also profitable businesses that don't offer value to a buyer. They have value to the current owner, but that value isn't transferrable to a potential buyer.

The projected or future value of a business is also transferrable if a buyer believes in that future.

My own business Diligent, Inc. (Diligent) is an example of a business with non-transferable value. Diligent is a small consulting business that my wife and I operate. My wife says I should call it a boutique consulting business! By design, Diligent has never had more than two or three full-time employees; we only take on one or two clients at a time. This is the business model under which I have chosen to work and that has supported me for years. We offer operations management services, positioning services, and due diligence services to our clients, who mostly come to us through referrals. We're not interested in growing Diligent into a twenty-employee consultancy.

Diligent was built on our personal experience, skills, and reputation for improving client operations while helping them grow their business. If we were to try to sell our business, we would have to remove ourselves, and there would be no transferrable value remaining in the business. Without us, Diligent does not have transferrable value that would interest a buyer. For some owners that's a tough admission. In our case it reflects the limits we established for our business. This allows us to do what we enjoy doing. Under a different model, if we choose to grow the transferrable value of our business, we would have to bring on staff and other consultants and focus on growing our own business instead of focusing on growing our clients' businesses. Personally, I don't need a gaggle of employees to feel successful. I have had the opportunity to manage a large staff several times in my career and choose not to do it any longer (managing employees takes a lot of time). When I have employees, my job becomes managing them, which doesn't allow me the time to be an advisor to my clients—the job I prefer to do.

Similar cases also exist where the transferability of value is constrained because the business requires professional licenses that are tied to individuals—for example, financial or real estate certifications; alcohol or other products needing extensive background checks, or agricultural licenses needing specialized training, for example. If the license is not transferable, then it doesn't add to the value of the business. It's important to know the local regulations for professional licenses because they change state by state or province by province (be sure to include the transferability of professional licenses in your discussions when you meet with your attorney). These businesses can be sold, but the new buyers must be licensed—meaning the transferrable value of the business comes from its assets. Because the rules for professional licenses are subject to frequent change, you should be wary of making assumptions about them. Also, be aware that there are regulations limiting the ownership of certain businesses only to licensed individuals. This could restrict the pool of buyers; you must see the potential buyer's license to qualify them as a buyer.

Look honestly at your business to determine whether there is value that can be transferred to a new owner. A business that is tied to a unique location, for instance, may lose a great deal of value or may not be salable if that location were no longer available. What gives your business its transferrable value?

Look honestly at your business to determine whether there is value that can be transferred to a new owner.

My wife and I like to eat out on occasion and had two restaurants we particularly liked. One was a seafood restaurant located on a pier overlooking the water near our home. The pier was damaged during a storm, and the restaurant was forced to close. The owners decided to sell the name and menu to a buyer who reopened the new business several blocks from the water. Even though the business had the same menu and the same cook, it had no water view, and their business never took off like the original one had. Without the unique waterfront location, the new restaurant was just another inland seafood restaurant among many others. The value of the original business didn't transfer. Dining on the water is what had attracted customers. Loss of their original location meant the loss of significant transferrable value regardless of the restaurant's past reputation or profitability.

The other restaurant was an Italian restaurant. It was owned by a couple who had operated the business for years. The restaurant had built a reputation for the high quality of its traditional dishes along with a reputation for great service. This business was popular for years and always drew a crowd on the weekends. Eventually, the couple retired and turned the operation of the restaurant over to their grown children. Their children, who had benefited from the business and had gone to college to earn business degrees, promptly put in changes they thought would improve the business, but it seems people preferred the traditional Italian dishes rather than the new menu that was served to lower the operating costs. As the quality of the food went down, so did the crowds. The children realized they were in trouble and decided it was time to move on. There was transferrable value in the business because of its prior reputation. The new owners understood this value. They immediately put up a sign saying "Under New Management" and returned to the original menu customers had known for years. Reputation and good will definitely affect the transferrable value of a business.

Look for any situations that limit the transferrable value in a sale. Many times, there is something you can do to improve the transferrable value of your business. However, not all businesses have transferrable value that can be sold. It's critical that you take the time to identify the true transferrable value of your business and be ready to take the steps needed to improve and spotlight that value as much as possible.

You must take the time to identify the transferrable value of your business. Be ready to take the steps needed to improve and spotlight that value as much as possible.

While you are operating your business, you are running a race to achieve success every day. When you sell the business, the race may be ending for you, but the buyer doesn't want the race to be over. They need to believe that, as you're passing the baton, the race will go on. They expect you to pass the baton on to them as efficiently as possible. Now it's time for you to look in the mirror and have an honest conversation with yourself about the value of your business. What exactly is it that you are selling? Does it offer something of value that can be transferred to a buyer?

"What value does my business have that I can pass on to a new owner?"

Can I Sell My Business If It Has "Warts"?

The nature of business is that things can and do go wrong. Keeping a business at its peak operating efficiency is difficult, because the business is impacted by things beyond your control, such as market changes, the loss of major clients, weather events that can disrupt a business's operation, and demands of key employees (e.g., unanticipated raises). A wise person knows: when you operate a business, doo-doo occurs—or similar words to that effect. Smart buyers also understand this and know that all businesses have warts. Buyers will use undisclosed warts as part of their negotiation strategy.

"We're lowering our offer because you knew this was a problem and didn't disclose it."

You are always better off acknowledging and disclosing your business's warts rather than trying to hide them. By exposing problems at your own pace, you avoid pesky ethical and moral issues and will be in a better strategic negotiating position than if the problems show up (which is usually when you least expect them). I'll repeat it: you must honestly disclose any known issues.

I find that businesses are typically sold the same way they are operated. If your operations are sloppy and you've done nothing to improve them, you won't achieve the same level of return you would from a highly efficient operation. If your business has warts you don't want to disclose, fix them. "Deny, deny, deny" may work as a political strategy, but when selling your business, a better strategy is to "admit, admit, admit." Follow each admission with a "but." Be prepared to take the high road. Be honest. There is no better way to kill a deal than by being caught in a lie. If I find a client is intentionally trying to mislead a buyer, I drop them immediately as a client. My reputation is far more important to me than any individual deal could be. Be prepared to discuss any due diligence discoveries during negotiations.

"Due diligence" is an umbrella term. It includes a hands-on, deep dive into your business that allows the buyer to collect information about the business and gain a detailed understanding of its past performance, current standing, and future potential. During due diligence, the buyer will assess three distinct facets of your business: financial, legal, and operations. We will cover due diligence in detail in Chapters 7 through 10.

"We tried something, but it didn't work, so we moved on."

Your goal is to negotiate from a position of strength. You can't do this if you ignore or hide an issue. Any such issue should have already been factored in your valuation.

"Yes, we introduced a loss leader product to see if we could sell into that market, but withdrew it when it became clear our price wasn't supported. It wasn't part of our normal operations, but we included the expense of our experiment as an adjustment when we valued the business."

The problem is that many business owners have trouble being honest about the condition of their business—especially to themselves. It's called "drinking your own bath water" or whatever phrase you wish to use when you delude yourself into believing you have built the perfect business. If you're trying to present your business as something it's not, then either change your presentation or change your business.

The problem is that many people have trouble being honest about the condition of their business—especially to themselves.

Be prepared for the buyer's due diligence to discover something. They will find something, and they will use what they find as a negotiation strategy. We will have more to say about due diligence later in the book, but for now, ask yourself this: if the buyer's due diligence will cost me something during negotiations, would it pay me to perform a due diligence on my own business? The answer: why wouldn't you want to do that? If you can't effectively perform your own due diligence (most people can't), then hire an independent third party to do it for you. The goal of a buyer's due diligence is to allow the buyer to enter a deal with their eyes wide open. The goal of an internal due diligence is to allow you to enter a sale with your eyes wide open. With your own due diligence in hand, you can either resolve any discoveries or prepare to discuss them, thus giving you a negotiation strategy.

> "Yes, we knew about that and already accounted for it in our valuation."

I sometimes think people leave obvious issues for the buyer to discover during due diligence, hoping it will distract the buyer from finding the real issues. Understand, I'm not advocating this approach as a success strategy, but it sure seems to happen!

Why Do I Need to Position My Business to Sell It?

Positioning means preparing the business to be presented to prospective buyers. Your business needs to be positioned to demonstrate its full transferrable value to a buyer. It's like priming a wall when you are preparing to paint it. You will need to take the time to touch up the rough spots and patch the holes to create a solid base before showing a buyer your business.

Your business needs to be positioned to demonstrate its full transferrable value to a buyer.

Positioning includes far more than the outside appearance of the business. You may need to put on a fresh coat of paint (and that's as far as the paint analogy goes), but more importantly, you will also need to be prepared to:
- Demonstrate the day-to-day operation of the business
- Defend the strength of its business model
- Declare and defend its financial performance
- Validate its legal status
- Explain the business's competitive and market position, in a way that creates a clear picture of the business's future potential

One of the best ways to accomplish this is to always operate your business as if it is for sale, knowing that someday you expect it will be. Think about the logic in this. Operating your business at its peak attainable efficiency, even if you're not ready to sell just yet, is exactly how you should operate it in any case. In the following chapters I will describe steps you can take to help prepare your business, by positioning it to maximize the return from its sale.

As important as preparing your business may be, the other important reason for positioning is that it forces you to do your homework and prepares you to drive the sales process rather than being a passive observer in what may be one of the most important transactions you will be a party to. It forces you to make the business operate efficiently. If your business is going to be prepared, then you must also be prepared.

My goal is to help you take on this task effectively. One important way to achieve this is to begin the positioning process well ahead of the anticipated deal closing date. The decision to sell a business should never be made on impulse. Plan, plan, plan!

The decision to sell a business should never be made on impulse. Plan, plan, plan!

If you have your back against the wall, you will be in the worst possible negotiating position. It's difficult to position a business for a fire sale. Selling a business is a strategic move that should be well thought out and planned well in advance of the actual event. Your business will be the product, and you need to take the time to market that product to get the greatest return for it. Operate your business as if it's for sale—that way it will be ready to sell when you are ready to sell it.

I'm Really Busy—How Much of My Time Will It Take to Prepare My Business?

Selling a business, in whole or in part, will take a considerable effort on your part—you will need a strategic plan, preparation, and commitment to execute that plan. You must be able to commit your time and resources for a successful sale if you want to maximize the return from the sale of your business. Regardless of how well your business has done, successfully closing a deal and putting together an optimal sale will require the same dedication and commitment from you in order to maximize your return.

Selling your business is a unique event in the life of the business. It is unique because many of the tasks required to maximize your return from the sale are outside the normal operation of the business. It will require additional effort beyond that needed for the continuing operations of the business, and it may include the addition of dedicated resources to effectively support the sale and supplement your time. You will want to limit the involvement of your employees to support these extra activities. Your employees probably don't have the right skill set; they may panic if they know you intend to sell; and your staff should not be diverted from their usual jobs (you need them to be busy demonstrating the value proposition of your business). You may want to consider hiring additional staff or contracting specialized help to form a team whose mission is completing the sale.

No matter where you plan to find the resources to prepare for the sale, you must keep the operation of your business running as efficiently as possible. Whether you're running a software development business or an ice cream shop, you must meet your development schedules. Someone must continue to scoop the ice cream, continue to order supplies and inventory, and continue to pay the bills and mop the floor. At the same time, you will need them to remain busy doing their regular jobs when a new buyer starts their due diligence. This is not the time for letting software releases slip or the ice cream cones melt Because you have re-tasked your employees to write a business plan!

This is also not the time to lose interest. You must take the necessary steps and provide any resources needed to demonstrate that there is continuous value. Remember, your goal is to pass the baton to a new owner and not let it appear the race is over. This is difficult if you take the runners out of the race!

Your goal is to pass the baton to a new owner and not let it appear the race is over.

If your business has been successful, then congratulations! But don't relax just yet. You still have some hard work to do to achieve an optimal exit. All the work you have been putting in to grow your business is about to pay off. Don't plan that fishing trip with your cousin just yet. Be prepared to postpone your vacation for a while and get busy working at your new job—preparing your business to be sold.

And while you're doing your homework and preparing to move on, keep this in mind. Expect that at some point your friends or family will look at the money you earned in the sale and tell you how lucky you are! Well, luck may have played a role in your success, but realistically, selling your business will require hard work, just like building it did. If luck does play a role, be thankful, but don't count on it. And be ready to tell your family and friends about the financial risks you have taken, the long hours and dirty jobs you had to do to earn your success, and the effort you put into sell your business. You will likely have to tell some of them that you're just not willing to give them the loan they may ask for to back their great idea. Closing a good deal with the right buyer takes planning and forethought.

If selling your business can best be described as "getting out from under," and you are in a hurry to move on, don't let the fact that you're in a rush to sell stop you from putting in the needed effort to position your business. Understand that, unless you are exceptionally lucky, your exit won't achieve the same kind of success as a business poised to continue to its next stage of growth. Understand that there are things you can do to improve your return. If you are holding a fire sale, don't be discouraged. Keep in mind that there are investors who look for fire sales. You will still need to be prepared if you hope to maximize the return from your sale. And if you are going to have to borrow the money to pay off those pesky creditors (and pesky employees if you owe them any back payroll), you will still need to maximize the return from the sale of your business. Now is not the time to quit.

How Long Will It Take to Sell My Business?

The expression "patience is a virtue" doesn't seem to apply when you're trying to move on from your business. Once an owner makes the decision to move on, they become impatient and want to make it happen as soon as possible. You could take the approach of just hanging a "For Sale" sign in the window or listing your business on an internet bulletin board to sell it—unless your goal is to maximize your return. Assuming your goal is to get the maximum return possible, you will need to prepare your business by positioning it to be sold. Planning for the sale of your business should start at least a year ahead of your intended closing (two years is not unreasonable).

Planning for the sale of your business should start at least a year ahead of your intended closing.

What? Was that a retching noise I just heard from the back row? You wanted to put the "For Sale" sign out tomorrow, didn't you? Of course you did, and I understand that many sellers will not be able to delay the closing for a year or more. One to two years is a long time when you are eager to move on (or need to cash out quickly). Can it be shortened? Three to six months is possible, but you will have to get busy and be willing to accept some risk. Keep in mind, when you shorten the positioning time, you may not have effectively prepared your business. You are constraining the amount of preparation you'll be able to do, and therefore you'll be limiting the amount of optimization you'll be able to accomplish. The steps you take to position your business, and the extent to which you are constrained from taking those steps, will affect the outcome of the deal. If you have been running the ideal business, maybe it won't take as long to position and sell it—or maybe you don't have the time and can't wait to get the optimum results. Whatever your circumstances, it's time to get busy.

And a Final Consideration

All businesses have one thing in common: to sell them, you need to show a buyer there is transferrable value and an opportunity for further success by acquiring (or merging with) the business. It helps to put yourself in the buyer's shoes by imagining what the buyer sees when they look at your business. Your job now is to create the image you want them to see. The race is on. You are preparing to pass the baton to the new owner.

Whenever I need to have a useful example or to clarify a point, I have referred to a fictitious business called "Jim's Bakery." Jim's Bakery doesn't exist, and it's not a pseudonym for any actual business. I use this example in the hope that many different types of small businesses will be able to relate to it, thereby helping you to apply the example to your own business. A bakery is a business most people can relate to. It is a retail store, a commercial B2B business, and a manufacturing business.

Jim's Bakery Example: Overview

Welcome to Jim's Bakery—combining the best of small-town retail friendliness with a large-scale regional baked goods distribution for our commercial customers. Jim's has been in business for thirty-five years and has a loyal following of retail customers who return year after year for personalized cakes and other specialty items, particularly around the holidays. Going to Jim's has always been the first stop for enjoyable family events, such as birthdays, graduations, and other happy occasions. Fifteen years ago, Jim's Bakery expanded its operations by adding a commercial bakery that supplies breads and other bakery items to local restaurants and other regional outlets. The loyal retail customers love finding Jim's Bakery breads and rolls in their local food stores because they know the quality for which the name stands. To help maintain their reputation for fresh baked products and to protect their brand, Jim's Bakery requires its commercial customers to remove any unsold products within twenty-four hours of delivery.

Jim's Bakery operates two facilities. The first facility is the original retail bakery, where they produce the cakes and specialty items, and the second is their commercial bakery that supports their "Bread as a Service" (BaaS) product line. The commercial bakery and the administrative offices for the business, located above the commercial bakery, are in a leased facility. The founder's office is located in the back of the retail store, which Jim owns. Jim likes to walk into the front of the store where he can greet people, as a way to remain close to his customers. This is not just nostalgia. Jim realizes that many of his commercial customers also started as retail customers.

After thirty-five years in business, Jim is ready to sell the business and retire to St. Thomas in the U.S. Virgin Islands. He is looking for a buyer who will continue to grow the business while maintaining its reputation for exceptional service and quality products. All rights to the Jim's Bakery brand and recipes, which have been used and improved upon for thirty-five years, are included in the sale.

Jim's Bakery Specification
Annual Revenue: $9.4 Million
Number of Employees: 24

Facilities:
- One leased commercial bakery.
- One retail store owned personally by Jim (negotiable in sale).

Retail Product Lines:
- Cakes: Customized birthday cakes made to order for walk-in and telephone customers. High margin product.
- Cookies: Sold in batches and handed out to children of all ages as loss leader samples in the retail store. Profitable stable product line with recurring sales.

- Bread: Baked fresh daily in five varieties. Aroma from baking attracts people from throughout the downtown area. Bread sales are constant but waste (leftover products) must be controlled.
- Rolls: Sold as a necessary staple of the business; however, it is not a profitable line.
- Gluten-free products: These products are custom-made and must be ordered in advance. Gluten-free products also represent a growing commercial bakery product line.

Commercial Product Lines:
- Bread as a Service: High recurring sales to contracted commercial accounts, including restaurants, schools, and industry cafeterias.
- Rolls: High-volume sales as expanded BaaS product offering for sandwich preparation.

Chapter 3
The Sales Process

At this point it will be helpful to understand the sales process itself. This will help to keep the chapters that follow in context and give you an appreciation for the task ahead.

The sales process usually seems a bit mystical when small business owners first encounter it. You may be familiar with some of the steps, but tying everything together and making it work can be difficult. Some of the steps seem tedious and appear to have been put there as hurdles just intended to slow things down. The process is usually loaded in favor of the buyer. If you take the time to become familiar with the process, we make some basic assumptions about your sales approach we will attempt to reverse that and make the sales process work in your favor instead of the buyers.

If your business presents a true opportunity, the first assumption we can make is that there will be buyers ready and willing to invest in it. Your goal will be to make that opportunity glaringly obvious. You will need to position your business to demonstrate its full value to a potential buyer. The trick is to make that value so noticeable that potential buyers won't have to dig to find it.

We will also assume the following: if there is only one buyer, that buyer will drive the process and will be in control. If there is more than one buyer, the seller will drive the process and be in control. Therefore, your goal will be to find more than one buyer. This can be accomplished by effectively marketing your business to identify and attract those buyers.

After making an initial offer to buy your business, buyers often use their due diligence assessment as an opportunity to lower the value of your business, allowing them to reopen negotiations and reduce their initial offering. To get the greatest possible return from the sale, your business will need to operate at its highest possible efficiency, and you must proactively identify risks before the buyer does. This requires optimizing your business's operation so that the buyer's due diligence assessment is a highly successful event for you.

There will be many people who are impacted by the sale of your business. Optimizing your return from the sale will mean understanding the roles and motivations of these people. These people can include professionals you will hire to help you with the sale; your vendors and your employees, who may feel they have a vested interest in your business; and your key employees and shareholders, who do have a vested interest in your business. All of these people may feel they are entitled to a piece of your business's "pie."

DOI 10.1515/9781547400249-003

Sales Process Tasks

While the sales process isn't fixed and generally includes recognizable tasks, it can change from situation to situation. The sales process may not move at the pace you anticipate, but keep this in mind: you are the driver. Take control and don't let others dictate your actions unless you believe they are required. Don't ignore the advice you receive from professionals either! You are paying for their help, but it's your show.

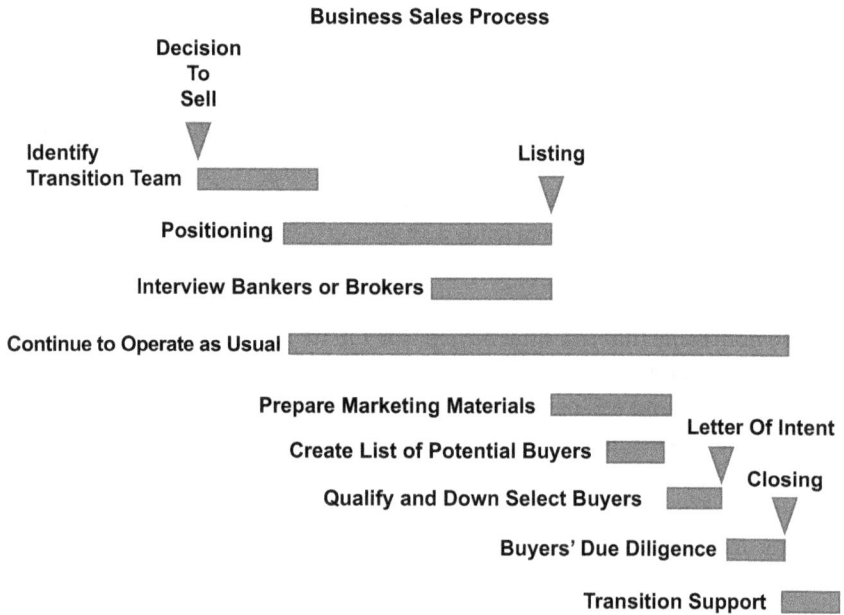

Figure 3.1: Business Sales Process

Because there are many things that need to happen at the same time, it's easy to get lost in the sales process. Figure 3.1 shows the milestone events you should anticipate in the sale of your business. I have attempted not to repeat information in multiple chapters, except where the information was needed for context to describe the steps in as logical an order as possible. Use Figure 3.1 as a roadmap to guide you through the process. A description of each of the steps follows and includes cross-references to chapters that describe each task in detail. For now, we will focus on understanding the sales process and its goals. We will discuss the requirements for each task by putting them into context in the later chapters. Each chapter stands alone, so don't hesitate to jump ahead if need be.

The length of each task in the process is variable depending on how well prepared you are before entering the sales process. For instance, if you already have an organization chart, then the positioning task suggesting the creation of an organization chart, will take less time for you to complete than for other business owners. You will be ahead, and that particular process will be shorter. But there are likely to be other processes that will take more time. The resources you are able to bring together to form your transition team, and the size of your business, will also impact the duration of these tasks.

There is a correlation between the level of effort you put toward positioning your business and the level of return you will achieve from its sale. Once you finally decide to sell your business, you will need to weigh these factors to establish a working schedule until you close the sale. You're just beginning the race to sell your business. Relax, do some stretches—and let's hope it's not a marathon!

There is a correlation between the level of effort you put toward positioning your business and the level of return you will achieve from its sale.

Breaking Down the Steps

I encourage you to manage your business's sale as you would tackle any major project—by establishing measurable milestones your transition team will use to target individual tasks on the schedule. If you don't set deadlines, the sales process can easily drift from task to task. Before you realize it, time will have elapsed; you will have paid a lot of money, and you won't have accomplished your end goal.

That beach may be calling to you, and you may be growing impatient to get there once you have finally decided it's time to move on. Listen to the call and respond to it by establishing a working schedule that will get you to the beach once the job is done, but don't compromise on your work or abandon the goals you established at the beginning of the project.

The use of an automated project management tool may be a good idea for a large business with complex scheduling elements. It is too easy for things to fall through the cracks. Holding weekly or monthly progress reviews and tracking assigned action items will be important. Hold people accountable for meeting their deadlines.

The Decision to Sell

This is the decision that will give you those sleepless nights. I show this as a milestone event, but it probably took some time to decide it's time to move on. This may be the starting point for the sales process. While you know you will sell your business someday, even if you haven't made the decision to sell yet, many of the tasks that follow can still be accomplished ahead of time. There is a benefit to improving your operations regardless. Go ahead and begin. The key to that decision is having "no regrets." You don't want to wake up the day after you sell your business with a bad case of seller's remorse. Once your decision is made, be prepared to put it behind you, and don't revisit it again. Move on.

Identify Your Transition Team

You won't be able to sell your business without help. For even the smallest businesses, the sales process requires resources. You will need to put together a transition team that consists of people you trust and who bring the skills you will need. This is the first step. Your transition team will act as advisors and should be prepared to take on some of the work. Some of them, such as your certified public accountant (CPA) and attorney, need to be specialists that you consult on a part-time basis. The other sales specialists you will need to hire will also have a price. In many cases, you can pay them a retainer and delay paying the bulk of their fee until after the sale closes, (the sale is completed). It certainly won't hurt to ask them! While you are putting this team together, do not forget to create a budget to pay for these services. We'll discuss the role that the transition team will play at crucial steps in the process throughout the book.

It is important to keep your business operating at peak efficiency while you are preparing to sell. You will need to have your employees working at their best. The more you can limit your dependence on your employees' time in the sales process, the better. Their ability to support the sale should be limited, although you will need their help, even if they may not understand why. Ask your employees to support activities that fall within the scope of their jobs. Improving the efficiency of the operations within their area takes time, but most employees would rather do it themselves instead of someone else telling them how to do their job. Your job will be to ensure your employees have a balance between supporting the optimization and doing their full-time job.

Ask your employees to support activities that fall within the scope of their jobs.

Position Your Business

This activity includes the optimization of your business to maximize its value in preparation for the buyers financial, legal, and operations due diligence assessments. This is one of those tasks you can do even if you haven't decided whether or not to sell yet. If you have run a tight ship, then the amount of preparation you will require may be limited; if you have been a "seat of the pants" type of manager, you may have some real work to do. Positioning activity is discussed in greater detail in Chapters 7, 8, and 9.

Some of the suggestions made in those chapters may seem like little more than basic management practices. In the context of this book, these recommendations are aimed at making realistic improvements that will help optimize your business's value and target your return from its sale. Some recommendations may seem overdone for very small businesses. Small businesses vary in size, but the process applies to all of them. If your business is very small, try to challenge yourself by taking the time to see how many of the recommendations can be implemented rather than finding ways to avoid them.

Try to challenge yourself by taking the time to see how many of the recommendations can be implemented rather than finding ways to avoid them.

Interview Bankers and Brokers

It's time for another big decision. Will you hire professional help to market and sell your business—someone who will act as an intermediary between you and your potential buyers—or will you go it alone? Most business sales require the use of a professional who is familiar with the sales process and whose job it will be to help you market and sell your business. These are professional sales agents who will also serve as intermediaries to assist you during your negotiations with the buyer. We will discuss the need for these professional services in Chapter 6 and describe the role they will play in Chapter 16.

At this point, you will need to work with your transition team to conduct interviews of these professionals (this task can be done in parallel with your positioning activities). Each person or company you interview should be asked for a written proposal that includes a definitive fee schedule. As the task progresses, you will select one of the persons or companies to represent you and participate on your transition team.

Listing

After selecting a broker or banker to act as an intermediary/agent, they will ask you to sign an agreement to list your business for sale and put it on the market. Your positioning activities should be completed before your business becomes an active listing. Your agent also has work to do before listing your business so continue to work on positioning and discuss with your agent the optimum time to make your business's listing active.

Most listing agreements are standard, but the terms they offer can vary significantly. Ask questions and don't hesitate to challenge anything you don't agree with. The agent may be in a rush to get a signed listing agreement, but don't hesitate to have it reviewed by your attorney if you're not comfortable signing it yet. The listing agreement will be for a specified time period and will delineate any special terms and conditions either of you want to include. Further information regarding the listing agreement can be found in Chapter 6.

Prepare Marketing Materials

Another activity you need to accomplish before you actively look for buyers is the preparation of your marketing materials. You must work with your agent to prepare these materials so they can be presented to potential buyers. You are paying for your agent's expertise, so don't hesitate to defer to them when they offer marketing ideas. Your agent will be prepared to take on this task; however, you should be prepared for this ahead of time by creating content and materials for them to use.

Your marketing materials will include a handout (see the example in Appendix A) and your draft "Book" (an example is provided in Appendix B). My suggestion is that you prepare a draft handout and "Book" for your business to present to your agent. Chapter 12 provides the recommendations for the format of your Book. By taking the time to create your own draft, you will be collecting your thoughts and driving the direction you want your agent to take. Be sure to retain final approval of these and any other materials created in your name.

Create a List of Potential Buyers

At this point in the sales process you may have been thinking about potential buyers—friends, competitors, businesspeople who are acquiring other businesses or expanding, and those people you think might be potential buyers. Make your list of potential buyers, or work with your sales agent to review their list, but do not communicate with *anyone* on your list about selling your business just yet. If you haven't done so, now is the time to discuss specific sales strategies with your sales agent.

If you and your agent agree that your best path to a sale is a public approach, then go ahead and put a "For Sale" sign in the window and start talking up your business. Make sure to give the contact information for anyone who expresses interest to your agent though. To all requests for information, your response should be:

> "Here is my agent. You will need to speak with them."

You want the agent to be your intermediary so you will always be in the position of negotiating through a third party. If your agent is openly advertising your business, then your business listing should be posted on a public, multiple listing "Businesses for Sale" website. Prepare to hold one or more open houses and let your agent filter the calls.

If you have decided to take a more stealth approach to selling your business, give your list of strategic prospects to your agent and don't do anything else with it. Don't reach out to anyone on the list. Don't try to "feel them out." Let your agent do the job you are paying them for.

Your agent should be doing industry research and developing their own list of potential buyers. They will begin contacting the people on the list once they have vetted them. If one of your competitors mentions to you that they heard a company in your industry is for sale, simply ask them to let you know if they find out who it is. Even if, at some point, someone correctly guesses your business is for sale, don't engage with them.

> "Gee Jim, I have it on good authority that your business is for sale."

> "You will have to talk to my consultant" (hand him your agent's card) "about that before you spread any rumors."

Your agent will ask the buyer or other interested parties to sign a nondisclosure agreement (NDA) before divulging any detailed information. In Chapter 6 we will establish some specific sales goals that will drive your marketing efforts.

Qualify and Down Select Buyers

At this point your agent will review a potential buyers list with you, and you will share your initial thoughts about who is a potential buyer and who is just "kicking the tires." Your agent will want to know about any buyers you already know or have insights into. After discussions with the potential buyers, your agent will bracket the potential buyers to see who has a realistic understanding about the value of your business (for example, if a potential buyer thinks its worth $800,000 and your price is $3 million, there is no reason to continue speaking with them). Your agent will also want a list of any potential buyers you have already spoken with or, in the situation where you might have had a prior listing with another agent where they may be an existing commission commitment. DO not assume that, because you terminated the listing, you have no further commitment when it comes to potential buyers they may have introduced you to. Be sure to read all listing agreements carefully if you decide to change agents.

At some point, your agent will invite a select group of potential buyers with real interest to submit a written offer (a proposal) with a draft letter of intent attached. The down select process can become iterative if you receive competing proposals. Ultimately you will ask all potential buyers for their Best and Final Offer (BAFO).

Assuming your effort to prepare and market your business has been successful, and you have achieved your goal of finding two or more buyers (if not, see Chapter 6), it's time to carefully review their offers to decide which one you will accept. Your agent should already have done a background check on the potential buyers and verified that they have access to the resources needed to close the deal. Everything you do from this point on should be reviewed and approved by your transaction attorney and reviewed by your CPA.

Letter of Intent (LOI) and/or Purchase Agreement

You will now receive a copy of the draft letter of intent (or another form of purchase agreement) from the potential buyer. The LOI should reflect all of your negotiated terms and conditions and the buyer's purchase price and payment schedule. The LOI states the terms under which the sale will be executed. Alternatively, your attorney can prepare the agreement or a purchase contract, as long as it accurately reflects the verbal agreed-upon terms. The principals from both parties must sign the LOI, and the buyer now provides the good faith funds to be escrowed. In general, the LOI is a highly conditional agreement (for instance, it will require performing due diligence). The documents required for the closing are complex and must be written and negotiated by the transaction attorneys before the closing. The LOI defines the terms of the deal while the closing documents are being prepared and due diligence is being performed. Even though it is conditional, the LOI allows the seller and buyer to declare their intentions while moving the deal ahead.

Signing the LOI means the "potential buyer" has now become your "buyer"— but don't start packing just yet. There is still work that needs to be done. Keep in mind that a signed LOI is not the end, but the beginning. This is where all of your preparatory work will come to light. Congratulations! The good news is you now have a buyer.

Signing the LOI means the "potential buyer" has now become your "buyer"—but don't start packing just yet.

The LOI is not a definitive agreement. It has conditions—for example, the successful completion of due diligence; verification of the detailed financial analysis; and the release of all those little details now that there is an actual buyer. Your deal is not closed until these steps have been satisfactorily met. There will be more discussions before you reach your final terms, conditions, and final renegotiated price.

The letter of intent is a legal document and should be prepared by an attorney. No example has been included in this book because I'm not here to give you legal advice. The length of the LOI is variable and can range from a brief statement to pages of detailed terms that must be met by both parties. All terms must be carefully studied and understood. If you don't agree with the terms, don't sign the LOI, no matter how eager you are to complete a deal. It takes much longer to work things out in court than it does to negotiate them in an LOI.

Buyer's Due Diligence

The duration of the buyer's due diligence can be variable depending on the size of your business, the depth of discovery the buyer wishes to go, and the number of resources the buyer deploys for the task. It is not an open-ended event, however, so ask for a tentative schedule at the start. It is in your best interests to keep this schedule as short as possible.

"I will be happy to support any due diligence activities you need but they must be wrapped up within 30 days."

The buyer will likely resist. You can push back and recommend they use more people to allow them to complete their assessment sooner rather than later. Remember, while the buyer is performing their due diligence, you cannot talk to anyone else.

Different buyers use different approaches when performing their due diligence. Some are very formal, and some are very informal. You should always treat a due diligence as a formal event. The activity will generally start with a request for a list of documents that can be reviewed by the buyers assessment team. Even today there are buyers who prefer paper copies to online versions. Some buyers will then provide a list of written questions they would like you to respond to in writing (and on the record). I generally advise my clients to be direct and truthful and to only answer the questions that have been asked (in other words, don't elaborate). This is not the time to show off your vast knowledge of why the market is dying and why you're getting out! You have an obligation not to mislead the buyer about the market, but the buyer has an obligation to do their market research homework.

At some point, the buyer will perform their financial, legal, and operations assessments. One of the goals of this activity will be to clarify and validate the responses your team has answered in response to the buyer's written questions, along with any claims you made in your marketing materials. Next will be the in-house assessment where the buyer will ask to spend time in your facility, observing how your business operates and getting to know your employees. After that assessment, some buyers prefer to return home to analyze the data they've collected, while others will be ready to immediately sit and discuss their findings.

If there are no changes to the LOI, the buyer will agree to finalize the closing documents. Your transaction attorney and theirs will begin the process of preparing the closing agreement along with any other documents that will be required to close. Typically, the buyer is not ready to go directly to closing. They will want to continue your prior negotiations.

"During our due diligence, our assessment team discovered the following items we were not previously aware of. . .."

"As a result of these discoveries, we are going to adjust our original valuation of your business and lower our offer to. . .."

Your choice is to accept their lower price, make a counteroffer, or refuse their new offer outright. The buyers know you are eager to get to the beach. They know you don't want to start the entire sales process over with another buyer. So, they are highly motivated to negotiate a lower price. That is why you limit the due diligence to thirty days as a term of the LOI. This may be a good time to call that buyer who was the runner-up and ask if their proposal is still valid! This is the point where many good relationships between buyers and sellers will fall apart.

"I thought we had already agreed on this number?"

"We did, but we had assumed that all of that equipment was included in the deal. That's not what we found out during due diligence."

Hopefully, you can come to an agreement and won't have to repeat the process with another buyer. This may be the point to consider looking at earn-outs, stock swaps, escrow to cover perceived risk, or other creative means to negotiate your price.

Closing

The day you have been working toward has finally arrived. Relax and let the attorneys run the show. Sign everything your attorney agrees to and, even if there is three feet of snow outside, wear your best flip-flops, shorts, and Hawaiian shirt to the event!

Remember that following the closing, your loyal employees will work for the new owner. If you plan to reward them, have the checks prepared and ready to distribute immediately following the closing, and get the new owner's permission to address your former employees. "Thank you for your loyalty" goes a long way when you shake someone's hand by putting an envelope into it.

Transition Support

If you are staying with your former business, you should have a good understanding of what your new boss or partner expects. This will be a good time to sit with them and start things off in the right direction. Rumors are very likely flying among the employees, so—with the new owner's agreement—introduce the new owner, explain what your new role is, and reassure them about their future. This will help to quiet the rumor mill. If there are going to be any changes to salaries, positions, or benefits, the new owner should announce them as soon as possible. Employees are always suspicious of and never like change. Nothing is ever gained by delay. The sooner the employees know the facts, the sooner things will quiet down.

If you are exiting the business, you should plan to work with the new owner to orchestrate how this will be done. You may want to shut the door following the sale's closing, but this is generally not practical. If you have a good relationship with your employees, you should be the one to announce the sale and do the introductions. All other announcements (salary, benefits, etc.) should be made by the new owners.

Plan to get calls from the new owner looking for information. Provide answers, but don't let this become a burden. Unless you have a contractual reason to do so, limit your answers and the time you spend at the business. You might also be contacted by former employees looking for advice or looking to complain about the new owner. If they are not happy, be supportive, but never undermine the new owner. Make it clear you will not comment and be sure to honor any "lock-up" terms in your sales agreement.

It's time to move on.

Chapter 4
Start Thinking about the Value of Your Business

So, you've lost some sleep, spoken with your spouse, and gone through whatever routine you use when you're about to make a life-changing decision. You've checked your emotions and know you're not going to suffer seller's remorse. And now, finally, you've made the decision. You're ready to sell your business and move on.

No matter what is driving your decision, your goal now is to maximize your return from the sale. Selling a business requires positioning the business to demonstrate its transferrable value to a buyer. Every action you take to position your business should be aimed at achieving that goal. Your value proposition should be obvious to a buyer.

> "Here is the opportunity when you buy this business."

The value needs to be apparent without having to dig too deep to find it. In this chapter we will talk about the initial steps you can to take to kick off the sales process. These are steps you will want to start now, even if you haven't quite decided it's time to sell your business yet. The actions recommended here may take some time so don't delay working on them. Hopefully some of the actions described here are already being done in your business (they are good management practices whether you are selling or not), which means you may already be ahead of the game. But if they're not something you regularly include in your operations, then don't delay—it's time to start.

Selling a business requires positioning the business to demonstrate its transferrable value to a buyer.

Make Sure Buyers Have the Correct Image of Your Business

Do you ever look in the mirror and wonder who that person is staring back at you? That person with an extra twenty pounds looking back at you probably isn't the image you have of yourself. But others see the twenty pounds when they look at you. The way we perceive something is not always the way others see it. You can't hide that extra weight for long, so you better start preparing to lose those extra twenty pounds by changing your routine.

DOI 10.1515/9781547400249-004

Buyers may also have a different image of your business than you have. You might be tempted to claim that your software developers turn out bug-free code, but that might not be the buyer's perception if your software has a reputation for failing. The buyer is likely to see through your claim (and, when they find your software bug list, it will become a negotiation item). You may need to make changes to the way you do business by hiring a software quality assurance person instead of making bold claims you can't defend. The way to improve the "curb appeal" of your business is to make changes to the business. There should never be a gap between what the buyer perceives and what the buyer is purchasing. What you tell prospective buyers must match what they see when they visit and must be validated through their analysis. What potential buyers examine cannot be a facade. Business buyers are going to perform a detailed due diligence and they will see through any facade. Improving your curb appeal means that even if your kitchen is small, it should be the best small kitchen a buyer can find—they will see the value your kitchen will give them. You should always assume that the buyer is looking at multiple businesses. This means you need to create a discriminator that makes them choose to buy *your* business. You must be credible and believable to potential buyers at all times.

You must be credible and believable to potential buyers at all times.

To maximize the return from the sale of your business, you need to start managing the image others see when they look at the business. Managing the image of your business doesn't mean creating a false image. It means pointing out the business's strengths, telling the truth about it, and making any needed improvements. It could be that your business already has the image you want buyers to see; but if the buyer sees an unrealistic image, then you need to change your business so that reality matches the image. If you want to change people's perceptions, you will need to be prepared to make changes to the business.

Does Your Business Have "Curb Appeal?"

"Curb appeal" is one of those terms that has become highly overloaded. "Curb appeal" has a different meaning in the sale of a business than it does in residential real estate sales. In residential real estate, curb appeal refers to what a buyer will see "from the curb" when driving by the property. There are no drive-by sales in business. Curb appeal for a business means demonstrating, to the greatest extent possible, why your business's value proposition makes buying your business a good investment and worthwhile opportunity. "Curb appeal" in business is when a potential buyer sees the transferrable value of the business demonstrated.

Improving the curb appeal of your business includes cleaning up and preparing the external image of the business so that it appears successful. It also requires being prepared to demonstrate all facets of the business's operation to a potential buyer. The business needs to be honestly positioned and appear as successful and professional as possible. For example, an online web business with no operating facility still needs to work on its curb appeal by making sure the image it presents to a potential buyer, based on its website and financials, demonstrates the transferrable value a buyer will be interested in. Business sales require a sufficient level of buyer analysis to entice them to look further—and hopefully, eventually buy. Your job is to prepare the evidence needed to convince the buyer that it's worth their time and money to look deeper. They should not have to dig too deeply to find value in the business.

In *Jerry McGuire* Tom Cruise and Cuba Gooding Jr. famously shout, "Show me the money."[1] What a buyer wants to shout at you is "show me the value." You can't just tell buyers about the value in your business; you must be prepared to demonstrate the value to them. That is how a business generates curb appeal. Unlike residential real estate, improving the curb appeal of a business requires going more than surface deep. I'm not knocking how difficult it is to sell residential real estate. I've tried it, and it's not an easy way to make a living. Residential real estate sells to a different market with different motivations than a business sale.

You can't just tell buyers about the value in your business—you must be prepared to demonstrate the value to them.

The sale of a business requires a clear understanding and demonstration of your business model. Even though you are in "selling mode," you need to limit the amount of puffing you do. Puffing means overstating the features or value of your business. When "we have the greatest kitchen in town" turns out to be a false statement, you have probably lost the buyer (who will be thinking what else you might be exaggerating or which is simply untrue). "Our kitchen is small, but we made it highly efficient to support our menu" is a much better selling statement. A bright, clean, highly efficient kitchen is a better marketing statement than anything you might say.

---

1 *Jerry McGuire*, directed by Cameron Crowe (Culver City, CA: Gracie Films, 1996), film.

If part of what you are selling includes the capabilities of your team, it's not sufficient to simply show a buyer the resumes of key employees. There should be a history of performance bonuses and creativity or other awards, acknowledgments, etc. hanging on the wall where buyers can read them while they are on tour. And yes—it's also good for employee morale, which is also a great selling feature.

As you start positioning your business by determining what potential buyers will be looking for, search for a way to put the answers to those questions in front of them. If your business is a retail store located in a strip mall, it should look like the most successful business in the mall. You want it to be obvious to a buyer why shoppers are attracted to your store, why these customers want to come into your store, and why it is more attractive than another store they might also be considering.

"We knew buyers would be interested in our production speed, so we posted production charts in the shop because we understood that would be a discriminator for our sale."

The answers to a potential buyer's questions should be obvious. If you're selling a restaurant, the kitchen, the dining room, and the restrooms should be sparkling clean, and the buyer should see how efficient your service is. If your business is a light manufacturing company, the shop should look well maintained and organized so a buyer can see how efficiently your assembly line works. If your business is a software development company with a staff of young, highly energetic engineers, it should be obvious you have created an energetic environment that challenges the staff's creativity. I had one client who put in a pool table and sponsored after-work activities for their engineers because they recognized that their team had more ideas in group settings than they did working at their desks. One of the greatest chances to make an impression on a buyer is when they first walk in the door. You know you've struck gold if their reaction is "wow, this is just what I'm looking for." That type of reaction doesn't come by building a fake facade over the front of the building like an old movie set. You must clean up, improve efficiency, and make changes that encourage creativity and motivate staff. Creating curb appeal for a business means painting, polishing, and cleaning, but more importantly it means preparing to demonstrate the transferrable value in the operation of the business.

Creating curb appeal for a business means painting, polishing, and cleaning, but more importantly it means preparing to demonstrate the transferrable value in the operation of the business.

Be Prepared to Demonstrate Your Business in Operation

In residential real estate sales, a technique called staging is often used to help create an image for a home buyer. Staging a vacant house, by minimally furnishing it, is a marketing technique that allows prospective residential real estate buyers to envision themselves living in the home. Since your business is operating and isn't "vacant" this type of staging doesn't work. When someone invests in a business they want to see products moving off the shelves and services being provided to customers, so they can observe firsthand how the business operates. You'll want to demonstrate and validate the value proposition of your business by showing it in operation so the buyer can observe it. Of course, cleaning and painting to freshen things up, particularly if the deal includes real estate, may make sense. Falsely staging a business or intentionally planning to mislead a buyer should never be your goal when positioning a business. I had a client who was selling a paint store. The buyer asked to sit in the store on Saturday and observe the store in operation. Knowing the buyer would be there, the seller arranged to have friends come by acting as customers and the buyer got to see a false image of a crowded store. It was so crowded in fact, that the buyer got suspicious. The next Saturday the buyer sent people in unannounced to observe the operation of the store and found it much quieter than the prior week. The buyer realized he had been given a false image the prior week and the deal died immediately.

Falsely staging a business or intentionally planning to mislead a buyer should never be your goal when positioning a business.

Positioning a business is similar selling a car. When you sell a car, you try to keep the car clean, waxed, and polished while you're also driving it to work every day. When a potential buyer is coming to see the car, you want to wash it and vacuum off the floor mats to make it more presentable . . . but like business buyers most car buyers will want to look a little deeper and open the hood to check the oil. It's hard to keep your business operating at its peak because, in business, things can and do go wrong. If you've been performing regular maintenance on the car you won't need to take the time to change the oil or do any of the other things that should be done as part of the routine maintenance you perform on a periodic schedule . . . and you should have those records to show the buyer.

A car buyer may look at the dipstick to see that the car has clean oil but showing the receipts for the regularly scheduled maintenance you've performed adds value. The same is true for your business. You need to demonstrate that the business has been routinely maintained as part of its ongoing operations. Showing the records for the normal operation of your business is a significant way to demonstrate value. If the car's oil is dirty or the level is low, the buyer is likely to try to use this to negotiate a lower price. The same is true for your business.

Demonstrate that your business has been routinely maintained as part of its on-going operations.

If your business uses specialized equipment, showing routine maintenance records for that equipment or a regular upgrade of your software says a lot about the operation and potential value of your business. Buyers expect businesses to run into problems, but they want to know how the business manages those issues and how it mitigates potential risk. Be prepared to have a frank conversation with a buyer when they ask about scheduled equipment maintenance and upgrades to keep these from becoming negotiation items used to lower your return.

If the business is operating well but starting to show its age you may want to improve its value by updating the operational software systems you use to the latest version or installing the latest industry machine tools. If you see changes to your operations that will add value, then now is the time to make the change. Just like you would improve the curb appeal of the car by adding a new set of tires, you may want to consider making some additional strategic investment to justify asking the top value for your business.

Effective positioning means you are prepared to make the trade-off between the expenses of an upgrade against your sale price . . . and keep a potential investor from negotiating the price down by saying it will cost them to do those upgrades. Positioning such as this needs to be performed with your anticipated negotiating strategy in mind and well before you get to the deal table. If you do perform regular maintenance and upgrades as part of the normal ongoing operation of the business this should be pointed out as a feature and used to add value to the sale of the business.

"Yes . . . our shop has the latest CNC milling machine software allowing us greater precision and putting us far above our competition."

Talking to Your Employees

It's difficult to find the right time to notify your employees that you are selling the business. Most advisors will tell you, the longer you wait the better off you will be . . . and in some cases, this can mean not saying anything until the deal has closed. "Hi, I'm your new boss" is the first hint they get of the sale.

Even if this is your plan (or the buyer's, which is more likely the case), it is rare that the sale of a small business can be kept secret from the employees for long. Employees sometimes see the sale as an opportunity to try to negotiate a promotion for themselves into the deal.

"Sure, I'll stay but I want a 20 percent salary increase."

You don't want to panic your employees into sending out resumes that flood the market . . . including places where your competition might see them. That would put you in the position of trying to negotiate a deal with someone who already has the ability to hire your key employees through a head hunter . . . you will lose that negotiation. The problem is, in most small businesses, the employees will pick up on the activity related to a sale well before closing.

You don't want to panic your employees into sending out resumes that flood the market... including places where your competition might see them.

Waiting to tell your employees about the sale starts to sound like a good plan but it's not an easy secret to keep. You will probably want to let the people who have supported you and been loyal to you know what's happening with the business. In practice it is highly unlikely you will complete a sale without at least some of your key people being aware of what's going on . . . because no matter how hard you try not to involve them, you may need their help to prepare for the sale. Besides, are you really ready to wait until after the deal is closed to tell even your direct staff? That would mean the first time they hear about it would be when the new owner calls them together and says;

"The business was sold last night and we, the new owners, are inviting you to stay employed with us and here is your new benefits package." "And if you don't like the package you are now unemployed."

Some buyers feel this type of approach immediately shows the employees who is in charge. In cases where the buyer has more interest in acquiring the product line than the employees, they have no fear in using these tactics. I have seen this happen and it is a cold dose of reality for the employees. Keep in mind, while this conversation is going on, and depending on the type of deal you make, you may be at the beach on your third rum punch, so you might not care . . . but those people who have been loyal to you probably won't be wishing you luck at this point if the sale truly came as a surprise to them. You may still be there to help with the transition of the new owners or have some thoughts of hiring your key employees again in the future, in your next business, but your agreement with the new owners will likely keep you from doing that for at least a year and will likely lock you out of the industry for some time. They may ask, but you may be constrained from hiring them again. No matter what the circumstances are, your relationship with these former employees will have changed.

In practice, you will need to decide if there are employees you trust enough to confide in and at what point you want to disclose your plans. Tread carefully. This is your life, but it is their job. You will be taking a risk when you disclose the sale so limit those who you talk to. When you speak with your employees and what you say to them may become one of the buyer's terms of the sale. If you speak with employees too soon it might have a negative impact on the deal. Remember that the buyers you're trying to bring may be the people your staff has been competing with and correctly or incorrectly, they may have some preconceived thoughts about each other.

"I've heard about the way they treat their people."

"I just can't work for them."

"I used to work for them and don't think they'll keep me when they take over."

Selling your business won't make your employee headaches go away. It will amplify them . . . for a short time. Putting employee agreements in place with your key staff may help to protect them . . . but don't wait until the last minute to do it.

In practice, you will need to decide if there are employees you trust enough to confide in and at what point you want to disclose your plans.

It takes committed resources to perform many of the tasks needed to correctly position a business. Collecting your records in preparation for due diligence, recasting your financials to identify valid financial adjustments, identifying potential strategic partners, reviewing the legal structure and ownership of the business, writing a business plan that will serve as a marketing brochure for the business are all positioning activities you need to undertake before you speak with any potential buyers. If your business is going to operate at its most efficient, your staff will be busy and may have limited availability for these additional duties and you will want to limit how many are exposed to your exit strategy. You need to consider bringing on a transition team that is committed to the success of the sale, hopefully one that has experience in mergers and acquisitions, at the appropriate time to handle the sale of your business.

Jim's Bakery Example

Jim had existing employment agreements with his CFO, Retail COO, and Commercial COO so he knew their compensation would be protected in the sale. This meant he could bring them in on his decision to sell early. He made it clear from the start however that there was no room for them to renegotiate those agreements. He explained that he would need to ask them to put in extra effort to support the sales process but assured them he would not forget about the extra effort. He planned to bonus all three, not just for their effort here, but for their continued loyalty and the roles they had all played in helping to grow his business. Jim knew he would need to bring in other professional help, but this was going to be his core team.

To kick off the team, Jim gave them some initial guidelines.
- No other employees were to be told about the pending sale at this time.
- A weekly team meeting was to be held that would track open action items and end each week with the four of them doing a walk around inspection of both the retail and commercial bakery facilities.
- A plan would be implemented to clean, paint, and create a fresh atmosphere for both facilities. This was to include all areas and not be limited to customer facing spaces.
- Both COOs were to ensure that all equipment maintenance schedules were being kept and records for that maintenance were being collected.

Chapter 5
Who Are Your Buyers?

Before you begin marketing your business, it makes sense to think about who the potential buyers for it might be. To begin, it's important to understand that you are *not* looking to find a buyer for your business. Your mindset, right from the start, should be that you are trying to find two or more buyers for your business. I warned you that selling your business was going to take a lot of work! Finding the second buyer is as important as finding the first buyer, because your goal is to maximize the return from your sale.

Your mindset, right from the start, should be that you are trying to find two or more buyers for your business.

Having only one buyer is like holding an auction with only one person is bidding. You'll have to take whatever you can negotiate, but the buyer knows they are your only choice and will have every incentive to bid low. If you have two or more potential buyers, they will both be forced to compete on price to buy your business. So, make it your goal right from the start to find two buyers. Damn. . .. Just when you were worried about finding one buyer, your problem just doubled!

Business Buyers Are Not Impulse Buyers

Consumers buy on impulse. In residential real estate they drive down the road and stop at an open house or form opinions about neighborhoods without doing much research in advance. The resale value of the house is a consideration but not a driving one. The aesthetics of the home and the neighborhood are far more important. That is why the curb appeal of a house is so important and the reason why real estate developers hang up flags and fly balloons aimed at attracting buyers as they drive by on the weekend. I am not saying the sale of residential real estate is easy—just that the marketing problem is different. Business buyers, by comparison, buy according to a well-thought-out plan that supports their investment or strategic goals.

Business buyers, by comparison, will buy according to a well-thought-out plan that supports their investment or strategic goals.

DOI 10.1515/9781547400249-005

This is true for small businesses as well as larger ones. Even when buyers are looking for an investment opportunity rather than a business they intend to operate themselves, they rarely purchase a business on impulse. Business buyers are looking for a capital investment opportunity or the chance to advance a strategic plan. They will want to analyze a business by reviewing its financials to determine its past performance, by performing a detailed due diligence, by studying the market for the businesses products, and by understanding the employees and operations of the business in detail. Because all business buyers are going to perform an analytic deep dive to discover as much about your business as possible before making the decision to buy it, you must position your business and be prepared to show them why your business is the opportunity they are looking for. It will help you if you understand the motivations behind these different types of buyers.

Qualified Buyers

Let's face it. There are buyers and there are buyers. Your cousin Jake has been "helping out" part time and would love to take over the business. He just doesn't have the resources (as in, no other full-time income), he has no inheritance, he doesn't understand why you can't go fishing with him on the weekends, and he wonders why you keep telling him you are tied up at work. You have lots of family and friends, but most likely they're not the qualified buyer you're looking for. And, more importantly, even if one of them does have the resources, you will still want to find two qualified buyers to ensure you are getting your best return. If you do decide to sell the business to cousin Jake and move to the beach (and you cave in to your mom and compromise on the price or the terms you offer to cousin Jake), you will want to do that from a position of knowing exactly what the value of your business is and what you are giving up instead of selling to another buyer. You may also want to seriously consider changing your phone number, so you won't be disturbed at the beach later when cousin Jake runs into trouble and is looking for help! A qualified buyer is an individual or business who has the resources to close a deal to purchase your business at (or above) its true value according to terms you are willing to accept.

A qualified buyer is an individual or business who has the resources to close a deal to purchase your business at (or above) its true value according to terms you are willing to accept.

You will likely have other considerations that drive your decision regarding which buyer to choose, and these will become the contractual terms in your deal. How will the buyer treat your loyal employees? Will the buyer move the business or change its name? You may not care about these things, but most sellers have some considerations that go beyond money.

> "We have been established in this location for years, but they were going to move the shop to another town."

Your business's cost also comes in different forms that may affect the buyer you eventually decide to sell to. Will your closing be a one-time event where you receive all the funds at once, or will it include some form of earn-out that pays you over time (more on earn-outs later in this chapter). Depending on the "earn-out" deal you may negotiate, will the buyer you choose demonstrate an ability to operate the business successfully after you leave? Will part of the payment be a stock trade for shares in a merged company in return for shares in your company? A qualified buyer in either of these situations would have to bring more to the table than the initial funds. Some buyers may only be interested in an asset sale while you are only willing to consider an equity deal (more on this in the final chapter).

You may need to perform a due diligence of your own to qualify the buyer. This is particularly true if your plan is to remain with your business. Are these the people you want to work for? Background checks and the services of a private investigator might be well worth the cost to qualify the buyer at this point.

Looking for Strategic Buyers

All buyers do not have the same goals, or at least they don't all have the same motivation, for buying a business. Some buyers are already in your industry and will be looking at your business because they have a strategic motivation for buying another business within the same industry. Strategic buyers often try to expand their current business by buying another business in the same industry. They may see your business as an additional outlet to expand their customer base; they may want to acquire your product line; they may want to take your business off the market to keep another competitor from buying it and entering the market; they may want to acquire one of your assets, such as your facility, or hire a key employee; or maybe you have always competed with them and they want to gloat that they have lasted longer than you. There are many things that motivate buyers, but you only care about one thing: a strategic buyer will see greater value in your business than other buyers might and therefore may be willing to pay more for your business than other buyers. One strategic buyer is good; two strategic buyers turn your sale into a competitive auction!

One strategic buyer is good; two strategic buyers turn your sale into a competitive auction!

Your goal will be to find strategic buyers, but beware—there is an inherent risk that comes with strategic buyers. Not all buyers, and in particular strategic buyers, are what they might appear to be. A potential buyer who is also a competitor may be a great strategic opportunity but may in truth be more interested in what they can find out about your business rather than having any genuine interest in buying it at all. The goal of a strategic buyer who is a competitor may be to gain insight into your business model, obtain your customer lists, identify key employees to poach, and tell your existing customers they can no longer rely on you. Strategic buyers are a great potential opportunity when they're truly motivated to buy, but they also present a tremendous risk when you open your doors and books to them. Risk and opportunity are closely related! Don't shut a potential strategic buyer down. Qualify them and take steps to protect yourself. Be sure to put a nondisclosure agreement (NDA) in place (you should do this with all buyers) and use great care when and how you release information to them prior to cosigning the letter of intent (LOI) with them for the purchase of your business. After an LOI is signed you'll have no choice but to be open and forthright, so take care beforehand and make sure your attorney pays close attention to the terms and conditions (often simply referred to as the Ts and Cs) specified on the LOI. Ask for good faith money to be put in escrow at this time as well.

So where does this leave you? You're not just looking for a buyer; you're looking for two qualified buyers. And you want both qualified buyers to be strategic buyers. How hard can it be after all? You can almost hear that calypso music and taste the Caribbean rum punch that is waiting for you. Well . . . in a perfect world, that's how it would happen. Even if you did have those two potential strategic buyers and they were qualified right now, you still need to negotiate the price with them and get through due diligence before they are ready to write a check.

You're not just looking for a buyer; your goal is to find two qualified strategic buyers.

Looking for Financial Buyers

Financial buyers are capital investors who are interested in acquiring all or part of your business because they see its growth potential. They expect the business to grow in value and hope to share in its future success. Sales to financial buyers include mergers and acquisitions (M&A) used to expand the portfolio of companies they may already own and operate. In a merger, these investors are seeking to acquire your entire business (or at least a controlling interest) and will absorb it into one of their existing businesses. In an acquisition the investors will want to keep your business intact as a portfolio holding but often have no interest in directly operating your business. If you're considering an offer from a financial buyer, you will need to understand the difference in exactly what they are offering from what other potential buyers are offering.

The answer to whether a financial buyer wants you to remain or to go after the sale depends on their financial objectives and strategic plan. If their strategic plan calls for radical changes in the operation of the business, they will most likely want you to exit once the sale is closed. If the buyer wants to become directly involved in the direction and operation of the business, they won't want you to stay in your current job. They might instead want to replace you with one of their own managers but may insist you remain with the business in some capacity for some period of time.

> "They bought a controlling interest in the business but then put a new president in charge."

> "It was difficult for me to remain with the business and take direction from someone after running the business for so long."

In an acquisition, where the investor plans to have the business continue operating the way it has been previously, they may not want to lose you and may insist you continue in some capacity, but you won't necessarily be at the top of the organization chart. If they believe your pro forma projections or they believe that, by investing additional capital into your business, they can grow it to another level, they may insist you remain in your current position. This is particularly true if the business developed some unique intellectual property under your ownership. If you're not looking for a full exit, this may be the type of buyer you are looking for, because they are acknowledging your success to date and will participate in it as the business continues to grow in the future. A financial investor may be willing to put additional money into the operation if you are willing to partner with them. They hope to accelerate the growth of your business by making more capital available to support the accelerated growth.

"If we put in additional money, can we accelerate your growth any quicker?"

Find out whether a financial buyer's strategic plan aligns with your personal plans early in the sales process. Remember, your life will change whether you sell part of your business and make them a partner, or whether you sell the entire business and make them your boss. The good news is that financial buyers who are looking to buy part of your business are looking for an equity deal rather than an asset deal, so their goals are more likely to be aligned with yours in that regard.

Taking on a partner is like getting married. Once someone invests in your business they are going to have a say in what you do with their money—even if they are a "silent partner." Silent partners tend to remain silent when things are going well, but they start to speak up if things start to go wrong. And that's where your partnership starts to look like a marriage. Enjoy the honeymoon, because if things begin to fall apart, the breakup can become nasty.

Find out whether a financial buyer's strategic plan aligns with your personal plans early in the process.

Financial buyers are looking for the transferrable value in your business and may even recognize value you haven't seen. By investing in your business, they have recognized your business's value and they want to "buy in" and become a participating member of your team. They may want to merge your operation in with one they already have, or they may strip out the value and throw the rest of the business out with the trash. If you're planning a full exit you might not care, but your former employees may well care. Be sure you take the time to fully understand the intentions of any financial buyer.

"They bought the entire business, but then moved our primary product line to one of their other businesses and shut the rest of our operation down."

Get to Know Your Buyer

You will want to know who your buyer is as soon as possible and certainly well before you drop your consideration of any other potential buyers. Whether you are a once-in-a-lifetime seller making a deal to exit a business you've spent years building from the ground up, or you're an entrepreneur who regularly closes deals and moves from one business to another, you're entering a high stakes game that you may just be beginning to learn the rules to, and you need to be prepared.

There are people who play this game all the time and who make their living taking advantage of people like you!

Given the stakes, don't be surprised to find that there are people who make up their own rules to the game (and who invent their own games). Selling a business—whether you sell businesses frequently or not, or whether you are looking for a strategic buyer or a financial investor—always includes an element of risk. When there are large sums of money involved, you are chumming the water and will likely attract "sharks" (the kind that will offer you a bad deal and steal your business—particularly if you show any signs of desperation to make a sale).

Selling a business—whether you sell businesses frequently or not, or whether you are looking for a strategic buyer or a financial investor—always includes an element of risk.

This is a case of "let the *seller* beware." Whether you expect to accept an "earn-out" or are seeking an investor in a business you will still own, you need to do your homework. Ask questions, do a background check, and check their references. Know who you are going into business with. Be prepared to walk away from any deal you're not comfortable with. Anticipate walking away from at least one potential buyer—maybe more. Even if you really like the sound of a deal, you cannot afford to be passively engaged in the sales process. Given the stakes, you should be prepared to drive the process, even if you seek out professional help (such as an attorney, investment banker, or a business broker) who gets paid when the deal closes, whether it's a good deal or not.

Even if you plan to exit the business at closing, some deals include a "tail," which means holding part of your payment in escrow for some period so the buyer has the chance to operate the business, verify your claims, and mitigate any risks. Before you accept these terms, you need to know who you are working with because the tail ties you to them after the closing. While they are willing to let you share the performance risk, they may be slow to pay. You need to retain the right to audit them to verify the business's performance while the tail is in effect and establish a set date for the funds to be released if there is no claim made on them.

Be Open to "Earn-Outs" and "Stock Swaps"

An "earn-out" is an agreement that lets the buyer pay the seller a percentage of the earnings of the business for a specified period of time. It is a vehicle for increasing the overall price paid for the business that allows both the buyer and the seller to share any future performance risk. It can be a device to allow a buyer to reach your asking price, and it can be a way for the buyer to raise their offer if you agree to accept some of the risk. Generally, an earn-out doesn't specify a minimum amount to be paid to the seller, but you can use this as a negotiating tool. It assumes the seller is absorbing some risk if the business fails to perform as the seller advertised it would.

> "OK, you claimed the business was going to produce this much revenue; back up your projections by keeping some skin in the game."

I have had owners say they would never accept any kind of an "earn-out." I find that extremely shortsighted. "Never" is a long, long time! Most sellers start out saying they are not interested in an "earn-out," but there are many situations where an "earn-out" makes sense, so be careful how firmly you resist accepting this type of deal. If all else is equal and you have the deal you want, then an "earn-out" is just icing on the cake. Also, when you have a buyer who is on the edge of the sale, having a seller who is willing to continue to hold onto a piece of the action and share the risk may put the odds in your favor—and be the thing that convinces them it is worth paying a little more for the business, as long as they can delay making those payments.

Let's assume you achieve your goal of finding two buyers, and they are each offering the million dollars you valued the business at. If one is also willing to offer 10 percent of earnings for the next two years above your asking price, why wouldn't you take it? Don't reject an "earn-out" off hand. Treat it as an opportunity by using it as a tool to sweeten the deal.

The same is true for stock swaps (where the buyer offers you stock in their business as partial payment). Rather than immediately rejecting a deal with a stock swap, look at the stock swap as a deal sweetener—after you get an acceptable cash offer. Don't forget to find out what stock they are offering you. It should be stock in their parent company. As part of your buyer due diligence, have your CPA review their annual report or financials of the business whose stock is being offered to in order to assess the true value of the swap.

Don't reject an "earn-out" or "stock swap" off hand. Treat it as an opportunity by using it as a tool to sweeten the deal.

If you are considering accepting an "earn-out" or a "stock swap" you should take the time to background check the buyer, because you are not only handing over control of your business to them but also agreeing to become a partner with them while the "earn-out" is in place.

If your negotiation includes an "earn-out" (that's not just icing) that allows the buyer to reach your price—for example, being paid 20 percent of earnings for three years—you will want to be sure the buyer has the experience to operate and grow the business. Your buyer's due diligence should include a review of the credentials of the new management (which may or may not be the actual buyer) because you are now betting on their performance. These deals can work for you, but you really need to keep your eyes open. In cases where the buyer is someone you know, such as a former employee taking over the business, an "earn-out" can be a powerful means of helping them while still helping you achieve your price. Make sure they agree with your "helping" them in the future, and their goal isn't just to see you gone.

A Word about Ethics

For some people, selling a business is about hiding the truth or somehow misleading potential buyers about a business's shortcomings. This sets up a "let the *buyer* beware" scenario. Hiding or falsifying information about a business is unethical and a fool's game that will likely be discovered during an effective buyer's due diligence. It will likely end, in the best case, in a blown deal and wasted time on your part as well as the buyers' part and, in the worst case, could result in expensive litigation. When problems are discovered during due diligence, the buyer may assume you knew about them and were not being up front with them. They may not walk out of the deal, but they may well lower their offer.

When problems are discovered during due diligence, the buyer may assume you knew about them and were not being up front with them.

Intentionally misleading a buyer is a stupid game to play. Even problem businesses can be sold honestly to a buyer looking for an opportunity to restore the business. Before you decide to throw out your ethics remember that, because of the widespread use of social media, reputations last a long, long time these days. The internet has made it easy to perform background checks and, if you're not planning on being honest when selling your business, you probably wasted your money in buying this book!

Be honest, take the high road and focus on identifying and demonstrating the transferrable value of your business to buyers who are looking for that value. Besides, it's nice to be able to sleep at night!

Jim's Bakery Example

Jim's Bakery was offered for sale and now had offers from three potential buyers. Jim originally wanted a straight up deal with no earn-outs; however, with an anticipated value of $20 million, he now sees anything above that as "icing on the cake." With everything else being equal, he has decided to look at the earn-outs as a discriminator in selecting a buyer.

- Buyer #1—Buyer #1 is a local competitor who has watched the growth of Jim's Bakery with envy for over a decade while trying to figure out what the key to Jim's success is. She has offered $18 million at closing with no additional earn-out and is eager to replace Jim's Bakery with her own brand in the region.
- Buyer #2—Buyer #2 is a group consisting of Jim's top-line managers, including his CFO who had been Jim's right hand man and who would now become the new president. The COOs and division managers on both the commercial and retail sides of the business will remain in their current jobs. Their offer consists of $16 million at closing and an annual payment of 20 percent of the profits of the business for the next five years (potentially worth an additional $6–$8 million over the five years). Because these employees have been loyal to Jim and helped to grow the business, he is confident they would be able to operate the business and sustain its current growth rate even if he's no longer there.
- Buyer #3—Buyer #3 is a financial investor who is seeking new opportunities in the food services industry and is planning to expand their existing portfolio of businesses with a line of bakeries. They are offering $20 million at closing plus options on an additional 50,000 shares of the new Jim's Bakery stock, worth about $5 million if executed at their current value. Buyer #3 plans to invest additional capital to greatly expand the commercial bakery and franchise the Jim's Bakery retail outlet into other regions by exploiting the Jim's Bakery brand name.

Jim will have to weigh the pros and cons of each buyer before narrowing down his selection and deciding which buyer to close a deal with. Even though the cash deal offered by Buyer #1 is tempting, Jim is suspicious that the deal will actually close. He knows of Buyer #1 from the local small business association and she has a reputation for not living up to agreements. Buyer #2 represents a group that has been loyal to Jim for years and had a direct hand in his success. He has little doubt they can continue to grow the business. Their offer may not be the best for him personally, however, because it has lower potential than Buyer #3. The business plan for Buyer #3 shows the investment of a great amount of additional capital to open five more retail stores and a large expansion of the commercial bakery through increased sales. This was a growth Jim had never envisioned. Over five years his options could be worth almost $25 million. One of the terms of the sale would be that Jim would remain as the vice president of marketing responsible for advertising his own name to help advertise the new stores.

Jim has already bought a condo at the beach so now he has a real decision to make.

Chapter 6
Marketing Your Business

If you are going to sell your business, you will need to find qualified buyers, which means you will need to find a way to effectively market your business. You need to find qualified buyers and then convince them to purchase your business instead of any others they may be considering. You need to understand where to market and how to market your business, and you need to understand the distinction between marketing the products and services of your business and marketing the business itself.

Where Are Buyers for Your Business Going to Be Found?

To begin marketing your business, you will need to identify the market where those buyers will be found. Most small business owners have trouble doing this. It amazes me how many business owners are not able to properly define a market for their business. They tend to confuse the market their product sells into with the market their business will sell into—which are usually far different from one another.

If you operate a business that develops software applications for the restaurant industry, you are not in the restaurant business.

"We develop software for restaurants, so we are in the restaurant market."

No! Your customers are in the restaurant business. You are in the software application development business. Your business is more likely to be sold to a software developer, not to a restaurant. Small business owners are usually comfortable and familiar with the target market for their products and mistakenly identify their business that way.

"I started out in the restaurant business and recognized the need for the software."

Yes, and that is when you stopped cooking and started writing code—and moved into the development market. Some owners will recognize the problem and try to answer it by saying,

"We are a restaurant supplier."

DOI 10.1515/9781547400249-006

Well that's closer to the truth but not quite the right answer. Small business owners often resist being identified outside a market they are comfortable being in and have identified with for years. Identifying with resellers in the supply chain doesn't help them (although the resellers may eventually become a source of leads).

"What specials are you running on wholesale vegetables this week?"

"Can I get a new frying pan from you?"

You are indeed in the restaurant supply chain, but you are not a restaurant supplier. You may sell through restaurant suppliers, but you don't have your own catalog of restaurant supplies. Someone who does have a catalog of restaurant supplies is not going to buy your business either. The prime target for selling your business is most likely to be an investor or application developer looking for a new software product or trying to expand in the restaurant software market. It will not be a restaurant or a restaurant supplier.

Small business owners often resist being identified outside a market they are comfortable being in and have identified with for years.

If you're still having trouble making this distinction between the market your products sell into and the market where a buyer for your business will be found, try thinking about the geographic area where your products are sold vs. the geographic area a strategic buyer for your business might be found. For example, in the case of an application developer for the restaurant business, restaurant patrons come from a regional territory (the communities that surround the restaurant), but an application developer that sells to restaurants would sell to restaurants across the country, so the business is in a national or even global market.

"Our restaurant clients draw their patrons from the surrounding communities, but we sell to restaurants all over the country."

A restaurants market is limited to the communities that surround them. The market for a development business is national. The distinction is an important one because you don't want to constrain the search for buyers for your business to the smaller market. If you run a wholesale business and sell products regionally, then your immediate market extends throughout that region. If you sell to customers throughout the state, across the country, or globally, then your market extends to those areas. The market you need to look for buyers in is defined by the territory your business sells products into. This may also be argued to be your minimum market. It is possible for buyers to come from beyond this market, trying to buy into it. When you are establishing your marketing budget, you may want to consider reaching further than this immediate market.

The market you need to look for buyers of your business in is defined by the territory you sell products into.

How Will You Market Your Business?

Now that you spent some time thinking about who you will sell your business to, you need to consider how you are going to reach out to that market. For most businesses it is better if your marketing is done quietly. This is different than most product marketing efforts where you want to make as big of a splash in the market as possible. I assume you have had plenty of experience with product marketing. That is why you were successful. But how much experience do you have marketing a business?

Getting Professional Help

You may have a contact list with the private numbers for most of the other owners in the industry, and you may know some of them personally. You may even golf with them or meet them at the club or other social events regularly but keep this in mind. You are the face of your business. If you talk to them about buying your business, you stand a great chance of devaluing your deal. Even if you are great friends with someone who was your college roommate, you may not be the right person to negotiate your best deal. You may get a deal and save paying someone a commission on the deal, but it may cost you a lot in the end. Maybe you're looking for more than one strategic buyer or an investor (or group of investors) who have the resources to back your strategic vision. Knowing when and how to reveal that you are selling your business or when and how to reveal your strategic plans means first finding the right buyers and then managing the disclosure process. You need an intermediary.

If you are serious about selling your business, you need to seriously consider seeking professional help. These experienced professionals will conduct a stealthy marketing campaign and will act as an intermediary in your negotiations. These are people who know when and how to reveal information about your business to potential buyers. There are different types of professionals who can assist you, depending on the size and type of deal you are seeking. We will talk about professionals more in chapter 16. As with most things in business you will need to decide whether the trade-off between their fees and the services they provide is worth it. But keep in mind, marketing your business is one of the primary services they provide; this is why you want this type of help.

If you are serious about selling your business, you need to seek professional help. These experienced professionals will conduct a stealthy marketing campaign and will act as an intermediary in your negotiations.

Selecting a Sales Agent/Intermediary

The types of sales agents and professionals and the role they will play are described in chapter 16. While you are interviewing these professionals it's a good time to find out what type of working relationship you will have with them as your sales agent. Are they listening to you and making valid observations and suggestions, or are they telling you what to do? Make sure they are prepared to give their best resources and attention for a deal of your size. They may play a critical role, but they work for you and are there to support you.

Don't hesitate to negotiate with them. Do you need them to do everything they are offering, or are there some things you can accomplish on your own? Some agencies will not take on smaller deals or, worse, will hand them over to junior representatives and let them get trained by learning lessons at your expense. Remember, the sales process is yours. One of the questions you should ask is,

"Who will be working on my sale?"

Business intermediaries work on commission and larger sales will get more attention. Is that top sales broker or banker you first met going to be the one working on your project, or will you be pushed off to a new agent or entry level rep with little to no experience?

After selecting a broker or banker—your agent—to act as an intermediary/ agent to represent you, they will ask you to sign an agreement listing your business for sale with them. One of the first discussions you need to have with your agent will be whether to list your business publicly (e.g., by putting a sign out front and posting the sale in online bulletin boards) or quietly (e.g., by conducting a stealth marketing campaign your customers won't be aware of). Listen to their recommendations and be sure you agree with their advice before signing an agreement. The listing will be for a specified period and should be performance based (that is, the agent will get paid when you sell your business). Occasionally a small nonrefundable upfront fee will be charged to cover material expenses. These fees also help to keep their clients from "agent hopping."

These agreements are generally written to protect the agent, so read your agreement carefully and be sure you understand all its terms. For instance, in a typical agreement, if they fail to sell the business, any contacts they bring to you during the listing period will remain their contact only. If you should drop them at the end of the listing period, they will be due a commission *if* a buyer they introduced to you decides to return later—even if the agent failed to negotiate an acceptable deal. They won't agree to drop this term (or others), so be sure you understand all the terms and use care not to violate them. You don't want to end up in a position where you could owe two commissions! You want to establish a strong working relationship with your agent. If the relationship becomes antagonistic (which is unusual), you have the wrong person working for you.

One term you should insist on is the retention of ownership of all materials related to your business. The cost for printing marketing materials can be high. Make sure your listing agreement defines who pays the cost for producing the marketing materials. Also, be sure it's clear who owns this material in case you decide at some point to find another agent. You don't want to have any constraints on the use of these materials in the future. The cost for printing marketing materials can be high. Make sure your listing agreement defines who owns the rights to this material in case you decide at some point to find another agent.

Having Your Say

Whether you take it upon yourself to market your business or you decide to hire a professional, at some point in time prospective buyers will want to hear directly from you. They will want to hear what you have to say and be able to ask you questions about your business. And, as you are having these conversations with potential buyers, you will need to be able to effectively answer their questions. Part of the positioning activities you will be going through will help prepare you with the information to provide those answers. You are the face of your business, and the impression you give buyers will have an impact on their impression of your business.

At this point you will need to have your marketing hat on. You will need to know what information to present to a prospective buyer and how to present it. Many small business owners are not good presenters. It's just not what they do. If this describes you, then you will need to overcome the problem. The way to do that is to prepare what you will say, and practice, practice, practice. Even if you are a comfortable speaker, then I offer the same advice. Prepare a brief ten-minute presentation and a thirty-minute presentation to be given to a small group of people. The exception to this is when you are fund raising. That presentation may be done in front of a much larger group. Have someone who will be honest with you listen to your presentation and make recommendations to improve it. I use my wife. She is generally willing to point out where I need improvement!

Marketing Materials

Marketing material must be created to support your marketing campaign, and this material will target two distinct audiences. One will be a one-page handout that provides an overview of your business that can be given to potential buyers who express a general interest, and the other is your "Book," which provides a greater level of detail in the form of a business plan for prospective buyers who express a specific interest in purchasing your business. The level of detail in these documents is carefully crafted to provide sufficient information to draw buyers' interest while limiting the level of detail you are providing to the public (including your customers, employees, and competitors). The requirements for creating these documents are covered in detail in chapter 13 and examples are provided in Appendix A and Appendix B. The material for these documents are the product of the positioning activities in the chapters that follow.

Market Relevance

All statistics are good statistics; at least that seems to be what many small business owners believe. They make the common mistake of using statistics that aren't relevant to their business in their oral presentations to prospective buyers and in their printed marketing materials.

> "There will be 2,500 new bakeries opened in the state this year."

Well, can you tell me how many are opening in this town next year? The buyer's response, even if not stated directly, will be "who cares." You must be prepared to describe market statistics that are useful to potential buyers, and you need to be sure the description is relevant to your business. Don't spout out statistics that don't relate directly to your business.

> "The demand for our baked goods continues to grow because the global demand for baked goods has gone up by 20 percent."

This kind of statement is just not relevant. Who cares what the global demand is, when the market for your business is only relevant in your town? By making the statistics you use more relevant, you provide a stronger argument that a buyer can hold onto (and use later).

> "The demand for baked goods in our retail bakery has continued to grow because there are 2,000 new families moving to our town each month."

This is a useful statistic because it is directly relevant and provides useful information a potential buyer can take to their bank if need be. Owners like to spout facts because it is a way of telling a buyer "I know my stuff" instead of providing information that supports the buyer's decision. If you want to show a buyer you "know your stuff," use relevant "stuff." Keep in mind that the potential buyer will very likely reuse your business plan and metrics when speaking with their partners and backers.

Be prepared to clearly state why your business model works in this market and then demonstrate that you understand the relevance of the market statistic. These statements can also be used as a "door opener," because they allow you to add growth opportunity statements such as:

> "And this business could be expanded to the next town or other regions."

Although you may have never acted on these growth ideas, you can now use them as an opportunity to plant the seeds of a potential idea the buyer may not have considered yet.

If your business has a national footprint, go ahead and use national demographics, but if you are a local business, make relevant, local demographics work for you. If you operate an automobile dealership, you no doubt know the technical specifications of the cars you sell, and you know how to market the cars by finding creative ways to advertise them as sexy, efficient, or affordable transportation. If you're trying to sell your dealership, you need to know the demographics of your customers, how many other dealerships there are in the area, and which local banks will finance your sales.

> "We're in a rural area so we sell a lot of pickup trucks through the local Farmers Exchange Bank."

You're looking for a different buyer for the dealership than you are for your cars. Explaining the demographics to a potential buyer provides rationale for the value of your business and tells them why your business emphasizes the sale of pickup trucks with customers who then return to buy their next vehicle.

"Because of our access to multiple fiber optic carriers, our data center provides virtual servers and hosting for customers throughout the state."

"We provide electric scooters on a temporary basis for visitors to the local attractions, which allows us to charge more for short-term rentals than we would for long-term rentals."

Your marketing strategy and business model need to go "hand in hand." This connection may not be obvious to potential buyers, and you may need to be prepared to point it out. (More on business models in chapter 11.) The statistics you use should be relevant to your business model and support your rationale for using that model. Your use of statistics should explain why your business model works and, more importantly, why it gives your business a discriminator over your competition. The following isn't a relevant statement.

"Buying our pizza shop is a good investment because there is going to be a 10 percent growth in pizza shops nationally."

The following statement has much more relevance because it cites a metric that has direct relevance for a buyer. The metric is easily verifiable and tells a potential buyer where the opportunity will be for the business in the future.

"Buying our pizza shop is a good investment because, based on open building permits, the local economic development council (EDC) projects a 10 percent increase in new families in the neighborhoods immediately surrounding our location."

The statistics you use should be relevant to your business model and support your rationale for using that model.

The internet provides a wealth of interesting information, including market reports from the world's top researchers, but a buyer won't care unless the information relates directly to your business. If your business sells to a national market, then an industry report—particularly one that names your business or products and discusses the growth in the industry—would be highly relevant.

Citing third-party references is important. "I think" is not a relevant or useful statement unless you are an acknowledged expert. A buyer knows you are in the "sell mode" and will automatically discount your opinion. Prepare by searching for relevant, third-party references that describe your market and competition.

"According to Investor's Business Daily there is a strong national movement by larger corporations to gain market share by buying early stage cloud software development businesses."

Know Your Competition

Knowing who your competitors are and being prepared to explain the competitive discriminators between your business and the competitors in your market helps to build buyer confidence and tells a potential buyer not only how strong the market for your products and services will be but why customers will buy from you before the competition.

Your list of competitors doesn't need to be extensive. Pick your closest three or four competitors and be prepared to explain why customers prefer your business over others. Think about the message you are giving a potential buyer. Occasionally I hear a business owner say,

> "We are the only business in this market and have no competition."

Instead of being a discriminator to buy the business this can be a "bell ringing" statement that scares the buyer away. The logical question becomes,

> "Well why are you the only bakery in town?"

We are the only business in town is not a good answer. It draws questions and leads a potential buyer to wonder if the town is too small to support two similar businesses—or even one. Hmmm. . .. Maybe that's why you're selling. Ding, ding, ding! I can hear the warning bell ringing as your deal dies. You better have some information ready!

> "The town grew by 15 percent last year and we are the only bakery in town, which means we are well positioned to capture the market."

If you claim to be the only business offering a product or service, be prepared to defend that position. Of course, there are occasions when you *are* the only business in the market. Most buyers would prefer to hear there are competitors, but maybe you have gained some defendable market advantage over the competition.

> "We have a breakthrough innovative product and have captured the intellectual property for it."

> "There were two bakeries in town, but two years ago we bought out the other one and opened our second store."

Be sure to remain professional whenever you describe your competition. Be sure to take the high road when describing your competition.

> "Oh, those guys treat their customers like #$@#, and everyone knows it."

Negative, personal comments may lead a buyer to see you as #$@#. In some industries word gets around quickly, so your reputation may suffer. No matter what your history is with a competitor, the buyer doesn't share that experience and there is no reason to bring it into your deal.

> "We have been working to grow our reputation for customer support by building greater rapport with our customers."

Point out the positives of your products and let comments about the competition be implied but unspoken. It's called "ghosting." You ghost your competition by pointing out their weaknesses without specifically mentioning them by name, prompting the buyer to recognize their competitive weaknesses (and ask them the tough questions).

> "Our product has won the national XYZ award for innovation."

Provide the questions you want the buyer to ask by letting someone else speak for the competition. Of course, you hope to be speaking with strategic buyers, so your potential buyer may be one of those competitors. Be careful not to become defensive if they don't see the market quite the same way and always be truthful.

If you think there is a real advantage to directly using your competitors name, one of the simplest ways to convey your strength in the market is with the generation of a bulleted functionality matrix (Figure 6.1). By using a functionality matrix like this, you can remain professional while directly comparing the features of your business or product with those of the competition. Be sure to use care with this approach, because it carries a level of risk. You must do your homework and ensure that the competitive statements you make are absolutely correct. Don't go by industry rumors or statements made by disgruntled past employees. A competitive matrix not only tells a buyer what the strengths of your business are; it gives them a ghosted message about the weaknesses of your competition. A good approach is to use functionality the competition states publicly on their website.

	Competitor 1	Competitor 2	Competitor 3	Your Business
Feature1	X			X
Feature 2	X	X		X
Feature 3	X		X	X
Feature 4		X	X	X
Feature 5		X	X	X

Figure 6.1: Competitive Matrix

Markets Are Dynamic

Markets are dynamic and change constantly. A market that is strong today can be gone tomorrow. Business buyers are leery of market change. The transferrable value of a business and the eventual valuation it receives are usually tied to the growth of the market its products sell into. This is particularly true of technical markets, such as manufacturing businesses and software development businesses, where today's hot product can become tomorrows "has been" overnight. This can make technical market leaders quickly turn into loss leaders—they are successful in kicking down a new door only to have competitors rush through that door with new features and product discriminators while the market leader is still trying to get their original bugs out. Market vision is often twenty/twenty for a competitor who can use your product as a model to grow their business.

Also, pointing out your market vision to a potential buyer will give you the opportunity to ghost the fact that your competition is still trying to catch up with you while you have already moved on to your next generation product. To do this you will need to predict what the future path is for your product, say where you see the market is going, and state your plan to stay one step ahead of the competition—particularly when your revenue growth curve is predicting a "hockey stick" in sales growth that you are using to justify a higher valuation. You need to have a plan for generating the increased sales leads that will be needed. Without a solid marketing plan, your predictions may not have much credibility. You don't need a crystal ball to make these predictions. You need a well-thought-out strategic path that continues to drive the market. Your goal is to add transferrable value to your business by establishing a track record as a market leader which is a sure way to justify an increased valuation.

Your goal is to add transferrable value to your business by establishing a track record as a market leader which is a sure way to justify an increased valuation.

To repeat an earlier caution: there is real danger when the potential buyer you are speaking with is a strategic buyer, particularly when they are one of your direct competitors. You need to balance the scales between exposing your plans to someone who is not really interested in buying your business but is using your sale as a competitive fact-finding trip to gather information about your business. They are hoping you will divulge the strong value drivers for your business so they can use them or the fact that you are for sale against you.

Your Business Is for Sale. Shhhh, Be Quiet, Shut up!

There are businesses that can be marketed by simply putting a "For Sale" sign by the curb or by posting an advertisement in an online bulletin board and then, after the sale, putting up a sign saying, "under new management" (which might be an asset in some cases). There are also businesses where that type of advertising would be ineffective and put the new owner out of business, because their customers would leave as soon as they heard about the sale. In most businesses, customers, particularly B2B customers, value business continuity. "Under new management" devalues the business.

If your business has gained a good reputation, if you are a critical supplier for other businesses, if your suppliers have given you deals based on years of established credit, they will see a new owner as a risk to their business. This may be a risk they are not willing to accept. There are a lot of reasons to make marketing your business a stealth activity. Imagine what your competition will say to your customers if your business includes recurring customer sales or long-term maintenance support. Customers may not be willing to pay the price for your products if they think you may not be there to support them in the future. You can bet your competition won't hesitate to turn this information into a discriminator for buying their products.

> "They have a great product, but their business is for sale. We're even talking about buying them, but no one really knows what they're doing. You can count on us to be here in the future when you need help."

A potential buyer will also understand the impact the sale of your business will have with those customers. The buyer will want to manage how that information is released and most likely want to make their own announcement at a time they find appropriate. If you jump the gun and make the sale public knowledge, then you have taken some advantage away from your buyer, which is another potential deal killer and a negotiating item they could claim devalued the business. Expect the timing and type of announcement of the sale to become a term of your deal, and don't risk the deal by making a premature announcement.

Expect the timing and type of announcement of the sale to become a term of your deal, and don't risk the deal by making a premature announcement.

Remember that people connect you with your business. You cannot have a beer at the club and have a discussion about the sale of your business because "keep this between us" never remains "keep this between us." Your best approach in discussing the sale of your business is shut up!

And then there is that pesky cousin Jake that works for you and who finally understands he can't afford to buy the business from you. He met one of your competitors at a trade show and thinks if he tells them he heard at a family barbeque that your business might be for sale he will be getting himself in good with a potential new boss. "I can set up a meeting for you with Jim." Nondisclosure agreement—what NDA?

Down Select

The goal of marketing is to identify qualified buyers. At some point you will have a list of qualified buyers to choose from. Even though this is where your active marketing campaign will end you will still need to have your marketing hat on for a bit. At this point you will begin to meet with each of these buyers, and while they are asking you about your business, you will be getting to know them. If you have had a professional working with you to market your business, they will be doing the research to determine who the buyers are and to ensure that they are qualified and have the resources to close a deal with you.

Following this you will ideally have a short list of qualified buyers to choose from. At least, this is the goal. In most cases you won't end up with a line of potential buyers going around the corner, but you hopefully have met your original goal of finding at least two qualified strategic buyers. If you end up with a mix of financial buyers as well as strategic buyers, that is okay because it will add some price pressure to the offers. The reality is that getting to the short list of the two buyers you started out to find is a significant accomplishment. If you get more than two you are ahead of the game. If you only have one buyer, you may be under a lot of pressure to go ahead and make the deal; hold out as long as you can and continue looking for that second buyer. Board members, creditors, the intermediary who is working for you, and even your wife who is eager to make the move to the beach may all want you to go ahead with the deal.

If you only have one buyer, you may be under a lot of pressure to go ahead and make the deal; hold out as long as you can and continue looking for that second buyer.

Your conversation with each potential buyer should quickly reveal which buyers have a true interest in your business; it will likely end with them making an offer, either verbally or in writing. Buyers will try to avoid being in an auction situation and will make their offer valid for a short period. Assuming you are speaking with multiple potential buyers, you will need to be open with all of them that you are "entertaining other offers." If you have not gotten interest from multiple buyers then you will need to decide when to stop marketing your business and resolve whether or not to move ahead and make a deal with the one you have in hand. It can be difficult to discontinue looking for additional buyers for offers when the beach is calling to you, so these can be tough decisions, particularly if the offers you get are significantly below the price you are seeking. It is okay to let potential buyers know you are speaking with other potential buyers but, since you should be under a nondisclosure agreement with each, you cannot and should not let them know who else you are speaking with or details from those discussions.

This down select process may be iterative, but at some point, with advice from your intermediary, you are going to have to decide when to end the marketing process and proceed with the qualified buyers you received offers from. It is time to down select to just one. Next you will ask them for their best and final offer (called a BAFO). After you receive their best offer, you can (and will) try to negotiate to try to improve that offer.

> "Yes, we received your final offer, but we would like you to consider adding an earn-out to get the offer where we can accept it."

This is one of those times where having a professional intermediary will be of great help. Listen to them and take their advice. This activity will end once you and a potential buyer have closed on the terms of your deal. These terms will be captured in a letter of intent (LOI). The LOI is a nonbinding agreement that now defines them as your sole buyer. Following this point, they will be ready to perform a detailed assessment of your business to verify that your claims about the business are valid.

Now you are ready to enter negotiations with the potential buyer. Your negotiations will include the price and any terms specified by either you or the buyer. The price and agreement about the form of payment (cash, stock, earn-out, etc.) and a schedule of any funds being held in escrow after closing, along with the conditions for the release of escrow, should be stated as terms. If you are going to remain with the business in any capacity, your compensation and employment agreement should also be included and stipulated as a term. Whether the potential buyer is a stranger, a close friend, or your cousin Jake, there should be no understanding of terms or side agreements that are not documented.

The buyer should capture all the negotiated terms and conditions from both parties and include them in their draft letter of intent. Review it carefully. It's not done until you agree it's done. If you find you have remaining questions or concerns, now is the time to raise them.

> "I was thinking about this before closing but hesitated to raise it and make it an issue since I knew I would have to work with these guys later."

Really! Now is the time. It won't get better once you're no longer running the business or working for them.

The Single Buyer Slump

If you have been hanging on, hoping for a buyer, but only one has come forward with an offer, you have a decision to make. You will need to decide to accept the offer, wait for another buyer to come along, or go back to chapter 1 and start over.

Preferably you will keep pushing to find that second buyer, but you will need to decide how long to wait. Some businesses are difficult and take time to sell no matter how much preparation work you do to get them ready. Make sure your sales agent is aware of your goal to find at least two qualified buyers well before you get to this point. They may want to push ahead with the sale immediately, once they have a buyer in hand, at a time when you want them to increase their marketing activities.

The location, the industry, the economy—are all external factors that can influence the sale. There is never a guarantee of success. Try to get as much feedback as possible and then step back and try to honestly understand why buyers haven't seen the transferrable value you believed was there. If it's a difficult market, you may need to allow more time.

Some businesses are difficult and take time to sell no matter how much preparation work you do to get them ready.

Jim's Bakery Example

Jim's Bakery has two divisions: the retail division—which was Jim's original store and sells to local customers in his town—and the commercial division—which sells to businesses on a regional basis. Jim's original thought was that he would have to sell the two divisions separately, looking locally for a retail buyer and regionally for a commercial buyer, but the operations of the two divisions were very interdependent and separating them would be difficult.

Jim met with several investment bankers and selected one that recommended that splitting the financial administration of the divisions would add a significant additional overhead that would have a negative effect on both divisions. He showed him that the value of the whole would be greater than the value of the parts—a fact Jim had not considered until they ran the financial adjustments for both scenarios. This understanding resulted in an increased valuation that more than covered the banker's fees. With that information in hand, the investment banker started meeting with potential commercial banker clients and eventually found buyers interested in both divisions. One was a strategic buyer interested in growing the business by opening additional retail shops throughout the region; one was a local baker who wanted to merge Jim's Bakery into their own operation (the banker advised Jim that this buyer was not qualified because they didn't have the resources needed to close the deal); and a financial investor who knew the reputation of Jim's Bakery and wanted to join what they believed was a sound investment.

Even though Jim has hired a professional—an investment banker—to help him market his business, he has now met with each of the potential buyers and answered their questions about his business and the potential strategic path opportunities he sees for it. He has down selected to a single buyer, whom he negotiated with to get better terms, and has now signed an LOI with that buyer.

Chapter 7
Preparing for a Due Diligence Financial Assessment

Once you have completed the down select and identified your buyer, you need to be prepared to let that buyer see and assess your business in operation—at its fully optimized best. In this chapter and the two that follow we will discuss the positioning process, which are the activities used to prepare your business for each of the buyer's due diligence assessments. As the term "positioning" implies, you are moving your business (figuratively) to improve its operations, because that is how you have planned to maximize its value. The goal of positioning is to make your business operate as efficiently as possible and by doing that, you are preparing it for due diligence. To have a successful due diligence, you need to make the changes that will help demonstrate the full potential and value of the business and will show the buyer that it is worth the price they are paying.

Unless your business is a "food truck," I am not talking about physically relocating your business (I'm not ruling that out either, if there is an argument that can be made for such a move). I'm talking about moving it to an improved level of operation.

> "Most buyers are looking for a restaurant with an extremely clean kitchen, so we changed our cleaning schedule and hired a specialized restaurant cleaning service."

During due diligence the buyer will assess in detail all aspects of your business while it is in operation. The more efficient those operations are, the greater the value the buyer will place on the business. To make sure you get the greatest value for your business, you will need the buyer's due diligence assessments not just to just go well; you need them to be a home run. Before we talk about the due diligence process itself, let's talk about how to prepare for the due diligence event.

To make sure you get the greatest value for your business, you will need the buyer's due diligence assessments not just to just go well; you need them to be a home run.

So, let's dig right in!

DOI 10.1515/9781547400249-007

If You Want to Sell Your Business Get Your Head out of the Financial Sand

If you came to this chapter expecting to find detailed charts and graphs with recommendations about the format of your financial reports or improving your profit and loss ratios, you'll be disappointed. There are any number of great accounting books available to answer those questions. My goal here is to help you improve your numbers, not just improve the way they are reported. Most owners can sense how their business is doing, even before they have the detail from the financial reports.

Financial reporting is one of the key areas where buyers will look at the maturity of your business. For very small businesses, the owners often start off keeping the checkbook themselves and only visiting an accountant at tax time. Larger small businesses may grow to the point where they have a finance department and an in-house CPA who functions as their CFO. The financial maturity of the business doesn't always keep up with its growth, which will become very apparent during due diligence. You will need to look at your business honestly as part of your preparation for a buyer's financial assessment. I generally recommend that my clients try to kick it up a level by implementing a financial infrastructure that will support their business at the next level. The rational for this is simple— you should be planning for your next level of growth and positioning your business to demonstrate that to a buyer.

In my consulting business, I often work with business owners who have an uncanny ability to understand the complex financial reports of their business, asking detailed questions in their monthly reviews that drive their bookkeepers, accountants, and CFOs to the edge.

"How did he know to ask that?"

I also work with owners who have risen through the ranks in their industry and are acknowledged subject matter experts at what they do, but who are absolutely bored to tears when they are required to attend financial reviews or review financial reports. They barely understand what their financial reports are telling them without an interpreter to explain what the reports mean. I've also seen both types succeed, sometimes despite themselves, and I've seen both types fail, despite their best efforts.

"I'll figure out how to make the technology work, you tell me if I'm making money."

My rule is simple. If you expect to sell your business, then don't treat it like it's a hobby.

If you operate a business with transferrable value, and you expect someone to be willing to buy it, then you will have to demonstrate that value to them. You need to regularly create and review your financial reports, meaning you should already have the financial data ready to present to a buyer. Financial data must be accurate and easy to interpret. What you present to a buyer can reveal a lot about your management style and ability. Relax and do the work necessary to have your financials prepared so they work for you and not against you; if you're not prepared to explain them, get someone who is able to help you.

Even if that data isn't in an optimal format to support the sale at this time, the data should already exist in some form. You need to gather the data and prepare it to be reviewed by your buyer. Whether you are intimately familiar with your business financials or are simply sitting through the reviews trying to keep up, your financial reports will be core to getting your deal done.

If you expect to sell your business, then don't treat it like it's a hobby.

Small business owners have a wide range of financial skills and use different management and reporting methods. Some owners are absolutely by the book financial managers who insist on a formalized financial management system, including a monthly income statement, balance sheet, and cash flow report prepared and reviewed regularly with their management team. These reports are tools used by management for their day-to-day operations decisions to help management identify trends and make sound financial predictions. In larger, more mature organizations, financial decisions can be delegated in this manner. Other methods, unfortunately common in many smaller businesses, are much less formal and are far less rigorous. There are owners who look almost exclusively at cash flow and others who manage by the shoe box method (they throw all their receipts in a shoebox and, if there is money in the bank after emptying the box and paying the payroll and bills, they are happy).

I am not endorsing either style. If your goal is to sell your business and get the maximum return for it, then it's time to apply some rigor in the generation of your financial reports. This may mean changing your financial operations going forward and (yikes!) re-creating and documenting some history. You will need to be prepared with at least three years of past monthly financial reports to satisfy most serious buyers.

You will need to be prepared with at least three years of past monthly financial reports to satisfy most serious buyers.

Unfortunately, preparing financial reports to be given to someone else to review is a task some small business owners fear enough to make them hesitate even putting their business up for sale. Some larger small businesses have similar problems producing past reports; just different rationale for not having the data.

> "We've never worried about preparing those reports and I wouldn't know where to begin, so maybe our business just can't be sold."

> "Our financial system isn't capable of going back that far."

These are all owners who fear discovery because they know it may disclose that the past performance of their business wasn't stellar (or their lack of understanding about how to read those reports will be exposed), or it may show their lack of financial maturity as the business grew. While they know they can't avoid it, they want to delay any financial discussions with a buyer as long as possible. Their hesitancy to discuss their numbers with a buyer could result in even more questions than answers. Get busy and start trying to recreate those reports for the last three years and put a system in place to produce reports every month going forward.

> "I requested a copy of their financials for the last three years but they're hesitating to provide them. What are they trying to hide?"

If you don't regularly review your financials and your financial data isn't readily available, then you have work to do. Financial archeology requires a lot of digging that will absolutely be required if you intend to sell your business. Be thorough, be accurate, and be as honest as possible. If you need to make assumptions to reconstruct your financials, be sure to document those assumptions. In these situations, worse case assumptions are easier to defend than best case assumptions. Give yourself credit by "taking the high road" when you make assumptions.

> "This is a worst-case assumption."

> "I no longer have our past utility bills, but I know the rates have gone up so I'm estimating the past expense using our current bills and assuming them as a worst case."

Warning: Nothing in this chapter is intended to reduce, replace, or discourage you from hiring a qualified CPA to advise you on the sale of your business.

Unfortunately, what many small businesses use as financials are actually cash flow statements and don't meet the standard of a true balance sheet or income statement. For that reason, the bookkeeper used by many small businesses to support their day-to-day operations is generally not the person they should use to prepare the detailed financial reports needed to support a buyer's financial due diligence. Your bookkeeper should be available to answer questions, provide the raw financial data, and support the CPA you will need to hire to correctly prepare the reports. Look for a CPA that has business transaction experience that matches deals the size of yours.

What many small businesses use as financials are actually cash flow statements and don't meet the standard of a true balance sheet or income statement.

If you can't provide even the raw financial data, your business may not be salable at this time. Waiting to sell until you are able to hire someone to implement a financial system that will be able to produce verifiable financials is a smarter business decision. Don't wait to find a CPA. The sooner you get one in place the sooner you will know how large of a problem you might have.

Putting your Financial House in Order

Even if you are one of those who treat their business like a business—meaning you have all the financial data you will need (or you have collected it since reading the last paragraph)—your financial positioning will still require formatting and recasting (making acceptable adjustments) to your financial reports, optimally for at least the last three years of operation, so that they can be presented to a buyer.

Financial reports need to be self-explanatory and easy to read to determine the past performance of the business. They should answer questions without the need for further explanation. You don't want your financials to become the source of additional questions. Reformatting and recasting of your financials should never be treated as an opportunity (or suggestion) to create an alternate set of books. This means you will need to use the past performance data as it exists— good, bad, or ugly—in the reports.

Financial reports need to be self-explanatory and easy to read to determine the past performance of the business.

Reformatting of your financial reports is done to put your current (and correct) financial information into an acceptable, standardized format that can be reviewed by the buyer's financial team—your CPA and theirs may need to be able to "mind meld"[1] to come to a common understanding about the financial data you provide.

Plan to provide a clean, freshly bound set of financial reports that a potential buyer can use to support their financial due diligence assessment. Ideally, your CFO or accountant is accustomed to preparing these reports as part of your normal operations and can produce them at any point for your own use. If you review your financials each month, supporting a buyer's financial due diligence shouldn't be a problem. Financial due diligence allows the buyer to analyze and validate your financial data to gain as true an understanding of the fiscal performance of your business as possible, so you must be prepared for the assessment. You cannot put this task off until the start of due diligence while hoping the buyer won't request the information. They will, so get busy. You can't afford to start stuttering when the buyer begins asking financial questions because it may appear you are trying to hide something.

> "Why doesn't she know what it costs to deliver that product, and why is she hesitating to give us a straight answer to our questions?"

If you don't know the answer to a financial question, try not to leave it floating. Send someone to get an answer as soon as possible; don't appear to avoid the question.

> "I don't have an immediate answer, but I will have it for you by tomorrow morning."

As a continuing financial operating practice your accountant or CFO should archive copies of each monthly balance sheet and income statement. If this isn't already one of your established business practices, this is a good time to start (and yes, prepare to enter the data for the last three years, month by month, if you don't have them). These reports can be produced using a spreadsheet, but basic accounting software, which is relatively inexpensive these days, really makes life easier. The method used to produce the report isn't as important as the accuracy of the reports you produce.

Small businesses that do their fiscal management strictly by watching their cash flow frequently run into financial due diligence problems. Avoid those problems by preparing now. Unfortunately, the conclusion a potential buyer may reach

---

1 The fictional "Vulcan mind meld" was a telepathic link between two individuals (e.g., "Dagger of the Mind," *Star Trek*, season 1, episode 9, directed by Vincent McEveety, written by S. Bar-David, first aired November 3, 1966).

is that you are trying to hide something (or worse, that you are not smart enough to read a standard report; either of these conclusions could kill your deal!). The quality of your financial reports and the accuracy of the data you provide will tell buyers a lot about the way your business has been operated (and may drive how they perceive your management skills) and could impact the value they place on your business. Keep this in mind if you are considering working for them following an acquisition. If you, or someone on your transition team, doesn't have an accounting background, spend a little money and hire a professional to prepare your financials.

Financial reports should not be prepared solely to get you through the financial due diligence assessment. If you are operating a business and not a hobby, there is no excuse for not knowing how to read a profit and loss (P&L) report or a balance sheet, so stop making excuses. I suggest reading *How to Read a Financial Report* by John A. Tracy.[2] There are usually inexpensive basic courses offered at most community colleges. By providing standard financial reports in a format familiar to a buyer, you are protecting your own credibility and removing the need to explain your accounting system or to explain its uniqueness. If you are not able to present these reports, then any accountant can help you and will be worth what you pay them. You must be prepared with the following reports:

- P&L reports capture the (actual) sales revenue and the incurred (actual) expenses of the business for a given period of time. The P&L report summarizes the performance of the business, generally on a month-by-month basis.
- The balance sheet summarizes the assets and liabilities of the business at a specified point in time. Assets include the means of production, such as the equipment and facilities used, and liabilities including payables, such as the amounts owed to suppliers. The balance sheet can be used as an indicator that the business is either under- or over-capitalized, supporting strategic decisions about the allocation of resources needed to support future plans, and is therefore of great interest to a buyer. For instance; did the business sell critical automation equipment recently to boost its cash reserves as part of its positioning for investors (a short-term tactical decision but not a good strategic decision)?
- The cash flow statement shows the cash reserves available to support the operations of the business. This report reveals a lot about the day-to-day fiscal management of the business. If it includes historic data (at least the prior

---

2 John A. Tracy, *How to Read a Financial Report: Wringing Vital Signs out of Numbers*, 6th ed.(Hoboken, NJ: John Wiley, 2004).

year's operations), it is an indicator of how well the business has planned and managed its cash.
– Make sure your accountant is ready to address issues such as bad debt (money that is owed to your business that cannot be collected for some reason) and asset depreciation (the declining value of assets shown on your balance sheet).

The Dichotomy Dilemma

The natural tendency in any business is to try to minimize the taxable income of the business by minimizing the earnings they will be required to pay taxes on. There are some owners however who attempt to avoid taxes by not declaring all their income. This is of course illegal, but what those who do this don't recognize, at least not at first, is that they are cheating themselves along with the government. Many small business owners learn this lesson early in the operation of their business. One day the business will eventually grow to the point where they turn to a bank for a business loan. The conversation with the bank will be short and go like this:

> "Can we have a copy of your tax returns for the past three years?"

And then the owner is surprised when they hear,

> "Gee, these returns don't justify all the income you listed. Loan denied."

This is when it dawns on them that they have been playing a fool's game.

The dichotomy occurs because, when they eventually reach the point where they want to sell their business, they want to do just the opposite. Now they want to justify maximizing all the income they possibly can and lowering the expenses. When they're selling their business, their goal is to try to maximize as much income as possible to get the greatest possible valuation for their business. A natural dichotomy exists between what owners declare on their taxes and what they are trying to state as actual income to the buyer. Note, I am not referring to valid, ethical recasting of their financials, which I will get to later in this chapter, but to an ethical issue that many small business owners face. This is the point where some small business owners end up with brown stuff on their faces and look like they have been "throwing stones at the outhouse."

A natural dichotomy exists between what owners declare on their taxes and what they are trying to state as actual income to the buyer.

So, you are a risk taker and your business has been doing well. You explain to your friends (with a wink and a nod) that it is a cash business and you bring in four times what you claim for tax purposes. They nod and think, "man, he sure is clever." But you are about to find out that clever person just outsmarted himself. They may have trapped themselves into devaluing their business. Let's say, for a simplified example, your cash business brought in $1,000,000 a year for the past three years. You, being a shady owner, only declared $250,000 of that. At a rate of 30% × (1,000,000 − 250,000), you saved $225,000 in taxes. Quite a savings, right! Let's continue the example. Suppose when businesses like yours are sold they are getting a multiple of roughly four times revenue. During due diligence your buyer asks for your tax returns for the last three years. 4 × $250,000 = a price of $1,000,000. Congratulations. Suppose however you had declared your true revenue: 4 × $1,000,000 = a price of $4,000,000. That $225,000 you saved just cost you $3,000,000. Was that a wink I just saw, or did you get something in your eye? The moral of the story? Be honest, take the high road, and pay your taxes. If you're looking for a near-term sale, you might want to talk to your CPA about filing some amended returns. If you have time, start doing things honestly (and still have that conversation with your CPA).

Now I can hear some of you saying—I inherited the business from my dad and he always kept his "other" book where he tracked his true income. Can't I just look for a buyer who "understands" that it is a cash business and show them the "other" book? No! No! No! Aside from the fact that it is dishonest, the buyers will know what you are doing—best case, they will never offer you the true value of your business; worst case, your negotiation could become a blackmail with some unscrupulous characters you don't want to know.

The owner responds to this situation by telling the potential buyer (with a wink),

"This only shows what we made on the books."

Yes, that buyer will want to do business with you now that you are an admitted liar and crook. And on that subject:

"Do you really want to do business with a buyer who is willing to accept this type of cheating?"

emma. It's not likely that buyer will offer you a fair price in any case so again, if you find yourself having this conversation with a potential buyer, you are playing a fool's game to its end. Fortunately, the solution to this problem is simple. Take what deductions you can legally take and pay your taxes.

Because the buyer also understands that this dichotomy exists, as part of their financial due diligence, one of the things buyers will request are copies of your business's tax filings for the prior three to five years. The buyer's negotiation strategy is to get to the lowest possible valuation, and they know you have already driven toward the lowest number when you did your taxes. You did part of their work for them!

The same dichotomy also exists on the expense side of your financials. You have naturally done your best to minimize expenses as you operated your business. When you do your taxes, however, you try to take every possible tax deduction to justify reducing your earnings. Your buyer will want to understand what rationale you used because they may also wish to use it—in their negotiations.

Recasting Your Financials

The next step in financial positioning is to review your financials and recast them to present a realistic valuation of the business. Your financial recast includes making honest, ethical adjustments to achieve a true valuation. Recasting of the financials is needed to determine what the normalized expenses and income are for the business by adjusting the financials to move any expenses or income that will not be normal to the buyers continuing business. Recasting removes any income or expenses that are incorrectly reflected in your financials—meaning eliminating those items in your financials that a new owner will not incur. These are the adjustments made when calculating an EBITDA (Earnings Before Interest, Taxes, Depreciation, and Amortization). EBITDA is a common determinate of business value.

Recasting removes any income or expenses that are incorrectly reflected in your financials—meaning eliminating those items in your financials that a new owner will not incur.

In many small businesses, for instance, the owner charges personal expense items to the business. Does the president receive a company car as a benefit? If so, that auto expense will lower the EBITDA if it is not moved below the line. This is a value proposition discussion, not a tax discussion. Remember, the profitability of the business will be used in negotiations to determine the value of your business, so you will want to eliminate any expenses that are not directly required for the operation of the business from the profitability calculation. A similar example may exist for others in the business who will no longer receive some "perks" after the sale.

The same is true on the income side. Did you spin off an asset or offer a product that you received income from, but which will not be part of the continuing business after the sale? That income can be reflected as a valid income adjustment. This is also a good time to have your CPA review what items have been capitalized vs. expensed as well as reviewing the value of deferred sales. Small, valid changes can have a large effect when a valuation multiple is applied, so decisions about these items need to be considered well in advance. This is one of the more critical areas that should be included when you are considering long-term vs. short-term strategic path analysis.

Third-Party Audits

Larger businesses generally involve more complex financial data and a much greater level of analysis than is done for smaller businesses (more product lines or sources of revenue and greater expenses or more employees). As a result, there can be more people involved in the financial operations of the business (more hands touching the financial data) and more room for error (and yes—manipulation). Because of this, and the large sums involved in the deal, buyers may require an audit of the financials by an independent accredited third-party accounting firm. This is common for high value deals.

Buyers may require an audit of the financials by an independent accredited third-party accounting firm.

The greater the value of your deal, the more likely it is that an independent audit will be a requirement and that a buyer will make this a term of your deal. If your financials are complex and will require some level of discussion or explanation, then you are far better off being preemptive and having an audit performed in advance of speaking with a buyer. Paying for an external third-party audit, performed by a reputable accounting firm, will tell a buyer you are serious, and your books have been validated. This lets buyers know that you are also serious about the deal and attempting to provide an honest picture of the business which will save you the time to have an audit performed as part of the buyer's financial due diligence. But, they may ask to have their own accounting firm perform an audit as well. Don't resist or complain. Just get it done—this time, at their expense.

Looking Toward the Future

In general, when a buyer looks at your financials, they are looking at the past performance of your business. The number one question any buyer really wants answered however is:

> "What is the future potential of this business?"

The person most able to predict the future performance of your business is you. The question may seem like a "crystal ball" question or maybe one for your "Ouija Board." Keep in mind that your answer may not be definitive, but you are still the best one to give an opinion on this.

> "How do I know what the future will bring?"

You may not have insights into things beyond your control (like the economy) or know about some radical innovation in technology that could disrupt the market for your products, and for sure you don't know what a new owner might do once they control the business. Short of that, you are the person who is best qualified to answer the question. Without using the "crystal ball" or "Ouija Board" methods, your answer may be a guess, but you are qualified to give the best educated guess about the future performance of your business, if nothing external impacts it.

The person most able to predict the future performance of your business is you.

Potential buyers will want to see your future projections, a "pro forma," early in the process, and you will need to be prepared to defend your pro forma during your initial discussions with potential buyers. If you don't have a pro forma when they request it, your discussions are likely to end there.

The Sales Projections/Pro forma Chart shown in Figure 7.1 is used to help potential buyers determine whether the business fits into the profile they may be looking for. In the end having this table available will save you from entering into a lot of discussions with people who really aren't interested in buying your business.

You need to create a pro forma that projects future revenues over the next three years. The most direct method of accomplishing this is to graph the actual past business revenue for at least the past three years, plot the curve of that revenue, and then project that curve forward for at least the next three years. If you have grown 10 percent per year for the past three years, then the curve will show 10 percent growth per year for the next three years. If things were just that simple!

Sales Projections/Pro forma

14,000,000

12,300,000

12,000,000

10,000,000

$11,400,000

$10,200,000

8,000,000

$9,400,000

$8,700,000

6,000,000   7,200,000 $7,900,000

Year-3   Year-2   Year-1   Year   Year+1   Year+2   Year+3

— — Projected   ——— Actual

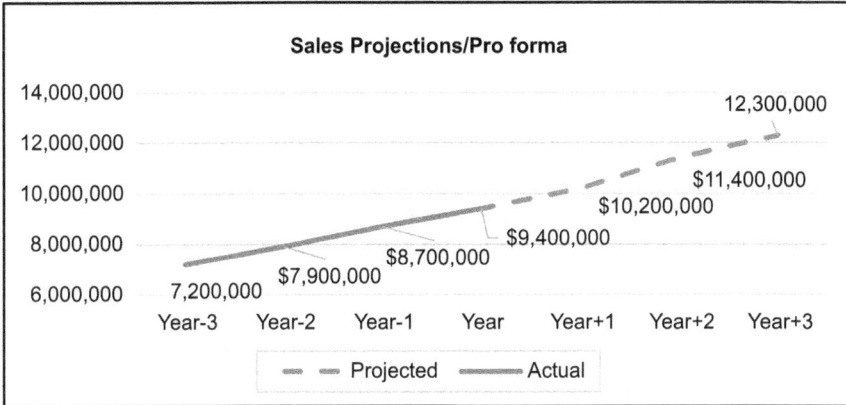

Figure 7.1: Sales Projections/Pro forma Chart

You might have a good reason to believe that the curve will no longer be 10 percent but 20 percent.

"Last year we put in new production equipment that will improve our throughput."

"Our staff has developed a newer, faster way to operate."

"An extra 10,000 new homes were just built in the area."

Each of these could be used as rationale for increasing the trend line and showing improved growth. Let's face it though—everyone also has bad years. Years when the business performance fell off for reasons beyond your control or which were only temporary.

"Our sales fell off two years ago because the town was widening the highway and our customers couldn't find parking, but we recovered last year and are back on track now."

"We lost one of our lead engineers, and it took six months to replace her and delayed the release of our new product."

"I was out on medical leave for a month and it took time for our new GM to come up to speed, but he has been running the day-to-day operations for the past year."

Any numbers you present at any point in the process must all match. You can't show one set of income numbers in one place and a different set elsewhere. If they don't match, the deal will die quickly. Future projections should always be put in context of the past performance because that makes the numbers more credible.

"I know we have averaged 10 percent growth each of the past years; I think we're due for a good year."

Any time your projections deviate from your past performance you will need to be able to offer solid rationale for the deviation. Any time you hear yourself using "I think," "I believe," "I feel," or "my cousin Jake says," you are not making a rational argument, and your opinion will not be credible.

Figure 7.1 is presented as a table that gives the annual revenue generated by the business for at least the last three years (but preferably the last five if the data exists). The annual expenses and gross profitability can also be added here if they support your rationale. The buyer may not agree with your rationale (and they may disagree to enhance their negotiating position), so keep in mind, the best person to project the future of your business is still you.

The numbers in this table are provided at the "20,000 foot" level, allowing potential buyers to bracket the business to determine whether they have any interest and form a basic understanding of the value of the business. From this they can determine whether the deal will be too small or too large for them. Your goal with these numbers is to bring a potential buyer to the point where they are willing to look deeper.

Draw a timeline in the life of your business from the beginning through the next five years. Financial due diligence will look at the past performance of the business, and operations due diligence will look at the potential sales and marketing performance going into the future. Developing a valid pro forma for the business can be done by extending the timeline into the future and placing your projections onto it. If the business has been struggling, then presenting a hockey stick growth curve will not be believable. If the business has a history of growth and can provide the rationale for continuing that growth with the addition of additional capital, then the growth will be believable. The financial positioning of the business requires showing the continuum of its past performance into the future projections.

Future Performance Should Be Based on a Solid Foundation

Look at the revenue curves in Figure 7.2 (these curves have been greatly oversimplified for the example). If you were a buyer, which of these curves would you be more comfortable accepting? Curve 1 is based on a two-year financial track record and shows that the pro forma projections are a continuation of the businesses demonstrated prior growth rate. Curve 2 doesn't include any history. Curve 2 says, "trust me, this is where we are today, and this is what I think the business will do in the future." No offense intended to your great judgment call, but if I'm the buyer, I'll have more confidence in the continuation of the actual performance demonstrated by Curve 1. If you are able to produce the past performance like that shown in Curve 1 then there is a good chance you can shorten the positioning time. If you don't have the data, then you have two options: wait one to two years to sell while you collect the data or start working on a truly convincing story as to why Curve 2 should be believed.

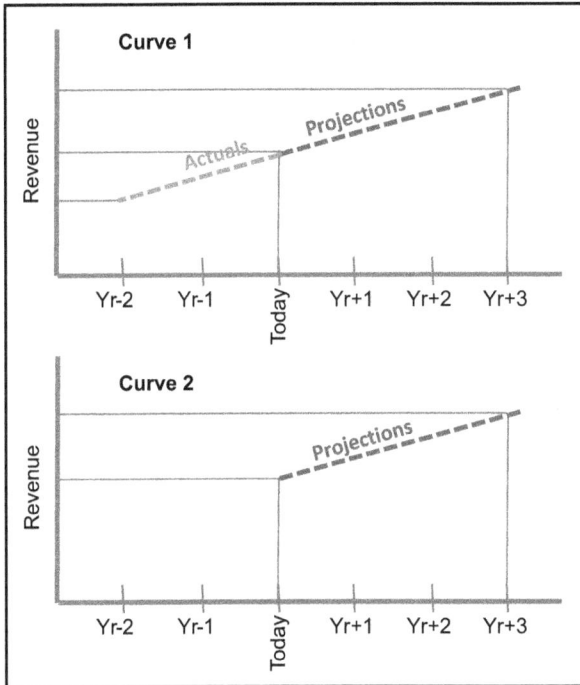

Figure 7.2: Revenue Curves

This is an example of why it takes time to effectively position a business. You can save the time and take the shortcut, but it will likely impact your sale. It's time to get busy.

Figure 7.3 is the well-known "hockey stick," because its shape looks like a hockey stick. While occasionally a business may see radical changes in their growth curves, you are going to have to tell a very credible story to explain your rationale for this type of accelerated growth projection. Causes of this type of growth include the addition of new product lines, added sales staff, or a change in the market. Whatever it is, you will need to be able to justify these radical growth projections to a buyer.

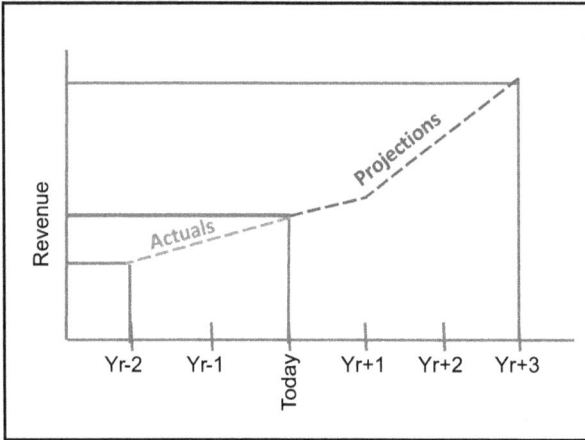

Figure 7.3: Hockey Stick Revenue Curve

The role your pro forma projections will play in valuing your business will depend somewhat on the type of business. For some businesses the value will be determined based strictly by your past performance. For some businesses, particularly some software businesses, your projections will become strong drivers of the business's transferrable value. More on valuations in a later chapter. For now, remember that positioning your business includes building believable revenue curves.

There is a school of thought that you should always operate a business as if it's for sale. I fully support that approach because it means optimizing the operating efficiency of the business and paying close attention to its position in the market. This also has the potential to reduce your positioning activities. In practice, however, it may not be possible to operate your business as if it is constantly for sale, because there may be differences in the long-term vs. short-term strategic approach you use when planning an exit. The argument is that continuing to emphasize a long-term strategy may enhance the value of the business. But, this assumes you are ready to make the same kind of long-term capital commitments to the business as if you intended to operate it long-term, when in actuality you're looking for a near-term exit. Realistically, you will be trading near-term financial performance against long-term capital improvements, and, unless there is a quantifiable value proposition improvement, it may not make sense to invest in long-term growth strategies.

Would you invest in a larger delivery truck if you're planning to sell the business? Strategic planning that includes the detailed development and maintenance of a roadmap with key decision points for the business, including both near-term and long-term goals, is an important tool in making these decisions.

Jim's Bakery Example

Jim's Bakery provides Jim with a high-end SUV as part of the compensation package he granted to himself. Jim's rationale for this "perk" is that he uses the SUV to drive between the retail and commercial bakeries and to visit some of his commercial customers throughout the region. Use of the vehicle is a "perk" Jim has enjoyed, but it is clearly more of a luxury he has allowed himself than a necessity to the business. The CFO has regularly deducted the allowable expenses for Jim's SUV on the financials for Jim's vehicle on the Jim's Bakery P&L.

When the Jim's Bakery financials were being recast as part of the financial positioning in preparation for the sale, the expense for Jim's SUV was removed as an EBITDA adjustment, lowering the expenses, increasing the EBITDA, and resulting in an increase in the overall valuation of the business. The adjustment was explained to the buyer during negotiations as an acceptable adjustment since the buyer didn't allow this type of perk for their senior employees.

Jim's CFO was a strict financial manager who kept detailed records and provided financial reports that were reviewed monthly. Because Jim wanted the financial due diligence to go smoothly and believed it was an opportunity to build buyer confidence, they hired a highly recognized third-party accounting firm to perform an independent audit of their financials.

Chapter 8
Preparing for a Due Diligence Legal Assessment

Let's begin this discussion by pointing out the not so obvious. You will need to conduct three distinct legal activities as you prepare to sell your business, and you will need (and want) to keep those activities on separate tracks, so now is a good time to start thinking of the activities in this way.

The first legal track that will need to be performed is the work required to complete the deal transaction. This track is necessary to complete the legal transfer of your business to the new owner. Once the deal is closed, you don't want there to be any strings attached that will pull you back needlessly, unless you have negotiated them in advance. The new owner will want to be sure there are no legal encumbrances or constraints on the business at closing. You will be asked to guarantee this in writing.

This track includes the cleanup of legal issues such as ownership, outstanding litigation, etc. These tasks generally take time, so this track may become a driver in your desire to get to the beach. The transaction attorney should begin working with the attorney that is representing you in any outstanding litigation. To handle the transaction and transfer of your business you will need to hire a competent, qualified transaction attorney. No matter what type of sale you are executing (equity, asset, etc.), the attorney you hire for this track will be given the responsibility for making the transaction happen and executing a successful closing.

Warning: Nothing in this chapter is intended to reduce, replace, or discourage you from hiring a qualified attorney to advise you on the sale of your business.

The second track is for planning your post sale taxes. How you are paid, when you are paid, and how much your closing expenses are (particularly payouts to other individuals) can all have a significant impact on how much taxes you will have to pay on the sale. You cannot wait until you are on top of the sale to begin forming a tax strategy. The type of sale (asset or equity) will become a large determinant of the tax burden resulting from the sale, so you need to begin planning now. The sale's type will impact your negotiations with a buyer, so you must know what the tax implications are well before you list your business.

If your personal attorney or your transition attorney are not tax attorneys or are not working with one, you will need to reach out to a tax attorney to develop a strategy before you list your business for sale. We will discuss this more in the

DOI 10.1515/9781547400249-008

last chapter, but don't wait until you are about to close the sale. Meet with a tax attorney and develop a strategy sooner rather than later.

Look for an attorney with experience compatible with the size deal you are anticipating. This will be money well spent. Even though you aren't anywhere near ready to close, don't hesitate to move ahead and engage this help now. Now is a good time to locate a transaction attorney and start a dialog.

The type of sale (asset or equity) will become a large determinant of your tax burden resulting from the sale, so you need to begin planning now.

The third legal track you will need is the continuing support for your day-to-day operations as you begin your legal positioning. The legal positioning tasks are intended to prepare your business for legal due diligence, and most of that work will not require an attorney. The legal operations of your business will include document collection and organization, contract review and verification, a review of your professional and business licenses, and a review of all customer and vendor agreements. As you review these documents, you should anticipate finding areas where problems exist (e.g., finding out that one of the documents you collect needs to be replaced or revised), and in these cases, you may want to use an attorney to make the changes to the document. As you begin your positioning, the level of support you need from your attorney may increase temporarily. One of the primary reasons for doing legal positioning is to identify potential problems and issues before your buyer finds them. Finding problems during the transaction could delay the closing or completely kill your deal, so the tasks you're going to take on now are intended to keep you from finding issues later in the process.

One of the primary reasons for doing legal positioning is to identify potential problems and issues before your buyer finds them.

When you do identify an issue, you may need to refer that issue to an attorney for resolution, but you may not want to pay your transaction attorney for this type of work. Check the hourly rates your attorneys are charging you. When your transaction attorney tells you what it would cost to handle the closing for your business, they probably have not included the resolution of operational problems you discover as you position your business. For operational issues, you may want to use the attorney that handles your day-to-day operations to handle this work. You will need an additional estimate!

"We thought we had cleaned up the ownership of the business, but we need to prepare a letter transferring shares we promised to our chief engineer. These shares will give him a payout after the closing."

"The contract with a critical vendor requires we notify them whenever there is a management change, and now they want to write a new contract with the new owners."

"I gave a personal guarantee to the landlord when the lease was written, and now it needs to be removed."

When you discuss the activities connected with any of the three tracks with your attorneys, you will need to have a clear understanding of who will handle the transition and your post sale tax planning and who will handle the operational issues and how they will be resolved. Keeping the legal tracks separated can become tricky. Maybe you need a fourth attorney to negotiate with the other three attorneys! No, no, no—just kidding! Three attorneys are probably enough.

Legal Positioning Casts a Wide Net

In the normal thrashing that occurs with the day-to-day operation of a small business, there are many things that come across the owner's desk that bind or constrain the operation of the business and commit the business contractually or financially. Think about the number of times you sign something or promise something to an employee, customer, or vendor. Anything that binds or constrains the way the business operates, or otherwise commits the business or costs the business money, is of real concern to potential buyers. The buyer knows it's not possible to remove these constraints but they want to enter into the deal with their eyes wide open as to what constraints and commitments already exist. Here are some of the day-to-day items that constrain or otherwise commit the operation of any small business:

- any known pending, threatened, or anticipated legal actions of any kind
- all contractual agreements currently in place or the contractual "tails"[1] related to any prior agreements that could constrain the ongoing operations of the business in any manner
- any known estoppel claims or waivers impacting the operation of the business
- all existing employment agreements (both written and verbal)

---

[1] A "tail" is a term that extends beyond the contract's close date.

- all professional licenses and certifications currently in effect, expired, or pending, either to the business or to the employees on which the business depends
- all titles and deeds to real property
- all property and equipment leases
- all outstanding customer warrantees, guarantees, and service agreements
- all outstanding (active) purchase orders and invoices
- all operating agreements such as nondisclosure agreements (NDAs) and letters of intent (LOI)

To prepare your business for legal due diligence, you will need to identify and find all these documents (and potentially many others). Include any other documents of a similar nature not specifically listed here. Include any items that put a burden on the business after the sale. Sit back, pour yourself a cup of coffee, and start making a list of where every one of the documents on this list can be found. Find out who has the original signed copy and identify where it can be found (both the hard [printed] and soft [electronic] copies).

If putting your hands on the documents containing all the information you need will be as difficult for you as it is for many small businesses, you will want to put on a fresh pot of coffee! After locating these documents, they should be gathered and put in a document repository where they can be tracked and controlled.

Legal positioning proves that the proverb "the devil is in the details" is certainly the case in business deals. There is no room for any gray areas when preparing your business for legal due diligence. Where financial due diligence will focus on the past performance of the business, legal due diligence will focus on the current position of the business. Assume current position to mean "on the day the deal is closed."

Where financial due diligence will focus on the past performance of the business, legal due diligence will focus on the current position of the business.

Create a Milestone Calendar

Finding all your documents and putting them in a due diligence file or in a virtual document repository is not enough. What commitments do these documents make? Are there critical dates where the business needs to do something? Financial payment schedules? You need to do more than collect the documents; you need to review the content of the documents to know what commitments they are making.

Legal commitments frequently result in critical milestone performance dates. One of the easiest ways to demonstrate to a buyer that you're ready to transfer your business to them is to create a milestone calendar that identifies all the critical dates that will affect the business. Lease and license renewal dates, key contract commitment dates—any dates that could significantly impact the business's operation should be tracked on a milestone calendar. If there are tasks associated with meeting a critical date, then the preparation start date should also be noted.

> "The application is due on June 15 but collecting the data for the application will take a month. So identify the preparation start date on the milestone calendar as May 15."

There should be a reasonableness to these tasks. If you have thousands of customers, then the sales department might want to maintain its own customer milestone calendar; but, if you have a client responsible for 20 percent of your revenue, you will need to be sure to include critical dates for this client on your milestone calendar.

Make your milestone calendar a rolling calendar (e.g., one that never ends). Of course, there is no excuse these days not to make it an online calendar. If your business conducts a monthly management review, then that is a good time to review closed items during the past month, look at near-term and long-term items, and assign appropriate action items to ensure you are prepared and not surprised by milestones.

Creating a milestone calendar will become a bit of a "thread-pulling" exercise. Once you review a document to identify commitment dates, you will also be able to identify other commitments, such as expense payments.

> "There is a balloon payment of $500,000 due in three years."

This may be something the buyer needs to know! That is a financial commitment you will want to make sure is noted on the calendar and in the budget as well.

> "I think our chief engineer's professional license runs out next March . . . or was it September? That's not far away. I hope she has the time to complete the continuing education requirements according to the state mandates."

> "We advertised lifetime repairs on that product, but it was so successful we sold 55,000 instead of the 2,500 we originally planned. Then the problems started. Each repair costs $100, and that totals to $5,500,000 that will be negotiated out of your price if the buyer discovers it before you reveal it."

> "Our salesman ran an extension cord across the showroom floor and that old guy with the cane tripped on it and fell. We paid his doctors' bills, but his son tells us he is still in pain."

A buyer will expect any dependencies such as these to be disclosed—along with any overdue commitments to be resolved—prior to closing. Sometimes, rather than walking away from a deal, the buyer will mitigate their risk by requiring sufficient funds be set aside for a specified period to protect them against loss from any pending or outstanding issues.

Sometimes, the buyer will mitigate their risk by requiring sufficient funds be set aside for a specified period to protect them against loss from any pending or outstanding issues.

Government Regulatory Compliance

Every business faces a mountain of government rules and regulations from all levels of government. Financial reporting, employment, environmental, industrial, privacy protection—never, even in jest, ask if the government has run out of things to regulate. They may take that as a challenge!

The government, at all levels, creates regulation to constrain the way businesses operate. Over time, the regulations change in response to many things. As a small business owner, none of this is likely to be news to you. You may even be one of the business owners that have decided it's time to move on rather than try to keep up with some recent change. This could be a costly decision, as a new buyer knows they will have to incur the expense for implementing the new change and will therefore devalue your business for not being up-to-date. Strategically, a better decision would be to bite the bullet, take the steps needed to become compliant, and then sell your business. There are process certifications that require the business to practice for a specified period. Buyers will try to qualify for the certification by buying a business that has reached some level of certification and use that business to umbrella their other businesses in.

> "To qualify for that contract, you had to have worked as a certified shop for two years. They couldn't qualify on their own, so they bought our shop because we met the certification requirement and they were able to bid under our certification."

If your competitors have not yet reached compliance or they decide to buy a compliant business to umbrella the buyer's other businesses, then the value of your business will go up—possibly significantly depending on your industry.

Some industries have certification and testing requirements controlling who can practice or operate a business in the industry. The certifications are often tied to individuals and sometimes tied to the business. You will want to help establish the credentials of your business by identifying all licenses and certificates held by the business and its employees. A list of these licenses and credentials will be requested by the buyer, so have copies available and make sure any pending renewals are taken care of. If your business relies on the personal license of an employee, be sure to have that employee under contract.

You will want to help establish the credentials of your business by identifying all licenses and certificates held by the business and its employees.

Along with reviewing all professional licenses, you need to make sure all of your registered business licenses and filings have been made and are up-to-date. Board minutes, information filings, and any state filings should be reviewed. Field sales offices that operate in a different state are a common place to find filing omissions and errors.

Intellectual Property

One sure way to increase the value of your business is to offer the buyer a competitive discriminator that no one else can legally offer them. This is done by capturing any intellectual property (IP) your business has created or is entitled to. A common mistake of small businesses is to avoid the cost of capturing their intellectual property. Unfortunately, this can turn out to be a penny-wise decision that will cost them when they are being sold. Intellectual property can be captured in the form of patents, trademarks, and copyrights.[2]

Patents

A patent is the public disclosure of a unique design or solution to a specific technical problem. In return for the disclosure, the government grants the inventor or their assignee the exclusive right to its use for some period of time. The patent creates value for a business because it allows the business to exclude others from using the solution and to license its use. Patents take the longest to capture and are the costliest. The international rules for obtaining a patent also vary greatly, but patents create real value for a small business because they tell buyers your business is unique and ahead of the competition.

---

2 For general information relating to Intellectual Property see the US Patent and Trademark Office's website, https://www.uspto.gov/.

Trademarks

Small businesses work hard to establish a brand and then fail to file a trademark to capture it as their own. A trademark is a word, group of words, or a symbol that uniquely identifies the source of a product. A trademark doesn't preclude one business from creating products similar to those of another business. The trademark is used to identify the business that is the true source of a product. When you make a product that is distinguished from your competition, because yours has higher quality, you want to be able to apply your trademarked label on your product so customers won't confuse them. Buyers will value your trademark and your brand because of the reputation that goes with it.

Copyrights

A copyright protects the author of an original intellectual work such as a literary, musical, or artistic creation or a creator of a computer program (among others). It gives the author or artist control of the publication and reproduction of the work. A copyright is the least expensive form of intellectual property to capture, and these days can be done quickly over the internet. The production cost for copyrighted material is comparatively low which makes it attractive for mass product sales (books, movies, music), and therefore also makes a business that owns the rights attractive for a buyer.

Intellectual Property (IP) Assignment

Patents are awarded to the designer who creates a new product design. The patent rights are then assigned to the business by the designer. Your chief engineer has been awarded three patents for work he did on your payroll and in your shop. You paid the patent attorney's fees. Did he sign a form assigning the patent to your business? If not, you may have an issue to resolve (and a negotiation to hold with your chief engineer). Maybe your chief engineer hasn't identified any patentable ideas. Have you asked her? Some small business owners fail to challenge their employees to identify intellectual property.

As you prepare to sell your business you will need to identify any patents, trademarks, or copyrights currently assigned to the business and ensure they are on your intangible asset list.

"We worked hard to release the product and moved on to start the design of the next one. We never had the time to file a patent, and besides, I knew the owners of this business weren't going to pay for a patent filing."

As you prepare to sell your business you will need to identify any patents, trademarks, or copyrights currently assigned to the business and ensure they are on your intangible asset list.

Capturing IP

While a lot has been done to improve the procedures and to lower the cost for capturing intellectual property, many small business owners still hesitate to seek these protections. The motivation that keeps small business owners from legally capturing their intellectual property may change or at least have different emphasis when they are trying to increase the value of the business they have decided to sell. Here are some of the common reasons:

- They forget to file. In the daily grind of running the business, everyone is so busy, and this is not an immediate task assigned to someone, so it is just lost in the hustle and bustle.
- They fear releasing their design solutions for public exposure in a patent where everyone else can see it, knowing that the technology life cycle is short, and the patent process is long. They choose instead to capture a market leader position over capturing the intellectual property.
- They do not want to pay an attorney to capture the intellectual property.
- They sell products in multiple country markets and the intellectual property laws and protections are different across jurisdictions.
- Many times, small businesses fail to train their employees about what constitutes intellectual property and fail to offer their employees an incentive for identifying it.

Many of these fears are based on fact; however, a lot has been done to resolve these issues and improve the process for capturing intellectual property. It may pay to look at the updated government processes before assuming how difficult or expensive it will be to capture your intellectual property. Patents remain the most difficult but also have the potential to significantly increase the value of your business. It takes time to file a patent, and yes, you should use an intellectual property attorney. The cost trade-off for the attorney might be worth it given the potential value increase. Even if you do not have the time to complete the patent process, being able to show a prospective buyer that a patent has been applied for may be a valuable discriminator for your sale. Trademarks and copyrights are much easier to apply for these days and much less expensive. Trademarks loose value if a buyer plans to merge your business into another or use their own brand.

It may pay to look at the updated government processes before assuming how difficult or expensive it will be to capture your intellectual property.

This might be a good time to hold an employee training session and to offer a bonus for anyone that identifies valid intellectual property currently existing within the business. You might be surprised what your employees produce. Aside from receiving a bonus, employees also like having their ideas acknowledged.

IP Violations Can Cost You

There are small businesses that have no value other than some old patent they still hold and may never have done anything with. Eventually others came up with a similar idea and developed a product based of their own without looking for existing patents. The business who owned the patent never challenged anyone for infringing on it. There are also buyers who look for just those businesses or just buy the patent outright.

In cases where a patent exists, even if it has been dormant, the value is not in the patent itself but in the money that can be made by going after other businesses who they find have violated the patent. Once a business has integrated the technology into their product, they are trapped. They can be sued for patent infringement and so are likely to pay to license the technology they are already selling to their customers. The term "patent pirates" has evolved because, while most businesses find the practice tantamount to blackmail, it has become a common practice. This doesn't just happen with technology. It's common for intellectual property (such as photographs and music) to be "pirated" off the internet as well. If there is any chance your business has infringed on someone else's intellectual property, now is the time to resolve these issues. Make sure none of your employees has taken any shortcuts.

"We didn't realize our web developer had illegally downloaded those pictures instead of buying them."

Jim's Bakery Example

Jim met with his transition team early in the process to determine their strategy for legal due diligence. He included the attorney who advises Jim's Bakery and his transition attorney. Together the team came up with a list of documents they anticipated buyers might requested during their legal due diligence. The documents include the service agreements the commercial bakery used for their recurring bread-as-a-service (BaaS) customers.

The commercial bakery COO took the action to review each of these agreements to ensure he logged the date each agreement ended on. He planned to back each date up thirty days so sales could start working with the customer to ensure all of the automatic renewals went smoothly and to try to upsell additional products and services for the customer. To his surprise, he eventually found that several of them had expired and needed to be renewed, as the contracts were an older version that hadn't included automatic renewals. They would have to resolve this by putting new agreements in place with those customers before they would be ready to be assessed during due diligence. If a buyer had found them, they might have tried to discount that income from the valuation. Jim contacted his attorney to review the agreement template and planned to have updated agreements sent to each customer thirty days before their renewal date.

The next action was a review of the intellectual property. To Jim's surprise they had not actually captured much of it. After offering to pay a bonus to any employee who could identify an intellectual property asset, he was surprised when one of his staff asked why there was no trademark on the Jim's Bakery logo. He knew that part of the value in his business was recognition of his brand name. His attorney was given the action to file the trademark as soon as possible.

Jim was actively driving his transition team. As a final action, Jim sat with a tax attorney who worked with the transaction attorney Jim had hired for the sale of his business. Working with his attorneys and his investment banker, they agreed that Jim's Bakery would only be offered to buyers who were willing to buy the business as part of an equity deal. Jim's banker pointed out that this approach might scare off some larger corporate buyers who would only consider an asset deal, but Jim insisted the tax advantages for him in an equity deal were too large to ignore.

Chapter 9
Preparing for a Due Diligence Operations Assessment

Positioning your business for an operations due diligence takes time and resources, but it is one of the key ways to justify a higher price to a buyer. Think about the difference between a Chevy and a Cadillac. They both meet the requirements to be on the road and provide reliable transportation, but qualified buyers are willing to pay more for the higher level of quality and comfort they get from the Cadillac. A buyer is going to invest a significant amount of money to buy your business. By optimizing the operations of the business, you are making it more attractive to the buyer who is willing to spend a little more to get a little more. They need to be able to see the difference when deciding which business to buy. Even though they may not be looking for luxury, they are still looking for a secure, quality investment.

Every buyer looks for different things when they assess the operation of a business. Some buyers like to say an operations assessment is about "management, management, management." Others believe it is about "sales, sales, sales." As a small business owner preparing for an operations due diligence, the first question you are likely asking is:

> "I know what legal and financial due diligence are, but I don't know what constitutes an operations due diligence."

Unlike financial due diligence and legal due diligence, which have the practices of accounting and law to guide them, "operations" doesn't have a similar standard of practice and often means different things to different people. There hasn't been a true consensus about the definition of an operations due diligence until recently, so knowing what the buyer's operations assessment might include has been a source of confusion. The only sure statement that can be made about an operations due diligence is that all buyers look at operations differently. Because each buyer usually has some unique concern (generally based on their personal experience or knowledge), they want to assess that function of the business and often do that while overlooking others. There has been some movement to standardize operations assessments, but many buyers are not yet familiar with this work.

As a seller, you will need to be prepared for the educated buyer who decides to assess the full scope of your business operations. When I published my book,

DOI 10.1515/9781547400249-009

Operations Due Diligence,[1] my goal was to create a standard for operations assessments that would make them more effective. I was looking at the problem from the investor's side at the time, and unfortunately, as a buyer, this may give you more work to do! Fortunately, you do have a guideline to go by that defines what constitutes an effective operations due diligence.

Unlike financial due diligence and legal due diligence, which have the practices of accounting and law to guide them, "operations" has not had a similar standard of practice until recently.

As a generalized statement, most people understand that a financial due diligence looks at the past performance of the business, while the legal due diligence looks at the current state of the business (i.e., at the time of closing). An effective operations due diligence by contrast looks at the future operations of the business.

"Will the products continue to sell?"

"Will the market change?"

"Is there growing competition?"

What these questions are all asking is what are the things that could go wrong with the business in the future? These are important questions for the buyer, but they only relate to a narrow sliver of the operating functions. To assess the operations of a business, you need to look at all of the functions that make up its operations—the entire "enterprise."

When you are trying to assess a business for future problems, by definition, you are asking about potential risks that might impact the operations of the business in the future. An operations due diligence therefore can be defined as an enterprise risk assessment. But there are two sides to that coin. Buyers also want to know what opportunities might exist for the business in the future.

"Will sales increase after we invest?"

"Will customers still come when we make a management change?"

"Can we use technology to improve production?"

---

1 James F. Grebey, *Operations Due Diligence: An M&A Guide for Investors and Business* (New York: McGraw-Hill, 2012).

An operations assessment looks for both risks and opportunities. Defining an operations assessment as an enterprise risk/opportunity assessment seems to be a radical idea for some people.

An operations assessment is an enterprise risk/opportunity assessment.

When I published *Operations Due Diligence* I didn't realize what a radical idea it would be to define operations due diligence as an enterprise risk/opportunity assessment. Many knew intuitively they were assessing the business for potential problems, but there wasn't agreement as to the method to use. By pointing out that it was an enterprise risk assessment, it was clear few were performing a full, effective assessment. They missed the need for an "enterprise-wide" risk assessment, until the benefit was explicitly pointed out to them. As I spoke with investment groups, I would see faces in the audience light up as they had a moment of understanding ("Of course I knew that!"), but it's clear they had never previously made the connection that performing an enterprise-wide assessment is the way to perform a truly effective operations due diligence. The next problem was to define the scope of the "enterprise."

An effective operations due diligence covers a lot of potential risk areas. Before they understood what an effective operations assessment required, most buyers and investors performed assessments in an ad hoc manner, assessing random areas based on who they currently had on staff or looking just in the places where they had had past problems. They would send an engineer to look at source code or a department manager to speak with the management team. Their assessment team was rarely trained to perform a true enterprise risk assessment.

I have not collected the data (I will leave that to some bright grad student looking for a thesis) but I believe there is a connection that can be drawn from this. The failure to perform an effective operations due diligence that spans the entire operations infrastructure of the business (the enterprise) to identify latent risk may be one of the leading causes of mergers and acquisitions (M&A) failures. The problem you face in the sale of your business is not knowing what your buyer's assessment will consist of. You must prepare and plan for a full assessment.

Start an Internal Risk/Opportunity Management Program for Your Business

As a seller, you want to anticipate the buyer's assessment questions so you can prepare answers in advance. You need to be able to respond well to those questions. You now understand that the nature of the buyer's questions will be risk/

opportunity based, even if they don't conduct a full assessment. The best way to prepare will be to implement an internal risk/opportunity management program for your business that continuously reviews the business for potential risk/opportunity areas. Once potential risks or opportunities are identified, plans should be put into place by implementing risk avoidance and mitigation strategies. Or, when a new opportunity is identified, strategies should be drawn to capture the new opportunity. This program is a good way to manage the strategic direction of a business, even if it is not currently for sale. Then, when you do decide to sell your business, this program will have improved your operations and will give you solid answers to a buyer's operations assessment questions.

To be successful, experience shows that either the owner or senior staff with the authority to implement the plans should be directly involved in the internal assessment.

"Jim, we are a small business and only have three employees. . ... This just won't work for us."

My response is that all businesses should watch for things that could go wrong and for new opportunities that might come along. Some just don't formalize their risk assessment process. If you truly don't look for risk or opportunity, it's like running a marathon blindfolded. Sooner or later you're going to run into something. At the beginning of the book I recommended that, even if an activity seemed too formal, rather than just blowing it off you should try it or modify it. This would be a good place to try it. Formalize what you do (e.g., write down a short procedure) and then try to do what you said you were going to do.

If you truly don't look for risk or opportunity, it's like running a marathon blindfolded. Sooner or later you're going to run into something.

In our two-person business, a mistake in bidding a job could be very costly. When an opportunity comes along my wife and I assess the schedule risk and adjust our proposal to mitigate the risk. Over time this has caused us to modify the way we charge our customers and the type of agreements we will enter into. We don't submit a bid or proposal unless we have gone through this risk assessment.

Buyers know there is risk in any business, and the fact that you have a process for managing risk shows them a level of maturity in the way the business is operated. It also creates a channel to talk about any tough issues that exist and any opportunities you may want to tell them about. Try it! You may like it.

What Is the Scope of the Enterprise?

Most small business owners don't think about their business in terms of its operations infrastructure, yet all functioning businesses have some set of guidelines that define the way they do things, whether they have formalized those guidelines or not. Bills get paid, invoices are sent, payroll is met, supplies are ordered, employees are hired (and fired), sales are made, and products and services are delivered, and if these things happen the same way each time they are done, your business has an operations infrastructure. A buyer will want to know what that infrastructure is, how your business works, and whether it will keep working.

When you look at your business in this manner you will realize there are many tasks that get done the same way each time they're performed. Preparing your operations to be assessed means organizing all those activities in a manner that will make sense to a buyer. Accomplishing that organization is also one of those things that will tell a buyer, "this business has their stuff together." It will reflect well on you as well as the business. To quote one bright young MBA graduate who sat in the front row in one of my presentations:

"OMG, this preparation includes a lot of stuff!"

Yes, it is a lot of stuff. I am often asked if the amount of work required for an assessment can be cut back. Yes, it can, but you may lose an opportunity to discover a latent risk (there's that pesky risk word again!) or an opportunity to optimize your operations. Even worse, the buyer may catch something you missed because it was too much work to fully prepare. I run into buyers all the time who want to "move due diligence along" and ask if it can be accelerated. When you are planning to invest a large sum of money, you might think it's worth the time to perform an effective operations assessment.

Since "operations" covers such a broad scope of business activities it is difficult to define exactly what the scope of the enterprise is. I recommend looking at the nine infrastructure areas that follow when preparing your business for an operations assessment. This will help organize the effort and allow you to assign employees in each area (as they are the ones who know how the job is done in any case) to identify risk and opportunity and find ways to optimize in their area. By breaking the work down into nine areas it minimizes the impact on the work any employee must do.

I recommend looking at nine infrastructure areas when preparing your business to be assessed.

Optimizing the operations of your business should include assessing and improving each of the following areas:

1. Customer satisfaction
2. Production/services
3. Sales and marketing
4. Organizational
5. Personnel
6. Financial
7. Legal
8. Information management
9. Institutionalized processes

Challenge employees to find improvements in each of these areas and formalize their findings by publicizing them internally. You will likely be surprised to see what they find. The most common response we hear is "no one ever gave us the chance to do this before."

Preparing for a Customer Satisfaction Infrastructure Assessment

The customer satisfaction infrastructure defines the role of functions such as product support, requirements definition, and quality assurance. One of the key questions a customer satisfaction assessment will ask is whether the infrastructure is an integral part of the business. It should be "built in" and not simply included like a facade over the front door.

Customer satisfaction drives recurring sales, and most businesses rely, to some degree, on making more than one sale to a customer. Recurring sales are the most direct form of marketing. If customers have a good experience and were satisfied with your product or service, they will come back the next time they are looking for a similar product. If they had problems with the product they purchased, or they didn't have a good experience with your business, they are less likely to return. Businesses that don't rely on return customers are the exception. Retail businesses, such as automobile repair shops, rely heavily on return sales, as do many technology businesses, such as software-as-a-service (SaaS) companies that count on customers who typically allow automatic renewal of their subscriptions—if they are satisfied with the product and supplier support they receive. When your customer satisfaction risk is assessed, the buyer will also want to assess the dependence level the business has on recurring customers.

To be prepared to tell buyers the percentage of your sales that are recurring, you need to start tracking which sales are being made to returning customers.

The customer satisfaction infrastructure should be "built in" and not simply included like a facade over the front door because it drives recurring sales.

Buyers frequently request to speak with some of your current customers to determine their level of satisfaction. This can be a tricky and dangerous step and in general, my recommendation is to say no. Bringing a buyer to visit customers can cause the customer to panic and start looking around for another company to fill your business's void. If it is a strategic buyer who is otherwise one of your competitors, you can offer to do an introduction after the sale. Keep in mind the customer may well have decided to buy from you instead of them for reasons you know nothing about.

If the buyer insists, I would first offer some alternate approaches. It is possible to poll customers through surveys and questionnaires but these items themselves tend to annoy customers. The people who respond are often not happy while those who are happy don't see a need to respond. This type of market approach requires real care in how the survey is constructed. Your best approach is to request testimonials from customers to post on your website and provide those to potential buyers.

Preparing for a Production/Services Infrastructure Assessment

The production/services infrastructure includes the methods that are used for the delivery of all products and services and ensures that this is being done in a safe, compliant, and consistent manner, capable of bringing all products and services fully to market. In preparation for a production/services infrastructure assessment you must be able to show that you either can deliver products to meet the projections you are providing to the buyer or provide a detailed plan to show how this will be accomplished. Optimize this infrastructure by improving your production efficiency.

In preparation for a production/services infrastructure assessment you must be able to show that you can deliver products to meet the projections you are providing to the buyer.

One of the key risks you may face in the production/services infrastructure results from the agreements many businesses have with suppliers for critical components and services that they have come to depend on. This risk occurs in almost any type of business that relies on critical vendors.

Of course, your buyer is calculating the new increased cost and adjusting your margins to account for the change. Lower margins mean lower earnings and a reduced valuation for your business.

When your buyer assesses production/services risks you want to be able to show that you have mitigated those risks. As you prepare, look for changes, such as vendor agreements, and don't accept margin reductions when you are holding the cards. Look for ways to mitigate or avoid risks now so you don't face reductions while you are trying to sell your business. This is where the effort to create a risk/opportunity management program within your business will start to make great sense.

Preparing for a Sales and Marketing Infrastructure Assessment

The sales and marketing infrastructure includes all the methods you use to identify customers (sales leads) who will be interested in purchasing your products, your services, and your strategies used to close those sales. It provides the guidance for your strategic planning, defines the sales process that guides the way orders are processed, and even provides the rationale for your future sales projections. In preparation for the sale of your business, you will want to optimize the efficiency of this process in any way possible.

Small businesses market and sell their products in a variety of ways. For example, the business I use for my home lawn care is a sole proprietorship with 135 customers. The customers come and go, and new customers are found strictly by referral. My neighbor recommended the service to me, and when there was an opening, the lawn care business owner started taking care of my yard. The owner does a good job and, as a result, people seek him out. He works mostly alone doing the outside work, and his wife supports him part time in running the office. The owner tells me that someday he expects to sell his business; I have found there is a healthy market for the sale of lawn care routes. His sales and marketing infrastructure isn't written down, but it is a very real, very tangible, and effective way of doing business. He doesn't change that model because it works for him. When he does decide to sell, the transferrable value of his business will be his client list (an asset) unless he finds a way to institutionalize his sales process, which would increase the transferrable value of his business.

Other small businesses simply sell over the counter to customers who walk in their front door. They offer coupons; advertise in local papers, local radio, and local TV networks; and have an online social media presence. Still other small businesses have outbound sales groups, inside sales groups, and telemarketers; they also market their products nationally and internationally through elaborate websites and search engine optimization programs intended to bring online customers to their website and establish extensive targeted lists of social medial followers. There are small businesses that rely solely on wholesale and reseller programs to sell their products and services, and they create a strong brand through events like industry conventions.

The sales and marketing infrastructure used by small businesses can include everything from the methods they use for pricing and lead flow (needed to support their sales pipeline) and the methods used to develop new product specifications, as well as their marketing approach, including the use of competitive and strategic analysis tools. By finding ways to improve the way you sell, you will improve your sales and marketing infrastructure and increase the transferrable value of your business. Can you find a way to improve the way you find sales leads and go to market with your products?

By finding ways to improve the way you sell, you will improve your sales and marketing infrastructure and increase the transferrable value of your business.

As you are preparing to sell your business, the sales and marketing infrastructure requires first that you document your sales process so that it can be explained to the buyer. Obviously, this will be easier for some businesses than others. Second, you must collect your sales metrics—such as, "how many customers," "average sale size (where possible)," and any other metric that can help you quantify your sales. And third, you must use these metrics to justify and improve your business model (see chapter 11).

It is easy to understand why buyers want to assess your sales and marketing infrastructure but be aware they may be asking about it for different reasons than you expect. You will benefit from knowing what those reasons are as early as possible. A buyer who is planning to continue the operations using your existing infrastructure will need to know how that infrastructure works. A buyer who is acquiring your business with plans to merge it into another business may be interested in picking and choosing which parts of the infrastructure to retain. Occasionally, when your business is being acquired by a larger organization that recognizes the value in your products, they may plan to increase the sales of the product by pulling them into an existing and larger established sales and marketing organization. They want your product to become another offering in their catalog.

"We were selling $7 million in our region; after the sale they began offering our product through their national sales channel and tripled that number."

This is a common practice of product resellers who want to acquire the supplier of a hot product to keep it away from their competition. If you have an idea of what the buyer's plans are this can help you in your negotiation. Buyers aren't always that forthright about their plans, unless of course they are trying to convince you to accept an "earn-out."

Preparing for an Organizational Infrastructure Assessment

The definition of the organizational infrastructure includes the formal and informal structures of the business. It includes the organization chart that forms the command and control structure plus the informal structure that becomes the culture of the business. The organizational infrastructure in most small businesses has grown in an ad hoc manner. Optimizing this infrastructure often requires looking at your organization for the first time and restructuring it by design. That may include finally deciding what to do with cousin Jake! Does he add transferrable value to the business, or is he just an expense?

The organizational infrastructure includes the formal and informal structures of the business.

A very small business, with one to five people, may find this definition difficult to apply. Take the challenge and see what you can do with it. An organization chart for a one-person business is pretty small and makes no sense. If you're going to sell your business to another individual, taking the time to write down a list of the jobs you do and a brief description of those jobs is probably something the new owner will find valuable.

Prepare an Organization Chart

The creation of an organization chart (an org chart) and defined position descriptions for (at least) the key employees is an important task that should be easy to accomplish. Creating an accurate organization chart "should be" an easy task but always seems to be difficult for small businesses that have previously avoided creating or regularly maintaining one. Putting your organization on paper the first time can lead to surprises your employees might not be happy with or want to acknowledge.

"You mean I work for her?"

Putting an organization down on paper can be stressful! It requires making decisions (and announcements) you may have been avoiding or putting off for a long time. I had one client who named each of his five key department managers a vice president (VP). The sales and marketing VP became upset. She thought she should have been named as an executive VP (EVP) because the EVP title "worked better with our customers." In truth she was trying to promote herself above the other managers. This created a problem with the other four VPs who didn't think she should out rank them. The client eventually solved the problem by naming all five department managers as EVPs (which didn't make the sales and marketing EVP very happy!).

Use a simple, hierarchical diagram to describe the command and control structure of your business. This is a place where the "KISS" (keep it simple, stupid) principal should be applied. The senior staff should report directly to the CEO or president (you) at the top. Each employee should have exactly one boss that they report to. Try to eliminate any dotted lines (often difficult to do). Supervisors report to you and their staff reports directly to them. When a buyer looks at this structure they see order, and it's clear who each person takes direction from. Unfortunately, this is not what happens in many small businesses. Their org chart looks more like the spokes of a wagon wheel where the owner is the hub of the wheel and everyone reports to him (or her). This works if the business only has five employees, but most business owners do not have time for a span of control greater than that, and it is a sign of immaturity and trust in the business.

Use a simple, hierarchical diagram to describe the command and control structure of your business.

When a buyer sees an org chart with more than five people, where everyone reports directly to the owner, they see a business that is fully dependent on a single person ("in the middle of the wheel"). This dependence is great if you are looking for an employment contract from the new owner, but not if your goal is to move on. Buyers won't want to see that dependence on you if you are exiting. It's also a sign that you haven't done a good job or been willing to delegate to your second-level managers. The buyer may start to wonder why. For a business to grow, the person at the top needs to be able to delegate, and the rule for delegation is simple:

"You can delegate authority, but you cannot delegate responsibility."

There are buyers who will insist that the senior management team remain with the business for some period (typically a year) after the closing. If being tied to the business after the sale is not consistent with your plan to move on, this may be a good time to promote someone else to the top position and remove your name from the management team.

The managers below you must also understand this rule and be able to delegate to their own staff. The need for this rule is easy to understand. It takes real effort to manage people, and the span of control for any one person limits how many direct reports can be effectively managed. During an operations due diligence one of the first things I ask for is a copy of the current organization chart because it reveals so much about the business.

To repeat an earlier caution, beware of potential strategic buyers trying to identify critical resources that they can poach from your business rather than honestly looking to buy your business. Your org chart makes it easy for a competitor to "cherry pick" key employees. Employee information should be held until you are well into due diligence. And remember, after your deal closes, your employees will be working for the buyer but you will probably owe your team at least some acknowledgment for the success of your business.

Don't Overlook the Informal Organizational Infrastructure

The informal organization of your business is just as important as the formal structure. What is your corporate culture? Do you run a very loose and casual business, or is it very rigid and formal? There is no right or wrong when you answer that question. There are however buyers who prefer one culture over another. A buyer who likes things run "by the book" may not value a very casual culture quite as much, and, more importantly, may be concerned about the resulting employee reaction when they try to "tighten things up."

Buyers know that culture mismatch is a leading cause of M&A failure. If you know the culture of your potential buyers or what is accepted as normal in your industry, then try to match the buyer's culture. This is not the time or place to start thinking out of the box. If people in your industry typically wear uniforms, then start measuring your staff and get them to wear uniforms. If you meet clients by appointment, then consider canceling your flex-time policy. If you do not know what the likely buyer's culture might be, your only choice is to drive your organization toward the middle of the road, reducing the potential that the culture will be a consideration. This is probably a case where being more rigid is better.

Preparing for a Personnel Infrastructure Assessment

The personnel infrastructure supports the human resources operations of the business. It defines the working relationship between the business and its employees and the relationship among the employees. It defines the strategy used for benefits and the compensation plan, and it dictates employee actions, such as the procedures for hiring, firing, and everything in between. Changes to the personnel infrastructure of your business is the area that will generate the most questions from employees once they are aware of the sale.

The personnel infrastructure supports the human resources operations of the business.

Dealing with employees is where most owners start to come off the rails when selling their business. Over time you may have become friends with some of your employees, made promises to some (promises they now want to hold you to), and have benefited from their loyalty. These are some of the things that can make dealing with employees so difficult.

"Will my pay change?"

"Will I get the raise I am due?"

"Will my benefits change?"

You want to and should be fair to your employees but the reality is that the new buyer will not be motivated by the same feelings of loyalty or friendship as you and won't have the same shared experiences with your employees that you have had with them. A buyer will want to understand what each employee's job is and will want to ensure that you aren't dumping problem employees on them. Buyers will want assurance that valued key employees aren't planning to leave after the sale and immediately go back to work for you.

Buyers will want assurance that valued key employees aren't planning to leave after the sale and immediately go back to work for you.

If this is true then it makes sense to portray your team in the best light possible. Even if you wouldn't describe your employees as your most important asset, you will still need to explain the role of each member of your team as succinctly as possible. A potential buyer will need to learn who your employees are and what each person's responsibilities are. Most small businesses claim:

"Our employees are one of our most important assets."

As they prepare to sell their business, owners occasionally find themselves in a position where they know someone has been a problem employee, but instead of solving the problem, they leave it to the new owner to solve.

"Cousin Jake doesn't actually produce much but Mom will be mad if I sack him, so I'll let the new owner deal with it."

Retaining a known problem employee may seem like a low pain approach for you. However, the cost for that employee can impact your sale, because you are still carrying them on your payroll (which lowers your profitability), and that can significantly impact your valuation. Do your own dirty work and clean up your staff as part of your positioning.

A word of caution here. It is not unusual for buyers to ask who your problem employees are or request to see your employee files—particularly for any employees that have had disciplinary actions. They then make the dismissal of those employees prior to closing one of the terms and conditions of their purchase. The intent of the buyer is to avoid inheriting problems after the purchase. That is why this is a good time to review employee personnel files to ensure they are accurate. You need to be honest with yourself and the buyer. Changing personnel files to protect an employee is not a good idea but be sure you have been fair. For example, someone might have had a problem and had a disciplinary action noted in their file; but since then, that person has become a stable contributing employee. So it's important to add a follow-up note stating that the employee responded to the disciplinary action; any evidence to that fact should be included in the file.

Retaining a known problem employee may seem like a low pain approach for you. However, the cost for that employee can impact your sale.

If your employee reaction to the sale is very negative, your buyer may decide their plans for the business won't work and back away from the deal. Your preparation for the sale should include a review of the personnel infrastructure and the impact the sale of your business will have on your employees.

Where is the strength in your management team? Buyers—or more specifically, investors—who want to hold onto a business "at arm's length" often say what they assess is "management, management, management." They intend to keep the management team in place; their approach to operations due diligence is to ignore almost everything but management in the belief that, if they get the management right, everything else will fall in line.

Maybe by now your mother has heard from her sister, and you have been pressured into promoting cousin Jake to VP of Employee Moral. Why? Because he leads in the company ping-pong championships, and you just had to find a title for him. Your best approach in this situation is to prepare a skills matrix that identifies the skills of the individual managers and indicates what they contribute to the combined skills of the management team. If cousin Jake's skills don't help the team, you may need to have a conversation with your mother and send flowers to your aunt after you either demote or fire cousin Jake.

Being prepared to hand the matrix to the buyer can build tremendous confidence in the buyer that the owner knows what they are doing and has their act together. It reflects that the business has grown by design instead of organically. Instead of just listing a set of skills, use the skills matrix to rank (with one being the best and ten being the worst) the management team member's skills in the nine operations infrastructure areas.

Preparing for a Financial Operations Infrastructure Assessment

The financial due diligence the buyer performs and the operations assessment of the financial infrastructure are two different activities. Financial due diligence assesses the financial status of the business (the content of its financial reports) whereas a financial operations assessment looks at the infrastructure that is used for fiscal control of the business. In chapter 7 we discussed the assessment of financial reports and the financial data that discloses the past performance of the business. In this assessment the buyer will look at the financial operations infrastructure that supports your business's day-to-day financial operations. There is a distinct difference between the financial reporting discussed in chapter 7 and the financial operations assessed here. Whereas the financial reports look toward the past, the financial operations infrastructure will also include forward-looking functions of the business, such as the preparation of budgets and sales projections.

"How do you arrive at your sales projections?"

Financial reports document the "actual" expenses and revenues incurred by the business in the past—last month, last year, or for however many past years you want to specify. Financial operations include the forward-looking functions of sales projection and budgeting because those numbers should be generated in the operational departments.

The financial operations infrastructure supports your business's day-to-day financial operations.

The financial operations infrastructure provides the framework for planning the continuing financial operations of the business and the financial support functions, such as the methods used for collecting the accounts payable and accounts receivable (AP/AR) and any other internal functions (such as issuing payroll checks). It also defines operating policies and procedures, such as specifying who has financial authority (Employee X can authorize that $50,000 purchase order). It includes functions that go beyond the finance department, such as cost account and project management and the generation of budgets and sales projections.

> "Wow, this sounds really complex (and for some large small businesses it really is) but we run a really small, small business."

> "I do the outside work and my wife does the administration, which includes keeping the books."

If you run a really small business where you do the outside work and your wife does the administrative functions, such as billing, your wife probably has some system she uses to track the bills, send out invoices, do the banking, and answer questions at tax time. There is the financial operations infrastructure in your business. If your buyer represents a larger corporation that is acquiring your business, they will have questions about your financial operations. Be ready to answer these questions in detail. It's important to show discipline in the management of your financial operations, regardless of the size of your business.

In addition to the "actual" expenses and revenues for the prior three years, you will need to project the revenues (a pro forma) the business will generate for the next three years and a budget for the expenses that will be incurred to achieve these sales. Rather than being prepared by the finance department, the budgets and pro forma should be generated by the operational departments responsible for managing to them. This is a case where some small businesses operate ad hoc and never create forward-looking budgets or projections. Some larger businesses create them in their finance department and force their operational departments to live by them. Other businesses formalize the process and ask their department managers to prepare their own budgets and projections, and then hold the managers accountable for performing against these projections. Buyers will see this as a sign of the maturity of the business. They will want to understand how budgets and projections were made because they will want to hold department managers accountable for the department performance you are promising.

> "Yeah, the former owner projected those sales, but the sales department never agreed to those numbers."

> "I never agreed I could run this department on that small of a budget."

Preparing for a Legal Operations Infrastructure Assessment

The legal due diligence the buyer performs and the operations assessment of the legal infrastructure are two different activities. Legal due diligence assesses the legal status of the business (e.g., are you involved in any litigation?) whereas a legal operations assessment looks at the infrastructure that is used for legal control of the business.

As you prepared your business for a legal due diligence, you collected all the contracts and agreements, any litigation documents, all your leases or other real estate–related documents, all your employee agreements or shareholder documents, and anything else that had a signature on it. Who is authorized to sign those agreements, and how do you manage them? Do you have a single repository where they are archived either in paper or electronically? How difficult will it be to build a due diligence file?

The legal operations infrastructure forms the framework for all legal operations of the business. It defines all legal authority, professional licensing, and controls needed to support the business on a continuing basis. It defines all activities used to protect the business from legal risk and liabilities and to ensure the compliant operation of the business.

The legal operations infrastructure forms the framework for all legal operations of the business.

Most small businesses don't have the luxury of a legal department. Instead they tend to leave the management of documents to the operational department that originates the document. The sales department signs nondisclosure agreements (NDAs) and customer contracts and maintains their current copies. But what happens when the engineering department sees one of the slick new functions in a vendor's prototype, and they can't wait to talk about it? They have divulged your vendor's new breakthrough product before it is announced to the public, violating that NDA. And this is how a business can end up in court. When the sales manager interviews a new salesperson and tells her he would be glad to discuss commission rates, but only over dinner, he may have more than the business in mind. And this is also how businesses end up in court. The problem is that many small businesses don't institutionalize legal operations guidelines or training programs as policies to guide the business. The legal operations infrastructure of most small businesses is treated in an ad hoc manner due to their inability to afford an in-house attorney or to pay the legal fees for an outside attorney. This becomes a tremendous source of operational risk that many buyers are not willing to assume.

If your business has grown organically and you haven't paid attention to its legal operations infrastructure, now is the time to do so. Prepare a brief but very pointed set of legal policies and procedures that include guidelines indicating who has the authority to sign various types of documents. Have your attorney draft a basic employment agreement that includes both ethics and confidentiality expectations for all employees. Have your employees sign the agreement now and have these signed forms ready to show to a buyer.

When a buyer sees a weak legal operations infrastructure, they become leery of unknown or potential legal actions and, to protect themselves, they avoid entering into an equity acquisition and may only be willing to offer an asset acquisition instead. That could reduce your valuation, because it eliminates the value of your brand name, trademarks, and good will. You will also need to discuss the tax implications of various types of purchases with your CPA and transaction attorney prior to entering any negotiations.

If you are in an industry that requires process certification or a professional license, this would be a good time to review your certifications and licenses to make sure they haven't expired. Be sure to review the requirements for renewal and verify that your business still qualifies. Plan to complete any necessary renewal requirements, such as continuing education, to ensure they can be completed on time. Some certifications include qualifications for upgrades, such as years of experience, dollars sold, quality records, etc. You may have achieved a basic level when you were first certified three years ago but qualify for a master level now. Achieving the higher-level certification may add value to your business. Keep in mind that some certifications and licenses are given to the individual rather than the business; use this as an opportunity to determine the status of certified or licensed individuals.

Preparing for an Information Management Infrastructure Assessment

It would seem like a tremendous understatement to say that all businesses are information intensive these days. The information management (IM) infrastructure includes all your business data, the electronic tools that support your operations and form the backbone of the business, and the documents and printed material and all other media that is used to support the business. The term information management is one of those umbrella terms that covers a lot of territory. We are familiar with the information technology (IT) groups that maintain our personal computers, but IM has a wider scope than that of the traditional IT group. IM also includes the business's telephones (fixed and mobile), document archives and records of all types, and any kind of media. In most small businesses the IM infrastructure growth occurs more organically than by plan.

The information management (IM) infrastructure includes all your business data plus all the electronic tools that support your operations and form the backbone of the business

---

Start preparing to answer due diligence questions about your IM infrastructure by preparing a diagram of your IM systems. Having this diagram ready to show to a buyer can answer many of their questions and will show them you are working by plan rather than organically.

In the age of digital everything, nothing is free from risk. Data can be lost, hacked, stolen, corrupted, and interrupted. Data isn't limited to what you have on your computer either. Your telephone system, alarm system, cell phone, facility power, car, and coffee pot are all likely to be hackable digital devices. Data that used to be stored in your desktop computer migrated to your server room and is now in the "cloud" (meaning you probably have no idea where it is stored or how it gets there). Whether done by accident or for commercial or even malicious purposes, you have good reason to protect the digital systems used in your business. The more data intensive your business is, the greater the risk. Even small businesses, however, have employee information, customer credit card data, contact lists, and health-care records. These days, with plenty of examples of huge fines being levied on businesses—not for stealing data, but for failing to take proper precautions for the data they have been entrusted with—buyers will want to know how your information management system is protected.

Buyers will want to know how your information management system is protected.

How prepared is your business to act as a custodian responsible for caring for of all this data? The bad press (and large fines) large and small businesses have received means that data security is an important issue and a significant risk that can impact any business. While you are justified in denying access to a buyer, it is becoming more common for buyers to request a security audit by an independent third party when the business stores privacy-related information.

The resiliency of data intensive businesses (i.e. the ability to recover from a man-made or natural disaster) is becoming a concern for buyers. The risk of data loss is extreme and can result in the loss of a business almost overnight. Buyers are concerned about the cost of implementing disaster recovery systems in such cases where even a short disruption in the continuity of the business is critical.

Your IM infrastructure includes all the personal privacy, security and disaster recovery controls that the buyer will want to assess. Note, we use the term "assess" not "access." In businesses that handle financial or health-care information data the system that hosts the data must be certified for this use. Buyers should understand the requirements for protecting that data and the reason you cannot allow them access to your IM systems. If they are not willing to understand this, find another buyer. Where large data servers are in use, penetration testing—to ensure the system is secure—may also be required. If your business is data intensive, don't wait for a buyer to make the request. Have the security test performed by a third party for your own protection and as one of your positioning tasks. Create a business resiliency plan and train your staff how to respond during business disruptions. This way, when a buyer asks, you can show them it has been done as part of your normal operations and increase the buyer's confidence in your IM infrastructure.

Preparing for an Institutionalized Processes Infrastructure Assessment

The institutionalized processes infrastructure includes the definition of all formalized policies, procedures, and methods that guide the business's operations. One of the resounding themes you may have noticed in this book by now is the need to define what you do, and write it down so that a buyer can understand how your business works.

The institutionalized processes infrastructure includes the definition of all formalized policies, procedures, and methods that guide the business's operations.

What I will add to that theme is this: once you create a procedure and write down what you say what you are going to do—do it. Don't have a buyer point out that you are not following your own published procedures or violating your own published policies.

Institutionalizing your processes is an absolute requirement in some industries. The International Standards Organization (ISO), the US's Health Insurance Portability and Accountability Act (HIPAA), Capability Maturity Model Integration (CMMI), Six Sigma, Enterprise Risk Management (ERM), and Lean or Quality Management Systems (QMS) are examples of industry standards that a business requires certification in to qualify for operation in a process-driven market. There are numerous other government regulations that set similar professional standards to be licensed to work in various industries. It's easy to see why large corporations with thousands of people want to define their processes and procedures. Everybody needs to have a road map to be sure they do things the same way. By improving their processes, they become more efficient, and nothing is forgotten. Process improvement programs can be expensive, and it is often hard to see the benefit. It's little wonder why small businesses would rather ignore this infrastructure area and not waste the time or money.

> "I have been doing this job for fifteen years and the only checklist I need is in my head."

> "It was only a problem when someone new started in sales, and I didn't get the orders the way I usually do."

> "Now that we're taking internet orders, someone needs to figure out what the commission plan is for them."

When a buyer starts to ask questions about the way your business operates, you don't want your answers to sound ad hoc or employee dependent. Employees should be told to write down what they do and how they do it. Assume that they are the experts at their jobs. Give them ownership of the job.

> "Your requirement is to write down what you do, and then do it that way."

Employees talk, and they will recognize potential improvements within their own work areas. They are often glad just to be asked, but rewarding them for improvements in efficiency isn't a bad idea and may bring change about sooner. What employees generally resist is someone else telling them how to do their job. It pays to make the ideas theirs.

> "We found out that customer contact information is entered into our systems at least three times before a product is ever shipped."

Jim's Bakery Example

Jim recognized that preparing his operations infrastructure would be a large, time-consuming activity. It was a good thing he hadn't decided to sell his business right away and closed in a month. The time it took to prepare his operations infrastructure had added tremendous value. Even though they didn't realize it at the time, it had also helped his employees. During the buyer's due diligence, it was clear the employees knew their jobs and had had an input in making the business operate efficiently.

Jim's Production/Services Infrastructure Preparation Example

Jim reviewed the 20 percent growth projections that the sales department for his commercial bakery had predicted and recognized that after next year he would need to almost double his oven space. He gave his commercial COO the task of researching how to fit the new ovens into their existing facility. Blueprints for the upgrade were completed so Jim could show them to potential buyers.

Jim's Sales and Marketing Infrastructure Preparation Example

As part of his preparations for a financial infrastructure assessment, Jim worked with the sales and marketing department to establish sales goals for the next three years. Once they agreed on these goals, they were broken down into a month-by-month projection over the three years. He allowed the entire sales team to contribute toward these projections and directed the sales managers to develop a sales commission plan to incentivize the team to meet these goals

Jim's Organizational Infrastructure Preparation Example

The organization chart (Figure 9.1) for Jim's Bakery clearly identifies the role each person plays in the business and the responsibility for each employee. Buyers will quickly recognize the straightforward efficiency of this structure.

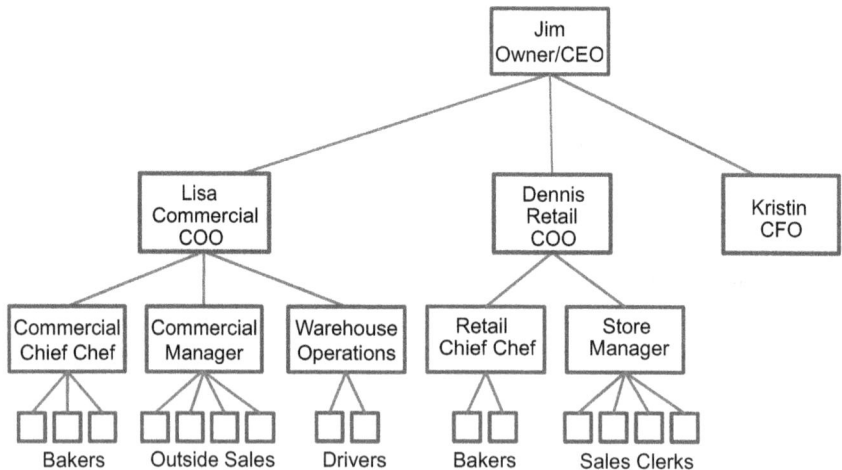

Figure 9.1: Jim's Bakery Organization Chart

Note: Without knowing much about Jim's Bakery, consider what the organization chart tells you about the business. How is the business structured? How many employees are there? How many employees are in management roles and what areas are they responsible for? How are sales supported? How are products delivered? Don't play down the importance of creating this chart.

Figure 9.1 supports your goal of making a prospective buyer's due diligence and deep dive analysis as easy to perform as possible. This shows why constructing an organization chart becomes a key to understanding the business. It can be used as a road map when trying to understand other areas of the business such as the structure of the financial reports and the different groups the expenses are allocated to. Put in the time, even if this is difficult or seems overdone for your business.

To demonstrate the business in operation, the buyer will use the organization chart as a simple road map to follow. The buyer will know that an interview with the three senior staff members (just below the owner) to understand the commercial operations, retail operations, and financial operations will achieve just that. If a buyer was considering growing the business, it would be easy to add a new catering operation, for instance, to this organization. Imagine a buyer's reaction if there were dotted lines of responsibility or if all bakery operations were not clearly identified.

Jim's Bakery Personnel Infrastructure Preparation Example

Jim's Bakery offers a wide range of benefits for its employees, including health care, tuition reimbursement, and flexible personal time off. As part of their preparation, the CFO was tasked with renegotiating the employer cost for their health insurance. He was able to find compatible insurance for a lower cost and signed a three-year contract with the insurance company.

Jim terminated cousin Jake. Jim's mom and aunt are still mad at him, but they were glad to see Jim gave his cousin a two-week vacation—on a beach far from where Jim was going to be.

One of the managers, whose department had a reputation for not performing, provided a budget input that Jim and the CFO agreed was way out of line. After meeting with the manager, it was clear to Jim and the CFO that the manager was not able to run his department effectively and the manager was terminated. A lead from within the department was promoted to manager, and the CFO worked with him to create the budgets. The department would now operate much more efficiently, and terminating the other manager actually improved the morale of the department.

Jim's Bakery Financial Operations Infrastructure Preparation Example

Jim had the CFO create a budget template to be used by each department head. Each department head was asked to provide month-by-month budgets for the next three years that would allow them to support the sales goals. Jim then negotiated the budgets with each manager and sent out a policy memo that identified the financial authorization of each manager.

As part of his preparations for the financial operations assessment, the CFO reviewed the commercial divisions accounts receivable (AR) and found that over time their collections had started to drag out. Some of their commercial customers were paying far too late. The CFO improved the collection process by implementing new late payment and bad debt (nonpayment) policies.

Jim's Bakery Legal Operations Infrastructure Preparation Example

Jim met with his attorney to review the various agreements and contracts Jim's Bakery uses on a regular basis. Quite often documents had come to him to be signed when he thought they could have been signed by his division COOs. He wanted to determine who needed to be delegated the authority to sign them. He had also had situations where documents, such as NDAs, had been signed by salesman who weren't authorized to commit the business. He implemented policies to clarify who had these authorities.

Jim's Bakery Information Management Infrastructure Preparation Example

Jim had the head of the IT department form a team with a representative from each of the other departments with the mission of identifying all support products they used. Sales had a tool they were using to track contacts and leads. Finance had a tool they were using to generate invoices and another one they used to create their financial reports. The administration department had a contract for the telephone system both facilities used. Marketing had a graphics product they used. The retail store had an inventory product they used. It seemed like everyone had purchased specialized products to support their needs.

Some of the products were backed up regularly, and others never seemed to have been. Some of the products kept credit card numbers and financial data, such as credit applications for the commercial customers, but the IT department hadn't been notified and had not installed firewalls to protect the data on some machines.

A project headed by the IT manager was kicked off to resolve all of the issues they had found. A second project was kicked off to establish a document repository that could be accessed by all employees.

Jim's Bakery Institutionalized Processes Infrastructure Preparation Example

Jim's Bakery had started with just two people and had grown regularly ever since. No one had ever taken the time to write down the policies and procedures they followed. New employees received no specific training. They just learned as they worked. Some new employees had introduced some new and creative methods when they started. But no one ever wrote them down. There were situations where two people were doing the same job but doing it differently. The commercial bakery had found some better ways to mix the batter for bread, but the retail bakery wasn't aware of it and was still mixing the old inefficient way.

After Jim formed a process improvement group that would bring employees together to document their methods, the employees found many more efficient ways to work. Jim offered employee bonuses when new work processes and methods were implemented.

Chapter 10
Due Diligence

In the initial chapters we talked about marketing your business to find a qualified buyer, and at this point you have completed the positioning needed to prepare your business for due diligence. You completed your down select to the buyer you hope to close a deal with. This is the buyer who offered you the most acceptable deal. Even though you have a purchase agreement or letter of intent (LOI) with them, the deal isn't done yet. Now you are at the point where your buyer will want to perform a detailed assessment of the business that goes much deeper than the marketing information you previously provided in your marketing "Book." The detailed assessment the buyer performs of your business is called due diligence.

> "Everything I have been telling you about my business is true. . .. Trust me."

Preparation for due diligence was done in parallel with your marketing activities and, by the time you get to due diligence you should have completed all of the work to fully position your business.

Due Diligence Is a Continuation of Negotiations

Don't confuse the fact that you have already negotiated a price and accepted a written offer from the buyer with the price you may eventually be paid for the business. You may find they are two different things. Your buyer will use the due diligence process to verify that all the marketing information you provided is true and that the business has the transferrable value you advertised to justify the price they offered. While the offer you negotiated with the buyer may determine where the bar is set and how high the price will be, many experienced buyers will try to use due diligence as an opportunity to further renegotiate in an attempt to drive the price down.

> "Based on what we found during due diligence we are going to lower our offer."

Your buyer will use the due diligence process to verify that all the marketing information you provided is true and that the business has the transferrable value you advertised to justify the price they offered.

DOI 10.1515/9781547400249-010

During due diligence, buyers will try to identify any warts your business may have (i.e., discover where the risks are). They will perform due diligence to ensure they are entering the deal with their eyes fully open, but that may not be their only purpose. They will dig to find areas where potential for risk exists, and they will use that information to help negotiate a better price (that is, better for them). Most people overlook the second part of that statement. If the due diligence team discovers a wart that you were not aware of, you will likely lose the discussion point during negotiations.

> "The buyer gave us a letter of intent with an offer of $10 million but during due diligence they discovered that a critical supplier was raising their prices and renegotiated the price down to $9 million."

Many buyers try to use due diligence to devalue the business and use that information to justify lowering their offer price. To avoid finding yourself in this situation, you need to identify any outstanding issues (all businesses have warts) and resolve as many issues as possible during your positioning to mitigate or avoid discovering any new risks. Then you should be upfront about any remaining known or outstanding issues. Be prepared to address any of the warts your business has well in advance of due diligence, and do not try to rationalize your way around them if they are raised first by the buyer. You also need to enter the due diligence process with your eyes fully open so that you can "take the wind out of the buyer's sails" during negotiation.

> "Yes, that is a known risk, but we are already taking steps to mitigate it."

> "Here is our plan, which is already reflected in our price."

The Due Diligence Process

In the prior chapters, we talked about some of the key things you can do to prepare for the legal, financial, and operations assessments of your business. But first you need to understand a little bit about the due diligence process itself.

Due diligence is sponsored by the buyers. It is their event, so they will provide you with a schedule and a request for the information they need to perform their assessments. It will include a list of documents to be reviewed and a schedule of any other activities the buyer wants to request. They will ask for a visit to the business to observe the operations first hand along with providing a list of questions they will want written responses to. They may also ask you to set up meetings with some of your customers either in person or by phone and possibly meetings with some of your vendors. Due diligence will kick off a flurry of activity that will make it difficult to keep the events secret.

This flurry of activity is usually the point where some of the employees first become aware that something is happening. News about this type of event will spread quickly in a small business so, even if you have tried to keep the sale from your employees up until this point, you should be ready and anticipate their questions. Without elaborating, a simple explanation that *"We are speaking with investors and appreciate any help you can give"* may suffice to answer their immediate questions.

This flurry of activity is usually the point where some of the employees first become aware that something is happening.

Document List

The buyers will request an extensive list of documents that can include all the legal documents, business plans, employee folders, customer agreements—and on and on. Any document with a signature or any existing agreements, policies, or procedures relating to the operation of the business may be on the list. Responding to the request for documents really exposes the business, so it is critical that the confidentiality terms in your agreement or LOI are able to protect you. Imagine the impact of releasing your customer agreements, including end dates, to a strategic buyer. You also must have your attorney review the confidentiality agreements between your business and your customers. Releasing those agreements to a buyer may violate your customer agreements.

At one time, sellers responded to a document request by creating a "due diligence box" that contained hard copies of the requested documents. Providing hard copies had some draw backs. It was inconvenient to copy that many documents (never give an original), and typically resulted in many physical boxes of documents and lots of "trees killed" to supply the paper. It was easy to lose track of things. Documents were lost, copies could be made and not tracked, and there was no record of who had read them. It was also difficult for the buyer to search that many documents when they needed to find specific information.

> "By the way, we know there are over 2,000 documents resulting from our request, so would you mind providing three copies of each for our review team?"

If the buyer does request hard copies of documents, specify that you will only provide one copy and that a record be provided of any additional copies the buyer makes (or prints). Technology has won the day on document requests and the due diligence box has given way to virtual data rooms (VDRs). VDRs are now being used to create reviewable document repositories (hard copies can be scanned into the VDR), which allow the buyer's team of reviewers to access your documents.

Technology has won the day on document requests and the due diligence box has given way to virtual data rooms (VDRs).

As part of your preparation for due diligence you should have already have collected all the documents you anticipate a buyer will want and created a document archive to put them in. That way, there won't be a delay while you try to find relevant documents after the start of due diligence. VDR services also offer a side benefit for buyers. The documents in the archive are now electronically searchable. Tools that were originally developed to support litigation discovery also work well for VDR discovery and allow the buyer to search all your documents for key words and phrases. This can work much more to the buyer's advantage than the sellers and enables them to look for trends. They may know more about your business than you do by the time they are done!

Preparing an Asset List

The buyer will request a list of all the assets that will be included in the deal. Review your asset list to make sure it only includes the items you intend to deliver. I had a client that had a large, high volume, very expensive printer they had leased. When their support staff inventoried their tech equipment they included the printer on the asset list. In fact, there was no intent to include the printer in the deal, but there it was, big as life on the asset list that had been provided to the buyer. The equipment lease for the printer wasn't identified (no one expected to deliver the printer) and the business ended up buying out the lease and delivering the printer to the new owner. Be like Santa—check your list twice, and don't give anything away you didn't plan on! There are numerous inventory applications that can help with this task, even some that are free. It makes sense to use one of these products since the list may be flexible during normal operations and your list will be easier to maintain if it is updated in the normal course of doing business. This activity will be needed whether you are entering an asset or an equity sale.

Review your asset list to make sure it only includes the items you intend to deliver.

The assets of your business include both its tangible and intangible assets. Tangible assets are fixed assets used to operate the business. Intangible assets are nonphysical assets that include the reputation of your business and its good will. Intangible assets also include intellectual property (IP) and add transferrable value—but you will need to discuss how they are valued with your CPA. Correctly identifying both types of assets is a critical value driver. Assets can also be categorized into fixed assets and current assets. Fixed assets include tools, equipment, machinery, property, plant etc. Current assets include accounts receivable, debts, stock, bank balances, and cash. Buyers will want to see these distinguished on your balance sheet because current assets generally change before closing in the normal day-to-day operation of the business.

Tangible Assets

Your CPA may already have a fixed asset list that is included on your balance sheet. If they have done a good job maintaining the list with sufficient detail, then you are ahead of the game. Experience has shown that the list your CPA maintains may not be of sufficient detail to satisfy a buyer. Creating a fixed asset list that inventories (and tags) every item that will be included in the sale may take some time and thought. It requires some care. It also has potential tax implications on the sale, so this is one of the areas you will need to discuss with your CPA and tax attorney. The good news is that it is a task that can be started early, before engaging with the buyer, and can be delegated to employees to complete. Depending on the size of your business, the fixed asset list can become excessive or it can be simple. Without a detailed fixed asset list, you will be taking a "what you see is what you get" approach.

What about the owner's Cadillac Escalade that is parked in a reserved spot by the back door? Is that included in the deal or will it be an adjustment you make on your income statement? The fixed asset list is a list of the hard assets, listed by model and serial number, which are used to operate the business. The Escalade may eventually become an adjustment when calculating your EBITDA.

Intangible Assets

An intangible asset is a nonphysical asset ("it is without substance") but which has value. It's easy to see how a machine or a building or even the furniture in the building has some value that can be assigned to it, but what intrinsic value do you assign to the goodwill you have established with your customers? Intangible assets include any stocks, bonds, or other assets held in a bank. They have value even if they can't be physically held.

Your customers continue to come back because they know the service they get from you will be better than what they get from your competition, so you know all the hard work you put in has some intrinsic value. When customers go to the store, they ask for products with your brand name, so you know your trademark on the package tells customers they can trust the product. Doesn't your trademark have value? You filed for a patent that has created a barrier to entry and keeps your potential competitors from creating a similar product. Doesn't that patent have some intrinsic value?

Of course, your intangible assets add value to your business. That is why small business owners work so hard to attain them. Assigning a value and determining how to treat that value for tax purposes can vary greatly from country to country. I find that most small businesses do not, for various reasons, take the time to consider what intangible assets they have. As a result, they fail to capture those assets and are not able to benefit from the value they could add to their business. As you start preparing for due diligence, an effort to identify, capture and value the intangible assets of your business should include professional help from both an accountant and an attorney.

Preparing for the Due Diligence On-Site Assessment

After completing their document review and analysis of your response to their written questions, the buyer will have a list of items they will want to observe and validate during their on-site visit. Some buyers perform due diligence in a very formal manner and others are much less formal. In either case, whether they are looking for specific items they want to verify, or they just want to do a walk around, whether this activity is scheduled to take a day, a week, or a month, be prepared to have the buyer under foot for a bit. Make sure you have an agreement with the buyer ahead of time regarding any employee or customer discussions and be prepared to be as open as possible with them. This is not a time for contention from you or your employees (it may be a stress-driven result, but it happens), so if you find any contention building you might want to take steps to end it immediately.

> "Hey boss, I know those guys who were visiting work for the competition and kept asking how we build these widgets so fast."

This may be the first real interaction the buyer has with your management team so be sure to give your employees a chance to shine—both for their potential new boss and for the value the team you built brings to the business you are selling. You want this to be a good experience for the buyer, too. You don't want the buyer's due diligence team to conclude that neither you nor your managers don't want them there.

> "Those guys clearly didn't want us there. We'd better plan to bring in a new management team after we close this deal."

This may be the first real interaction the buyer has with your management team so be sure to give your employees a chance to shine.

The buyer may bring in one or more people to do the on-site assessment, depending on the size of your business. At Diligent we tend to use two to three people with a mix of skills (mainly financial and operations); our assessment is what would normally be termed as an enterprise risk assessment. We have found it pays to take the time to reassure the employees that we are looking for risk and not assessing their individual performance.

The buyer's team will want to sit with individuals (but not necessarily everyone) and ask what people do and why they do it. It is easy for these questions to sound like the buyer is critiquing rather than clarifying during these interviews. This is particularly true if the buyer is a former competitor who is using their employees as assessors rather than trained assessors. Keep an eye out for this and prepare to explain to your employees that the buyer's questions are clarifications. If you feel the assessor is critiquing, then bring it to the buyer's attention immediately. These misunderstandings can quickly "derail" a deal or give the buyer a permanent bad taste for the deal that will show up when you complete your final negotiations.

> "Oh yeah, we're interested, but from what we've found out, we're only offering $8 million instead of the $10 million we originally agreed upon."

It's a Good Time to Build the Relationship

You are trying to *sell* your business. The best way to sell is to establish a relationship with the buyer. Allow plenty of time to visit with the buyer, offer to answer any questions, and in general, make yourself available.

"Hey, these are good guys; I look forward to working with them."

As the on-site assessment ends, it is a good time to host a dinner with your management team and the buyer, pay for a round of golf at your club, take a day off for offshore fishing, or whatever venue works best for your area. Your goal is to build a trust relationship. If nothing else works, make it a barbeque in your back yard.

The best way to sell is to establish a relationship with the buyer.

If you have two or three customers that you trust will not panic at the news of the sale and who will be willing to say why they use your products or services rather than a competitor's, consider asking them to join you and the buyer.

Post–On-Site Activity

After completing the on-site visit, the buyer's due diligence team will leave to prepare their due diligence assessment report. Less formal buyers may simply use a "thumbs up/thumbs down" method but more formal buyers will have their team develop a risk/opportunity assessment report where they document their findings. The advantage of the more formal method is that the report can be used by the buyer to optimize resources to mitigate identified risks following the purchase. You, as the seller, will likely never see this report.

Following their analysis, the buyer may request a second on-site visit to verify some of their findings. Their activity during the second visit will give you some indication of where they may have some concerns. You may also get some additional document requests or questions. Don't panic. These requests are normal. Remember, the assessment is looking for opportunities as well as risks.

"On our first visit we thought we saw an area for improvement, so we went back to satisfy ourselves this was an oversight of the seller and would be a real opportunity for us."

"I guess after running the business for twenty-five years he was just too close to see the opportunity."

At some point following their assessment, the buyer will notify you of their findings (positive and negative) and what their intentions are. Some buyers will provide feedback in the form of a letter where others will want to have a sit-down meeting. Neither by itself is a sign of success or failure. Attend these meetings, learn what you can, and don't get defensive. Have your attorney and your CPA attend with you to take notes

"Based on what we found during due diligence we are prepared to move ahead, pending discussions about our original letter of intent (LOI)."

Read that as "we want to negotiate the price." It may be inconsequential, and you can agree to accept their modified offer and shake their hand on the deal or you can accept their offer for consideration. Of course, you also have the option to dig in your heels and take the position you're not ready to change their last offer. They could also say:

"Based on what we found during due diligence we are not prepared to move ahead and are going to rescind our original offer."

Well, that's a "bummer"! You had more than one offer and after selecting them and dropping the other offer(s), they have now decided they are dropping out. For this reason alone, when you write the agreement with them, you need to specify how long the buyer will have to complete their due diligence as one of the terms. You may be able to return to your second choice (if they haven't moved on to another purchase), but even if you move quickly the deal may already have gone cold with them.

You need to specify how long the buyer will have to complete their due diligence as one of the terms in the LOI.

Jim's Bakery Example

After agreeing on the terms of their deal, Jim signed an LOI with one of the buyers. He was anxious to have the buyer begin their assessments. The buyer sent him a due diligence schedule they intended to follow along with requests for a list of documents for review, a list of assets to be included in the deal, and a list of questions they wanted written responses to.

The schedule showed a sixty-day due diligence period, which seemed excessive. Jim worked through his intermediary and was able to reduce that to forty-five days. Part of the justification was due to the asset list request. Jim's Bakery had prepared a list and hadn't waited until a request arrived to prepare one. The same was true of the document request. They had already created a document archive, so most of the requested documents were already in a secure online repository. The buyer asked for a couple of documents Jim's team hadn't thought to include but it was an easy task to add them to the existing repository. Jim had his CFO and COOs provide written responses to the written questions.

An office was set aside in the commercial bakery for the buyer's due diligence team to work. Employees were simply told the due diligence team were from investors who were assessing the business without elaborating anymore and the employees accepted this explanation. The employees were asked to cooperate as much as possible with the assessment team. The work they had been doing to clean up and improve the efficiency of their operations seemed to have positioned the business perfectly to impress the due diligence team.

Chapter 11
Describing Your Business Model

How does your business make money? This should be the easiest question you'll be asked when selling your business and you need to be prepared with a solid answer. The answer you give should be the description of your business model. The description of your business model should cause a potential buyer to have a real "Aha!" moment. And that's when you will know they understand the transferrable value of your business.

> "What a great idea! Someone really thought this through."

Unfortunately, the response given by many owners doesn't sound like it has been thought out very well at all. The owner hesitates in their response, or makes a statement in a manner that sounds weak, or even worse, risks sounding flippant and comes across at about at the same level as "buy low, sell high." The saying "If it were this easy anyone could do it" applies here, so if you give this type of answer, don't be surprised when the buyer's response is:

> "Well if it's that easy (or obvious), why do I need to buy your business?"

Do you have a unique approach to generating revenue? Unless you're a stock broker, "buy low, sell high" (or some similar pithy remark) is probably an understatement of your business and not the type of answer you want to give. There is a difference between being pithy and being direct and to the point. "Buy low, sell high" is a pithy statement. It doesn't convey much information a buyer can use. "We sell high volume products at a small margin" is direct and to the point. If you want to hear a great business model, ask a Girl Scout how they sell cookies: *"I wear my uniform and Momma and I set up a table outside the grocery store."* No doubt at all that their business model is one that works well for them!

DOI 10.1515/9781547400249-011

Prepare an Elevator Speech

The response you give when asked to describe your business model is the "elevator speech"[1] for your business. Practice it. Get it right and use it to quickly grab a potential buyer's attention.

The response you give when asked to describe your business model is the "elevator speech" for your business.

Providing pithy answers, or answers that haven't been thought out, are a lost opportunity to highlight the value proposition of your business, demonstrate the uniqueness of your business, or explain why customers turn to your business when they have other choices. It's second nature for some people to hold back, or maybe even feel they are bragging when they resist making claims about their business. Avoid the temptation to understate your business model. Practice making short valid statements regarding the way your business makes money.

> "This is a small business and my business model is simple. . .."

If you want to grab a potential buyer's attention, deliver this sentence well because it may be your one chance to tell them why this is such a great opportunity.

> "Our business is small, but we have developed a unique market approach. . .."

Prepare a Written Description of Your Business Model

A business model tells the buyer how you "do what you do" and how you make money doing it. Your business model needs to be thought out in advance, rehearsed, and then clearly, completely, and succinctly written down and targeted toward potential buyers. If your model is unique, you want your answer to be different from anyone else the buyer may be speaking with to convey the inherent value of your business when compared to others. It is your business's

---

1 An elevator speech is a clear, brief statement about your business (or in some cases, about yourself). It is a commercial that communicates what your business does, how it does it, why clients select your business and how it creates value for the owners. It must be short in duration—about the time it takes someone to ride up in an elevator (hence its name). It is important to have your speech memorized and practiced.

value proposition and you should be eager to explain how your business makes money. But keep in mind—even if your business model is complex you need to explain it in a manner that allows the buyer to have that "Aha!" moment. Your business model should start with a bold definitive statement about the business.

"Our state-of-the-art computerized milling equipment allows us to manufacture components faster and more affordably than other competitor in the region."

"We patented the process for manufacturing XYZ long before anyone else thought about entering the market."

I have heard busy investors say they would rather see a definitive business model than a full business plan. After your meeting ends and the buyer is asked why they are looking at your business, you want them to be excited and talk about how smart your business model is and how they can benefit from it. If they remember nothing else about you or your business, you want them to remember your business model—and then they'll come back for the rest.

If the buyer is asked why they are looking at your business, you want them to be excited and talk about how smart your business model is.

Your business model should be a written statement about a page long that explains how your business enters and competes in the market. It is a competitive statement that tells the buyer how money flows into and through the business. Your business model needs to tell the buyer how customers are attracted to the business, what their product options are, and why they might return. What are the discriminators that bring customers to you? What attracts them?

"We are a family-owned pizza shop that customers return to because the recipe for our sauce is unique and has been passed down for generations."

"We are a web development company that has teamed with a local university to employ part-time college students because of their creative designs and competitive wages."

"We are an IT company that offers live 24/7 support services from trained technicians."

"We are a SaaS product development business with a self-propagating product that drives new subscriptions."

Each of the preceding statements is a competitive discriminator because it implies (insert descriptive words here) and our competition doesn't do that. More importantly, each of the preceding statements, while brief, is likely to draw further questions and discussion from interested buyers.

> "Tell me more. . .."

To grab a buyer's attention and deliver a message that sticks, add value to your description by including graphics that explain and clarify your business model. Add any graphics, diagrams, or other descriptive material that enhances their understanding of how the model works. Flow diagrams that depict how your "sales funnel" works or how prospects are attracted and brought into the "sales pipeline" should be included.

> "Customers are attracted to low end products, but we are able to demonstrate our other options and upsell them once they are here."

You will eventually include the written description of your business model in the "Book" (described in the next chapter) you will prepare as a marketing tool for your business, but also be prepared by having a stand-alone version ready for the busy buyer who may be reviewing multiple plans, wants to save time, and asks, *"Just let me see your business model."*

Beware—Business Models Change

Some business models have lasted for a long time and can be considered classic, but the popularity of some business models has changed over time. At one time shopping malls were the hot business model, but today malls are closing as people turn more and more to online shopping. Even business models that were once considered "standard" and were sought by investors have eventually fallen out of favor with buyers. There are a lot of "brick and mortar" retail stores who found out too late that they hadn't gotten online fast enough once Amazon. com changed the retail sales model.

Savvy buyers will want to understand your business model in detail because they know business models change along with the markets they support. There are business models that buyers are familiar with and try to avoid and others they seek because the model has been proven and produces exceptional value.

Classic business models once included the ice cream truck that sold door to door throughout neighborhoods and generated sales by attracting children right out of their living rooms; door-to-door salesmen selling beauty supplies and vacuum cleaners to stay-at-home housewives—until women moved into the workforce; and manufacturers whose business model was to give away the razor, so people would buy the blades—until disposable razors took over the market.

Technology quickly changes business models and enables them to evolve to meet the needs of changing markets, making what was once a strong business model suddenly irrelevant. Buyers know that business models change, and the associated markets can also change quickly, making industries disappear overnight. The term "radical innovation" is used to describe products that completely disrupt a market, but radical innovation can also be used to describe changes in a business model used to sell a product. Mobile phones were a radical innovation, not just because they changed the wall-mounted communications device into a portable computer, but also because they changed the business model and disconnected the device's sale from the phone company as the business model evolved to include the newer concept of mobile carriers. "Ma Bell" never saw that business model change coming. Buyers want to know that you're not selling them a business that is based on a dinosaur business model.

At one time people went to "filling stations" for gas because it was also the place where they had their auto repairs done. And at one time the attendant even came out and pumped the gas for you. Today people buy gas from a convenience store where they can get a quart of milk on the way home, and people have learned to use self-service pumps. Technology has made cars much more reliable and much more complex. Auto technology evolution now causes people to turn to specialty shops for most of their car maintenance. These examples may seem like ancient history for some but there are even more radical business model changes taking place today. The old business model for airlines was based on the comfort and service they provided. That model changed when the discount airlines abandoned comfort and service as a competitive discriminator.

Spend time making your business model a strength rather than letting it appear as a weakness of your business. Your business model must be relevant to the current market. If a buyer recognizes that the model is changing and you're still operating the same way you did for the past thirty years, they will either not be interested or will greatly devalue the business. Which of these businesses would you want to buy? Be prepared to sell the strength of your business model.

"All of the diners in the area serve 'food to order' but the construction workers we were serving didn't have time to wait for those meals to be prepared on their lunch breaks."

"Our business model was to pre-make sandwiches and other meals that are 'grab and go' without waiting."

"When the bulk of the construction work moved across town, our business model allowed us to follow them with food trucks that went directly to their construction sites and provided the same ready-to-go meals."

The Franchise Business Model

One of the reasons for buying a franchise is its proven business model. Franchising is based on operating a business according to a business model established by the franchisor. The security of using an established business model is one of the compelling reasons to choose to buy a franchise. If you are selling a franchise business, it makes sense to claim your business model as one of your strengths. Even a franchise business model doesn't come with a guarantee though. With a franchise you are working under the license of a franchisor and the terms of your agreement usually makes it impossible to change your business model. When was the last time you rented a movie from a video store or bought something from a music store? Selling a franchise, with a business model that potential buyers know is failing, is extremely difficult and is often impossible.

If you are selling a franchise business, it makes sense to show its business model as one of your strengths.

It is no wonder buyers want to ask a lot of questions about the business model before an acquisition. They know what can happen. You need to be prepared to explain the value of your business model and to defend its uniqueness. To sell any business, you will need to sell your business model. This doesn't change just because you're selling a franchise.

Strategic Decisions Should Be Tested by the Business Model

A well-defined business model can serve as much more than a commercial for your business. It can also serve as a framework that can be used to test your strategic decisions and support financial projections and growth rationale provided to prospective buyers. Telling a prospective buyer *"We thought about doing that, but it would change our business model and impact our sales"* tells the buyer you are focused, know what you are doing, and not just chasing revenue. A stronger message might be,

> "Here is how our business model supports the kind of growth we are projecting."

Your strategic plan and business model should go "hand in hand." Together they define how your business captures value from the market and the ability of the business to continue growing that value into the future. Buyers need to fully understand your business model, not only to understand the current value of the business, but also to understand the rationale behind your projections. Potential buyers will bring ideas of their own into the business.

"We would like to do this with the business; do you think that will work?"

When the business model is a strength of the business, it can also be used to test ideas for new products and services. This can include testing to see if a new strategic business acquisition would add value by enhancing the business further through its business model. Products and services are added because they add strength to an established business model. Projections for strategic growth can be justified by showing how the new product fits into the business model and ensuring that the rationale for the product makes sense when measured for impact within the context of the model.

"The new products (or services) meet additional needs of our customers and are within our skill set to support."

Small businesses tend to become defocused by chasing much-needed revenue that divert resources from their business model. When small businesses are struggling, they go after low-hanging fruit even though it takes resources away from their established business model and has a negative impact on their strategic goals. Long-term plans get traded for near-term revenue. Chasing revenue can have tactical value but may result in a loss of strategic value for the business.

Small businesses tend to become defocused by chasing much-needed revenue that diverts resources from their business model.

If you have added (or say you are planning to add) a new product line that falls outside of your business model, buyers may challenge your business model or, worse, choose not to purchase that business line or portion of the business.

"We're interested in buying this half of your business but not that."

If you are hoping to find an investment partner and stay in the business, you will need to show how you will use any additional capital funds they invest to strengthen or grow your business model and provide the rationale for making changes to the model.

"That potential product fits our business model because it can be delivered through our existing channels."

You want your business model to be a strategic guide to your business decisions, but at the same time it shouldn't be a monolith that is cast in stone. As the prior examples have shown, when the market changes, your model may need to change in response. Business models (and strategic plans) need to be reviewed regularly and changed when justified. Be prepared to explain your rationale for past changes to a potential buyer. Explaining those changes is a great platform for showing a buyer how the business has evolved. Just be sure to put it in that context.

> "We were able to take advantage of our existing sales channels which made it easy to integrate that new product line."

If you are changing your business model simply to chase revenue, potential buyers will see this as a sign of desperation and react accordingly. You are much better off when you're presenting the strength of your business model and can demonstrate how adaptable and responsive it is.

> "Well the market changed, and we couldn't adapt to it so we're selling" vs. "Well the market is changing but we changed our business model in advance of the changes and increased our customer base."

You want your business model to be a strategic guide to your business decisions, but at the same time it shouldn't be a monolith that is cast in stone.

Business Models Affect Valuations

The business model you use will have an impact on the valuation of your business. Buyers develop strong preferences for businesses that adopt certain business models. As the popularity of an older model begins to fade, the valuation of a business continuing to use the outdated model will begin to decline. As various models come and go over time, businesses must change their methods accordingly. Some owners, who are accustomed to the old way of doing business, may have trouble implementing new methods and will begin having trouble competing. The owners of these businesses frequently decide it's time to move on and let the new guy figure out how to make the changes. If that's the position you find yourself in, then you should also be ready to acknowledge that you have decided to accept a lower valuation for your business. Even if you're not a software developer, read through the following example that shows how the business model can directly impact the valuation of a business. Later, see if you can spot how we adapted this model for the Jim's Bakery example.

Make an aaS of Yourself

The legacy business model for software companies first relied on marketing their software as a "one-off" sale. In order to advertise their products, businesses used traditional marketing methods such as attending trade fairs, advertising in trade journals, or advertising in any place where new users were likely to be found. Customers purchased software products "off the shelf" in a box that contained a CD and the technical manual for the product. The customer paid the full asking price and used the product as long as it continued to meet their needs. The sales department booked the sale and went out looking for the next new customer.

The business would add newer, updated products with more functionality, but this was mostly an attempt to keep up with the competition. The percent of customers that returned to repurchase the product (recurring sales) was a small percentage of the business's revenues and projections going forward. Customers who paid the entire price for the software weren't in a hurry to buy it again soon. Maintenance and licensing have always been problems, and numerous schemes have been used to resolve them. If the sales department sold products to 2,000 customers this year, to keep even, they would then need the marketing support to sell to another 2,000 customers next year. If they wanted 10 percent growth next year, they either raised their prices or sold to 2,200 additional customers next year. This caused an increase in marketing expense, and now they had to pay the maintenance expenses for 4,200 customers.

As the technology improved to include faster computers and increased internet volumes and speed, it also enabled the business model to evolve. Software could now be delivered without the need for the box, the CD, or a printed tech manual; it could just be downloaded online. Bug fixes were no longer a problem because the software could be easily upgraded, and maintenance migrated to online support centers that could remotely access customer machines to solve problems. As the new business model evolved, so did the way customers paid for the products. The new model now enables monthly subscription pricing.

The new business model, known as software as a service (SaaS), has revolutionized the software business and caused radical changes to the way the software industry operates. The change wasn't due just to the new technology, but to the new business model it enabled.

If 2,000 products are sold this year, the sale is no longer a "one-off." The product is downloaded, and the customer is charged a prorated monthly fee (effectively leasing the product and giving the customer an easy step into using it). If the product meets the customer's needs and the software business provides reasonable service, the customer will continue paying on a monthly subscription basis for years. The new business model relies on the business retaining a high level of recurring revenue so that the customer is automatically renewed at the end of the year. They have already effectively "rebooked" those sales without having to market for new customers. To grow 10 percent, they need to find 200 new customers, not 2,200, and they only need to provide maintenance support for 2,200 customers.

Investors became so enamored with the new SaaS model that it became difficult to find funds or sell a software business that had not implemented a SaaS model. If you were selling a software business, you had great motivation for changing your business to include a SaaS model. SaaS businesses are now valued based on their projected—rather than actual—revenue. "We did $2 million in revenue this year but are confident we can do $3 million next year, because we only need to sell to half the customers we did last year. Two million dollars is already under contract." Compound that growth for three years and you have significantly increased your valuation over the traditional model. Under the original model, 2 × revenue is $4.4 million, whereas under the new model a 2× valuation becomes $6 million, with half the projected sales risk. The model became so effective that many other industries are now trying to emulate it. Buyers place great value on a business that can demonstrate a working SaaS model.

Jim's Bakery Example

The business model for Jim's Bakery mimics the model followed by many SaaS software development businesses and is now being adopted by many other industries. It relies on the generation of long-term recurring revenue, based on an established monthly fee that automatically renews on an annual basis. Jim's Bakery is leveraging their retail business to draw commercial clients into long-term recurring relationships.

Within Jim's retail store they advertise their catering services for specialty events to single customers for holiday parties and weddings, and to commercial customers for business events and conferences. This gives Jim's sales team an opportunity to assess the customer's potential long-term needs for Jim's products and results in a targeted list of potential commercial clients. Jim's commercial clients include restaurants, schools, nursing homes, and health-care facilities. Jim's sales team can propose entering commercial clients into a bread as a service (BaaS) program that charges them a monthly fee for the delivery of baked goods for an agreed-upon periodic schedule (daily, weekly, or monthly programs are available). By using Jim's BaaS program these customers know they can count on Jim's Bakery's reputation for quality, dependability, and exceptional service on a continuing basis for a fixed monthly fee. Some customers never progress beyond the basic product while others become long-term commercial BaaS clients.

Jim's Bakery Business Model

The Jim's Bakery business model (Figure 11.1) relies on our well-established reputation for quality baked goods and exceptional service to draw retail customers into the store (the top of the sales funnel). We do this by first inviting customers to sample our bakery products for "free," enticing potential customers to purchase products and converting them into paying customers for our retail products. The goal is to drive commercial customers down the funnel over time. We know that everyone will not transition to the bottom, but we believe that even large commercial clients are likely to become familiar with Jim's Bakery first as retail customers at the top of our sales pyramid. This approach allows us to cast a wide marketing net, first by making customers aware of our products, and then making them aware of the service we provide.

At Jim's, our sales strategy is best seen as an inverted pyramid or funnel where a high number of low-value retail customers enter at the top of the pyramid and a lower number of high-value commercial clients are driven down the pyramid to become committed long-term commercial clients. The goal is capture commercial clients with less expensive products and services that meet their needs and then to migrate them down the pyramid toward higher value products and services. This approach makes tremendous sense when applied to a recurring revenue model. Clients can (and do) enter at any level but we take advantage of the nature of our products and services to attract a targeted commercial audience.

Lower Value, Easy Entry Sales
Many Retail Customers

Free Samples

Basic Retail Product Sales

Specialty Retail Products
and Catering

One-Off Commercial
Orders

Bread as a Service
(BaaS)
Contracts

Higher Value, Long-Term Commercial Contracts
Fewer Client Sales

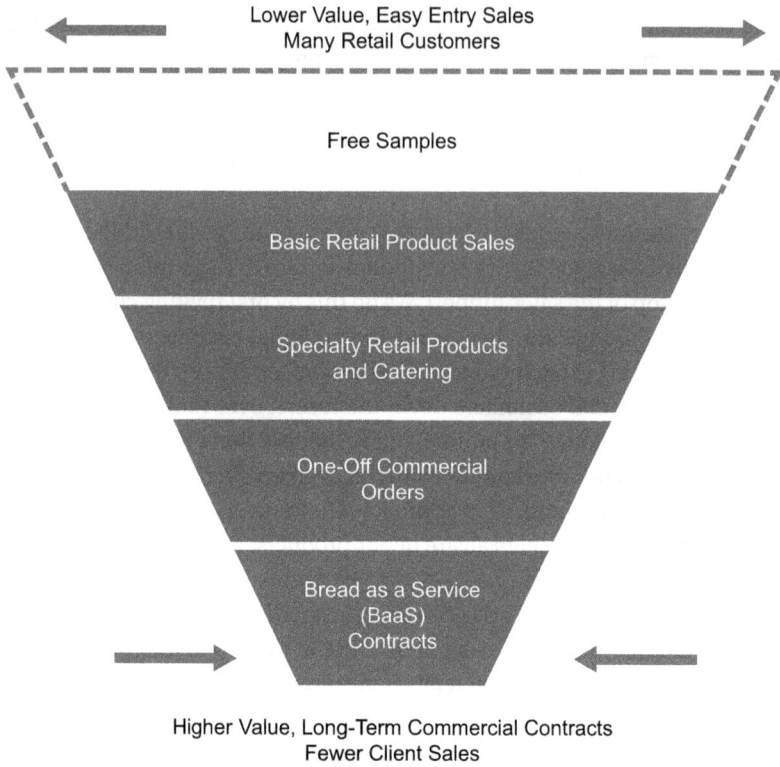

Figure 11.1: Jim's Bakery Business Model

Chapter 12
Writing Your "Book"

Once a small business owner decides it's time to sell their business and move on, they are all eager to jump right in and start writing their "Book" so they can begin handing out copies as soon as possible. Everyone knows about the Book. It's where you write the story of your business, put it down on paper, and tell everyone about it. Hold on—don't send your Book out just yet!

> "My cousin Jake says he has someone he could hand that book to today if I had it written now. I could save all that time and expense doing all that other stuff to position my business."

Ready . . . shoot . . . aim!

Your Book Is a Business Plan and a Marketing Proposal

Your Book should be written as a cross between a business plan and a marketing proposal and should describe where and why your business will grow and be a great opportunity for a buyer. Whether you are talking to buyers or trying to raise funds from an investor, they need to understand your vision for the future of the business and understand how you see that plan being executed. Your Book is the medium for conveying that information to the buyer. It should provide potential buyers with the essential information they need to move ahead with an offer, while controlling how much you divulge to competitors who pose as strategic buyers.

Expect your book to be parsed and studied in detail by the buyer. Frequently, particularly for larger deals, a potential buyer will have different people review the various sections of a Book. Anticipate questions regarding the claims you make in your Book. There are occasions when you will have to answer a question by stating "that information is available but will not be provided until we have a definitive agreement or until you perform your due diligence." Some buyers will respect this, and some will resist. In those cases, you will need to decide how much risk you are willing to take by divulging information early.

Your Book should be written as a cross between a business plan and a marketing proposal and should describe where and why your business will grow and be a great opportunity for a buyer.

DOI 10.1515/9781547400249-012

Your Book may be a marketing tool, but it also needs to be a business plan that you have enough confidence in to be willing and able to execute (particularly if you intend to remain with the business or are being partially compensated based on the future performance of the business). Even if you don't expect to execute the plan, your goal is to convey your vision of the future potential of the business. You may end up with a stake in its success. When you put growth projections into the plan, be ready to defend them. This is an area where "puffing" (overstating the features or potential of your business) can get you in trouble. Be honest, be direct, and take credit where it is deserved by focusing on the positives when writing about your business.

Of course, if you are talking to investors and expect to remain with the business, the execution of your plan will be as important to you as it is to them. At some point they are likely to hold you to your plan—so be careful what you promise! When you're talking to a buyer—particularly a strategic buyer—they may have a plan of their own in mind, but they will still want to understand your thoughts for the future. Don't be surprised and don't become defensive if they have more confidence in their own plan than in yours. Your job now is to give them accurate information they can use to take the business where they want to go.

> "Our Book has a summary of the financials for the past three years, and the detailed backups of our financial reports are available once we enter due diligence."

> "The organization chart in our Book shows the reporting structure of our management team."

Using a Third Party to Write Your Book

One of the questions you may have by now is:

> "Why do I have to write a book at all? The investment broker I hired includes that as one of their services."

Using a third party (typically the business broker or investment banker you hire) to write your Book is a good idea, but they will still need your draft as an input. There is an additional benefit to having an independent pair of eyes work on your book. They can add the marketing polish you need and have more experience writing this type of document which is designed to attract buyers. The problem is that an independent third party doesn't know your business and may only have a passing understanding of your market. They will need to get the information to write a Book about your business from you. By writing your Book, even if it is only used as a first draft, you will have a vehicle to transfer the information they require to produce a polished Book, and it will give you the opportunity to document your thoughts. One of the ways you drive the sale is by driving the Book. It's the place you will tell them "Here is the valuation of my business."

Using a third party to write your Book is a good idea, but they will still need your draft as an input.

Generating Content for Your Book

The content included in your Book should be available as a direct result of the work products you generated as you went through the positioning tasks we described earlier. This is one of the reasons you took the time to perform as many of the positioning tasks as possible. The business model you created and the organization chart you made earlier will now be incorporated into your Book. Of course, if you skipped those tasks, you will want to go back and complete them (or complete the alternative you decided to use). The description of your business model, your organization chart, and the financial information you collected will all become part of your Book. Your Book should clearly convey the transferrable value the business offers a potential buyer.

Your Book Provides the Pith of your Business

After reading your Book a buyer should have a strong understanding and appreciation of your business, of its employees, how it operates, and mostly, how it makes money. You need to accomplish this without providing the finite details. Your goal is to present the pith of your business. The buyer should be able to feel the opportunity owning this business would bring. You want them to "need" to know how this story comes out in the future and to have a strong desire to be a part of it. The buyer should be drawn toward your business instead of going the opposite direction to another business they may be looking at; you want them to envision themselves in your position. Your Book is a marketing tool used to convert a potential buyer into a buyer.

Your Book is a marketing tool used to convert a potential buyer into a buyer.

There is a tendency on the part of sellers to try to put everything into their Book. When you write your Book, your goal is to give the buyer a compelling picture of the business but not necessarily every little detail. A successful marketing document should sell the benefits of the business rather than directly selling the business itself, and your Book is no exception. This is difficult to do in a business plan. If your business is a pizza shop, you want them to smell the pizza without giving them the recipe for your special sauce. The buyer should understand the essence of the business (its pith) and be eager to ask more questions. To get these questions answered they will have to become a buyer.

"How can you afford to develop that software?"

"Do you go offshore for developers?"

"Who are your key clients?"

These are all valid questions that should be answered—after you have agreed on an offer and selected them from among all the potential buyers. You may have peaked their interest, but you don't want to give too much away to a potential strategic buyer who hasn't yet become a buyer. Your Book should say,

"We have very low development rates."

"Our client list includes several Fortune 500 users."

"We have already negotiated advantageous long-term rates with our key suppliers that are transferrable to a new owner."

Your organization chart, for instance, should convey titles and not names. Don't be confused by the example in Figure 9.1. Separate the positioning task of creating the full chart by only using the appropriate level of detail in your Book. Creating the entire chart does not mean it must all go in your Book. After all, you don't want a potential buyer to start calling key employees with job offers. The exception to this is the inclusion of short biographies for your management team—if those biographies are seen as a strength of the business. You want your Book to provide pith without seeming pithy.

How Long Should Your Book Be?

Have you ever run an employment ad and received a stack of resumes you had to wade through? Unless someone is exceptionally experienced with a long list of previous jobs, most people understand that a resume shouldn't be five pages long. The readers are usually short on time (which is why they are hiring someone) and just don't have the leisure to read an excessively long resume. They will put an unnecessarily long resume at the bottom of the stack to read later—effectively putting the candidate at the end of the line. If a candidate can't crisply convey why you should hire them, you lose interest quickly. The same is true for your Book.

You need to quickly and crisply grab a potential buyer's attention. I advise clients to keep their Book under twenty-five pages. Fifty pages may be acceptable for a large or complex business with many products. This is a marketing document and, if a potential buyer needs to read through unnecessarily long pages of "boilerplate" you're not helping them understand your business. You're drowning them in information they don't need at that point and probably won't retain their interest. Some investors receive stacks of business plans every day and just toss away any that don't quickly grab their attention. If you have trouble keeping your Book short, try giving it to your marketing department—or whoever writes your advertisements. They should be able to help.

Your Book needs to quickly and crisply grab a potential buyer's attention. I advise clients to keep their Book under 25 pages.

Think about the marketing brochures written by automobile manufacturers. They are short, but they are classic in their ability to convey pith. When we see pictures of that off-road four-wheel-drive SUV driving through the surf or that luxury sedan stopped in front of a fancy restaurant while the driver helps a woman we can only see by her shapely legs and the high hem of her little black dress exit the car, we understand what this vehicle is being used for. They are selling us a lifestyle, not a car. Auto manufacturers are champs at giving us the car's pith. If the sales brochures were long and provided only pure specifications, no one would read them. The essence of the vehicle is how much fun it is to drive or its sex appeal. After they get our attention we can ask about the 5.0-liter engine and soft leather seats.

If your business is a bakery, don't show pictures of the ovens; show pictures of the bride and groom cutting the wedding cake or a family fighting for the last roll over the dinner table. If your business is a secure data center, don't show pictures of the backup generator; show pictures of the lights on during a hurricane. Your Book should be long enough to sell a potential buyer on the essence of the business, but be short enough not to lose their attention (or to divulge too much information to a strategic buyer). Be ready to answer the detailed questions, though, once they have become a qualified buyer. At that point they shouldn't feel that your Book or your answers have misled them. Now you should only need to fill in the blanks. If you have misled them, the deal will die, and you will see a qualified buyer walk away from the deal.

Book Outline

This is the outline I prefer to use when writing a Book. Again, it is a business plan, so there is no harm if you decide to add other sections that make sense in that context. You might find it helpful to refer to the earlier chapters to see what content can be applied when writing your Book. I have included references to help you with that. Appendix B includes an example of a Book written for Jim's Bakery. I have attempted to track the Jim's Bakery examples from the earlier chapters back into the example in Appendix B.

Overview

The overview should be one to two pages long and should briefly describe why you are selling the business. This is the section of your Book that will determine how well or whether you get the buyer's attention. Try to put yourself into the buyer's shoes. Why do you think they are looking at your business? What are the burning questions they want to have answered? Is this a real opportunity and, if it is, why is it being sold?

"Because of a pending retirement."

"Due to failing health."

"To raise the capital to take the business to the next level."

Next talk about the previous success of the business. What is the one thing the business is known for? What is its star accomplishment?

"After twenty-five years as a key supplier to the industry, . . ."

"With a well-deserved reputation for quality. . .."

"After releasing a breakthrough product. . .."

Tell the buyer where the business is at today. What one thing stands out about the business today or sets it aside from the competition?

"We currently have a staff of twenty-five highly skilled employees."

"Our sales team currently works across the southeast."

"We are already seeing the results of last year's tooling upgrades."

Give the buyer your vision. What is the seed you would like to plant in a buyer's brain that you want them to hold onto when they think about the future path of your business?

"Because of our current success we would like to open two new stores."

"Our projections assume that a strategic buyer will provide. . .."

"A buyer who removes our current capital restraints can accomplish. . .."

Market

This section of your Book should be two to four pages long. In chapter 6 I explained that there are two distinct markets, and you should be careful not to confuse them here—the market you sell your products into and the market you expect to sell your business into. In this section of your Book you need to focus on the product market. If you are a software application development company making products for the restaurant industry, do not talk about software application development here. Talk about the restaurant market. Describe how strong the market is for your products.

"There are 5,000 restaurants in our region with a 10 percent growth rate, creating a strong opportunity for selling our application products."

Remember to describe only the market that is relevant to your products. If you sell products in one town, it's not relevant to tell the reader about the statewide market for similar products.

Describe only the market that is relevant to your products.

It is important to quote relevant metrics from acknowledged third-party experts such as the local economic development corporation (EDC), the state labor bureau, the census bureau, and industry analysts and research organizations, particularly if you sell your products into a national or international market.

Competition

This section of your Book should be one to two pages long. You want to use care in discussing your business discriminators without being an advertisement for the competition. Focus on the strengths of your business buy letting a buyer know what makes buying your business the best opportunity. Also assume they are also looking at other businesses.

In chapter 6 we discussed methods for creating a competitive matrix. This is the section where you include the matrix. Pay attention to the type of language you use. Be sure to take the high road when you write this section. Your statements shouldn't say the competition is bad. They should say, "they're good, but we're better."

Business Model

This is where the "other" market—the one you will sell your business into—should be described. If you develop software for the floral industry, this section of your Book should tell a buyer why the software development methods and sales strategies you use are superior to those used by other software developers. Maybe your business is better because you adopted a business model some developers have only just begun to look at. In chapter 11 we discussed the creation of an effective business model. The activity described in chapter 11 should have produced the content needed for this section of your Book.

Your business model describes your strategic approach to sales. This is an important concept to convey to a buyer. There are lots of small businesses with great people and great products who just don't know how to sell. If you have a strategic sales approach that works well, this is the time to brag about it a little. But be aware that some strategic buyers will have their own ideas. I had one client who got red in the face arguing with a potential buyer about whose sales approach was better. I asked him later why he was so adamant, and his answer was that it was the principal of the argument. If the buyer has a different approach, be sure not to become defensive. After the sale they can use any approach they choose. If you argue your approach you may win the argument but lose the sale. Capture your approach in your Book. Be wary of employees with big egos who will be remaining with the business. It could cost you the deal, or it could cost them their job with the new owner.

Product Descriptions

This section of your Book should be three to four pages and describe your product lines, the strategy behind them, and what each line contributes toward the success of the business. Note this is not a catalog. If your business is a manufacturing company that makes nuts and bolts, this section needs to give a generic explanation of the purpose for a nut and for a bolt and not the specification for a ½" 8/32 thread hex head bolt.

> "We manufacture specialized hardened bolts for use in environmentally hazardous applications, such as the building of bridges."

> "We provide bonded cleaning services for high security facilities."

If your business sells many products, then this section should focus on your product strategies such as your requirements for taking on new products. This is also the place to talk about quality standards and policies.

> "We are a regional reseller of automobile parts. Our catalog features only high-quality parts that we have tested in our own shop."

Sales Performance and Projections

This section of your Book should be one to two pages, provide a summary of your past sales growth and performance, and a summary of your projected growth (your pro forma) for the next three years. Charting the past and future performance of your business is a good approach for this section of your Book.

> "Over the past five years our revenue has grown an average of 5–10 percent per year. As shown in the attached figure we are projecting an increase in our growth rate to 15–20 percent per year. Our basis for this change to our growth curve is the addition of three additional salespeople (effectively doubling the size of our sales team) to support the productivity increase from our new CNC milling equipment."

Operational Description

This section of your Book should be one to two pages long and provide a high-level narrative of your operations—particularly, any unique aspect to the way you conduct business, such as a unique labor strategy, a unique application of manufacturing technology, high data security protection—anything that might be a discriminator for the purchase of your business over another. Providing your organization chart on this section of your Book will help a potential buyer better understand the structure of your business—for example, how work is divided among your management team.

This is a good place to describe any unique operating policies you have instituted.

> "We have instituted a 9–80 policy for our professional employees."

> "We buy a car for employees with twenty years of service."

> "We give supervisors the ability to pay a spot bonus for exceptional employees."

If you are a wholesaler, this is a good place to describe your requirements for signing new resellers and describing how you have deployed your sales staff. If your industry depends on cleanliness and you have instituted a specialized cleaning program, this is the place to talk about it. What puts your operation ahead of the competition?

Financial Summary

This section of your Book should be one page long and should provide a summary of your current financial position. It should include a brief description of your financial strategy—for example, the fact that you or your senior management team reviews the balance sheet and income statement each month and that you work against a fixed budget.

> "We are currently ahead of plan and will earn. . .."

> "Our revenues this year are anticipated to be . . . and will result in an EBITDA of. . .."

I don't recommend including detailed financials in your Book, but this is a subject you may find is of some discussion. I prefer to say, "Financials are available upon request." Wait until there is genuine interest before handing out financials and avoid papering your financials around the market for just anyone to request.

While you're not going to include your detailed financials here, you do need to include specific financial data such as financial performance curves. Give exact numbers to gain the confidence of potential buyers. If you have had financial performance issues, take this opportunity to briefly explain any setbacks.

"We had a brief setback two years ago when the real estate market dropped but have recovered since and made corrections to our sales strategy."

Protecting Your Work

All copies of your Book should be serialized and only provided to serious potential buyers who have agreed to an NDA with a receipt for delivery. A recipient should sign for each Book. This little bit of formality tells potential buyers you are serious and makes them think twice if they are strategic lookers that aren't really interested in buying.

Your Book is your story. You don't want a strategic competitor to show up in the future, using the information you created to tell a similar story for their business. It not only explains how you go to market but why and how what you do is unique.

"Gee, that business model they created was so slick, I thought I would use it as well."

You need to ensure you are retaining control of the material in your Book when you are supplying it to third parties such as sales brokers and investment bankers. Your Book may seem like creative writing, but it is *your* creative writing!

One sure way you protect your Book is to formally copyright it. Copyrighting a document these days is very simple and inexpensive. In the United States, you do this through the US Copyright Office.[1] This process is intended to help anyone who creates original material to apply for a copyright. If you need assistance, get advice from your attorney. You will need to identify any material in your Book, such as pictures and market material you purchase from another source (including those copied from an *internet* source), so they are excluded from your copyright. The process takes some time before a certificate is awarded. Even though you expect to give the draft copy of your book to a broker to update at some time, it makes sense to first copyright your draft. In addition, you can also add a copyright line to your Book before you formally copyright it—for example, "Copyright © [year] by Jim's Bakery." This line can go on page 2 of your Book or the last page of your Book.

---

[1] US Copyright Office website, www.copyright.gov/.

Create a Short Handout

There is no need to hand a copy of your Book to just anyone who expresses interest. After you complete your draft Book, it's time to create a one-page handout that summarizes the major points in the Book. A sample handout, based on the Jim's Bakery example, is included as Appendix A. The handout has an abbreviated overview and bullet points that list the significant features of the business. While your Book will be handed out only when requested by a potential buyer (and only under an NDA), the handout can be freely distributed to those you think might have interest. The content in the handout will not require an NDA. The "call to action" in the handout will be to invite interested parties to call and discuss the opportunity with your intermediary. If you feel the need to start the ball rolling on the sale of your business, this will be the tool you can use (rather than handing out copies of your Book).

Jim's Bakery Example

Appendix A (a sample handout) and Appendix B (a sample "Book") are included and are based on the Jim's Bakery model. Look at these samples closely. You should recognize that the content used to create the "Book" was developed as part of the positioning activities used as Jim's Bakery examples in the earlier chapters. Chronologically, the handout is used first in the sales process; however, the best way to create the handout is to write your "Book" (Appendix B) first and then paraphrase the content of the "Book" to create the handout (Appendix A).

Chapter 13
Create a Virtual Model of Your Business

Selling your business is a big deal and may be one of the most important life events you will ever experience. You have been working toward this event for years, and you're willing to put in any effort to make it a success. After you have diligently worked through all the steps in the sales process and you've put in the time and effort to prepare your business to be sold, you may find yourself looking for anything that will make your sale a success. At this point you don't want to leave any stone unturned when it comes to the sale of your business. You want to know:

"What else can I do?"

"Is there anything else I say to a buyer to convince them this is a good deal for them?"

Here is the answer—keeping in mind that business buyers don't buy on impulse. When someone is interested in your business, they want to gain as much understanding about the operation of the business as possible. They want to touch it, feel it, and "kick the tires." They want to be able to answer questions like:

"What if I changed something?"

"What would happen if I cut some expenses?"

"Suppose I made more capital improvements?"

Buyers are looking for more than a tour of the business. Curb appeal is not a driver. To take that next step, the one that will take you above and beyond in preparing for a sale, try providing your buyer with a software model of the business that will give them the ability to play "what if." By modeling your business, you create a planning tool for yourself (and therefore makes it a good idea for yourself whether or not you sell), and you offer your buyer a chance to "reach in" and get to know the business. This may also be the differentiator that builds the trust and confidence an investor needs to commit funds to you, if that is your goal.

Business buyers don't buy on impulse. They want to touch it, feel it, and "kick the tires."

By using this model, the buyer will gain a true "hands-on" understanding of the business, giving them the confidence to move ahead with the purchase. Creating a tool like the one described here will take you above and beyond. A buyer can

DOI 10.1515/9781547400249-013

use it to see what effect the changes he may be contemplating would be and what effect they would have on the current and future value of the business.

"What would be the impact of increasing the size of the sales team?

"What would the cost/revenue impact be if we increased our manufacturing capability?"

The ability of the model to support this type of decision is directly related to the fidelity of the model. To be useful, the model must integrate the past performance of the business with the future projections you developed for the pro forma; integrate the past expenses of the business with its projected budgets; and finally, show how these can be used to predict the impact any changes will have on the future value of the business.

Your Financial Reports Should Be Your Greatest Sales Tool

The approach described here improves the simple preparation of your financial reports because it creates a useful tool that changes those static financial reports into a dynamic instrument the buyer can experiment with. This step may be too much for some businesses; however, as I have previously recommended, try it before deciding it's not needed for your business. You may find it's not as difficult as it sounds.

This step represents the final level of financial positioning that you should consider taking—particularly if the discriminator for the sale of your business is its financial performance, or if you are trying to convince a buyer that potential changes justify a higher valuation.

You should consider taking this step if the discriminator for the sale of your business is its financial performance, or if you are trying to convince a buyer that potential changes justify a higher valuation.

If you find yourself trying to verbalize the great financial opportunity your business offers the buyer, and they just don't seem to be getting it, this is a tool that will help you drive that message home.

But suppose your business hasn't quite had the performance you would like to advertise, and now those financial problems you wrestled with for so long are in the rearview mirror. You solved the problem that was holding you back and driving your expenses too high; now you can see that the business is about to turn around, and positive performance is in the near and achievable future. How can you credibly explain it and prove it to a potential buyer? How do you give that message believably to a prospective buyer with a measure of confidence they can believe in and commit to? You need them to value the business on its future potential rather than its past performance. By creating a software model of your business, you can show the perspective buyer not just how the business has done in the past, but more importantly, how it is likely to do in the future. You need to provide future projections in a format the buyer can analyze and trust in. Your model must place them in a continuum from the actual results of the past continuing through today and on into the future. By creating a software model of your business, you are helping them mitigate the risk they are concerned about. Even if you don't believe the risk actually exists, they will be asking you to prove it's not a risk.

Creating a Spreadsheet Model of Your Business

This tool is implemented using a multipage spreadsheet.[1] Figure 13.1 is the summary spreadsheet for the tool and provides a snapshot of the current position of the business. The first thing you should notice is that using this model will require you to update the data with the "actual" results (taken from your financials) each month. The example shown (Figure 13.1) is for one year and goes through June of the current year. The summary spreadsheet you create should be wide enough to cover seven years of data. The model needs to be updated with inputs from your financial reports each month so that it remains accurate. You will also include similar spreadsheets for the three years preceding this one and the three years following this one.

Actual financial numbers (taken from your monthly profit and loss statements) are shown going out through June in this example. The values are not entered directly on the summary spreadsheet. They are entered on the linked spreadsheets (Figure 13.2) that contain the sales and expense detail. The monthly projected revenues are shown as are the monthly expense budgets. By integrating the actual income and expenses for the business, an actual EBITDA can be calculated and is also shown. The revenue curves shown in Figure 7.2 and Figure 7.3 can be charted directly from these spreadsheets. The summary spreadsheet becomes a dashboard that integrates inputs from linked spreadsheets that contain the breakdown of the detailed data.

---

1 I will post a template on www.diligentconsulting.com at some point.

	A	B	C	D	E	F	G	H	I	J	K	L	M	N	O
1	SUMMARY														
2		Jan	Feb	March	April	May	June	July	August	Sept.	Oct.	Nov.	Dec.	Totals	Annualized
3	INCOME SUMMARY														
4	Projected Product Line 1 Revenue														
5	Projected Product Line 2 Revenue			Month by Month Proforma Product Projections											
6	Projected Product Line 3 Revenue														
7	PROJECTED INCOME TOTAL														
8	Total Monthly Revenue		Actual Results (Shown To June)												
9															
10	Cost of Good Sold														
11	Budgetted Product Line 1 COGS														
12	Budgetted Product Line 2 COGS			Month by Month COGS Budgets											
13	Budgetted Product Line 3 COGS														
14	Total Projected Cost of Good Sold														
15	Total ACTUAL COGS		Actual Results (Shown To June)												
16	Total Gross Profit Budget														
17															
18	BUDGETt SUMMARY														
19	Product Line 1 Budget														
20	Product Line 2 Budget														
21	Product Line 3 Budget														
22	Sales Budget			Month by Month Expense Budgets											
23	Marketing Budget														
24	Administration Budget														
25	Employee Overhead Budget														
26	EXPENSE TOTAL														
27	Enter Actuals on Expense sheet		Actual Results (Shown To June)												
28															
29	NET INCOME														
30	Actual Income		Actual Results (Shown To June)												
31															
32	Adjustments														
33	Management														
34	Depreciation														
35	INTEREST														
36	TAXES														
37	EBITDA					Yellow Are Calculated Values									
38	Actual Adjusted EBITDA														
39	YTD EBITDA														

Microsoft® Excel™ screenshot. Copyright © 2018 Microsoft

Figure 13.1: Summary Spreadsheet Example

Now that may just sound confusing! Try this:

- Create one or more spreadsheets that lists all your sales income by product line.
- Create one or more spreadsheets that lists all your expenses by product line.
- Create a separate spreadsheet for overhead expenses.
- Create a spreadsheet with labor expenses broken out by employee.
- Link all those spreadsheets to the summary spreadsheet, which acts like a dashboard.

Use Linked Spreadsheets for Greater Fidelity

The model is created by the integration of these specialized income and expense spreadsheets. Through the use of individual spreadsheets, it is possible to add greater fidelity to the detail of the model. By linking the spreadsheets in the manner shown in Figure 13.2, it is possible to isolate various parts of the model into manageable and useful components and allows each component to have a greater level of detail. For example, the Product Line Income/Expense Spreadsheet is in fact an income statement that can be used to determine the profitability of each product line. This can be highly useful information when trying to determine where to apply limited capital resources. Buyers can play "what if" by changing these numbers to see what the impact of the change might be.

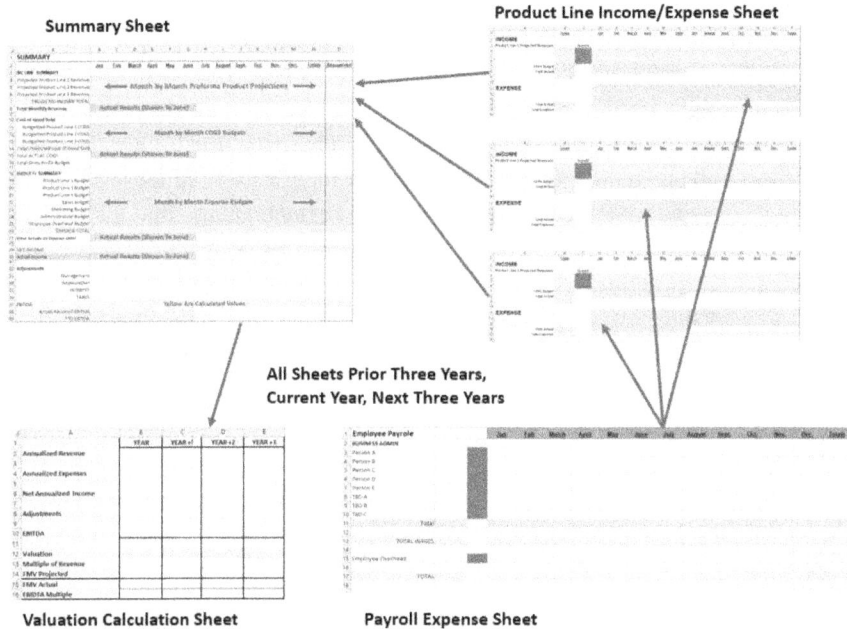

Microsoft® Excel™ screenshot. Copyright © 2018 Microsoft

Figure 13.2: Linked Business Spreadsheets

Actual and projected values are input to the summary spreadsheet from linked income/expense spreadsheets containing the lower level detail. The projected, budgeted, and actual detailed values are integrated on the income/expense spreadsheets shown in Figure 13.2. Expense inputs, such as labor expense, could be integrated from a separate employee expense spreadsheet (Figure 13.2) that can track the salary history for each employee and project the impact of future budgeted employee raises plus the impact of adding additional staff. Similarly, separate income/expense spreadsheets could be integrated that depict unit production cost vs. revenue generated on a unit by unit basis. This is a critical metric in some businesses.

A separate valuation spreadsheet can be linked to the summary spreadsheet and uses the integrated numbers from across the business to calculate the resulting valuation. The strength in this approach is the ability to model several valuation methods and see them side by side. You (or the buyer) can change the multiplier values or modify the basic calculation as desired.

Income/expense spreadsheets can also be created to reflect overhead expenses such as sales, marketing, and administration functions which are budgeted but reflect zero income. Overhead values can then be allocated as an overhead expense across the product lines. The benefit of this approach is the visibility it creates. Suppose a buyer (or you) are looking at the expense for the rent (by looking at its monthly actual values) they can compare any changes they are considering making. This is a definitive number which will be reflected in the actuals and taken directly from the financial reports. Now suppose the buyer wanted to see what the affect would be of moving the business into his existing facility where the rent would be only half the current rent.

By changing the budgeted value for the rent going forward, the model will reflect these values by calculating the revised EBITDA and reflecting this in an increased valuation. This is a straightforward example. The power of the tool can be seen when the buyer is deciding things like whether to lease a major new piece of equipment or purchase it and see what the impact is of depreciating it over the next three years.

Monthly "Actual" Input

To have the necessary fidelity, the model needs to be updated each month with the actual values for both the income and expense items. These numbers should be taken directly off your financial reports. This is a task easily assigned to your bookkeeper. It may be possible to automate this, but I am not aware of anyone attempting this yet. There may be an accounting system that provides the functionality of this tool but, in my experience, most accounting systems make it difficult to easily play "what if" or to create simple charts or even integrate other sheets. The pain of having to input the values monthly is well worth the utility the tool provides.

Jim's Bakery Example

The sheets for the Jim's Bakery Example follow. Figure 13.3 is the summary spreadsheet (the dashboard) and inputs to it come from the linked spreadsheets.

SUMMARY	Year Jan	Year Feb	Year March	Year April	Year May	Year June	Year July	Year August	Year Sept.	Year Oct.	Year Nov.	Year Dec.	Year Totals
INCOME SUMMARY													
Commercial Rolls	148,830	148,830	148,830	148,830	148,830	148,830	148,830	148,830	148,830	148,830	148,830	148,830	1,785,960
BaaS	372,945	372,945	372,945	372,945	372,945	372,945	372,945	372,945	372,945	372,945	372,945	372,945	4,475,340
Commercial Catering	70,180	70,180	70,180	70,180	70,180	70,180	70,180	70,180	70,180	70,180	70,180	70,180	842,160
Retail Products	178,652	178,652	178,652	178,652	178,652	178,652	178,652	178,652	178,652	178,652	178,652	178,652	2,143,813
INCOME TOTAL	770,607	770,607	770,607	770,607	770,607	770,607	770,607	770,607	770,607	770,607	770,607	770,607	9,247,278
	787,245	792,643	790,492	797,286	806,080	803,255	0	0	0	0	0	0	9,400,640
Cost of Good Sold													
Total COGS	159,986	159,986	159,986	159,986	159,986	159,986	159,986	159,986	159,986	159,986	159,986	159,986	1,919,837
Actual	159,739	156,385	159,386	159,243	156,455	159,908	0	0	0	0	0	0	1,911,034
Total Gross Profit Budget	627,506	636,258	631,106	638,043	649,625	643,347	610,620	610,620	610,620	610,620	610,620	610,620	7,327,442
EXPENSE SUMMARY													
Commercial Rolls	39,042	39,042	39,042	39,042	39,042	39,042	39,042	39,042	39,042	39,042	39,042	39,042	468,506
BaaS	199,868	199,868	199,868	199,868	199,868	199,868	199,868	199,868	199,868	199,868	199,868	199,868	2,398,410
Retail Products	22,418	22,418	22,418	22,418	22,418	22,418	22,418	22,418	22,418	22,418	22,418	22,418	269,010
Sales	14,438	14,438	14,438	14,438	14,438	14,438	14,438	14,438	14,438	14,438	14,438	14,438	173,250
Marketing	7,875	7,875	7,875	7,875	7,875	7,875	7,875	7,875	7,875	7,875	7,875	7,875	94,500
Admin	192,308	192,308	192,308	192,308	192,308	192,308	192,308	192,308	192,308	192,308	192,308	192,308	2,307,690
Employee Overhead	44,925	44,925	44,925	44,925	44,925	44,925	44,925	44,925	44,925	44,925	44,925	44,925	539,104
EXPENSE SUB-TOTAL	520,872	520,872	520,872	520,872	520,872	520,872	520,872	520,872	520,872	520,872	520,872	520,872	6,250,469
ACTUAL EXPENSE SUB-TOTAL	501,299	501,585	500,193	503,777	502,686	502,067	0	0	0	0	0	0	6,136,842
TOTAL EXPENSE	680,859	680,859	680,859	680,859	680,859	680,859	680,859	680,859	680,859	680,859	680,859	680,859	8,170,306
TOTAL EXPENSE ACTUAL	661,038	657,970	659,579	663,020	659,141	661,975	0	0	0	0	0	0	8,047,876
NET PROJECTED INCOME	89,748	89,748	89,748	89,748	89,748	89,748	89,748	89,748	89,748	89,748	89,748	89,748	1,076,972
Actual Income	126,207	134,673	130,913	134,266	146,939	141,280	0	0	0	0	0	0	1,352,764
Adjustments													
Retail Rent Adjustment	20,772	20,772	20,772	20,772	20,772	20,772	20,772	20,772	20,772	20,772	20,772	20,772	249,266
Depreciation	57,694	57,694	57,694	57,694	57,694	57,694	57,694	57,694	57,694	57,694	57,694	57,694	692,332
INTEREST	10,500	10,500	10,500	10,500	10,500	10,500	10,500	10,500	10,500	10,500	10,500	10,500	126,000
TAXES	0	0	0	0	0	0	0	0	0	0	0	0	0
Total Other Expenses	88,967	88,967	88,967	88,967	88,967	88,967	88,967	88,967	88,967	88,967	88,967	88,967	1,067,598
EBITDA	178,714	178,714	178,714	178,714	178,714	178,714	178,714	178,714	178,714	178,714	178,714	178,714	2,144,570
Actual Adjusted EBITDA	215,174	223,640	219,880	223,293	235,906	230,247	0	0	0	0	0	0	2,420,362

Microsoft® Excel™ screenshot. Copyright © 2018 Microsoft
Figure 13.3: Jim's Bakery Summary Spreadsheet Example

One of the reasons for creating the model as linked spreadsheets rather than trying to draw the information from an "canned" accounting tool application is the flexibility it provides for playing "what if." Look at the Total Income line in Figure 13.3. It projects a total income of $9,247,278 for the current year. The example however assumes that the actual values have already been entered through June. Because the actual sales for Jim's have exceeded projections through June, there is an adjusted actual projection of $9,400,640 total revenue for the year. That is the number that should be shown to a buyer, particularly if there is a revenue multiplier being applied to it to determine value.

Figure 13.4 is an example income spreadsheet for Jim's Bakery and is the source for the revenue numbers shown in the summary. Note the level of detail found on this sheet adds a higher level of fidelity than would have been attained if the numbers had simply been entered on the summary spreadsheet. The column titled growth allows the user to set the value for the BaaS product at 15 percent growth while only predicting 5 percent growth in the retail products.

INCOME		Year Jan	Year Feb	Year March	Year April	Year May	Year June	Year July	Year August	Year Sept.	Year Oct.	Year Nov.	Year Dec.	Year Totals
Commercial Rolls	Growth													
Sales Revenues	10.0%	148,830	148,830	148,830	148,830	148,830	148,830	148,830	148,830	148,830	148,830	148,830	148,830	1,785,960
Total Projected		148,830	148,830	148,830	148,830	148,830	148,830	148,830	148,830	148,830	148,830	148,830	148,830	1,785,960
Total Actual		151,847	152,488	152,455	160,253	162,941	160,111	0	0	0	0	0	0	1,833,055
BaaS														
Sales Revenues	15.0%	372,945	372,945	372,945	372,945	372,945	372,945	372,945	372,945	372,945	372,945	372,945	372,945	4,475,340
Total Projected		372,945	372,945	372,945	372,945	372,945	372,945	372,945	372,945	372,945	372,945	372,945	372,945	4,475,340
Total Actual		385,286	387,230	385,592	382,153	388,794	386,299	0	0	0	0	0	0	4,550,824
Commercial Catering														
Sales Revenues	10.0%	70,180	70,180	70,180	70,180	70,180	70,180	70,180	70,180	70,180	70,180	70,180	70,180	842,160
Total Projected		70,180	70,180	70,180	70,180	70,180	70,180	70,180	70,180	70,180	70,180	70,180	70,180	842,160
Total Actual		71,657	71,980	71,400	71,400	72,000	72,645	0	0	0	0	0	0	852,162
Retail Products														
Cakes	5.0%	93,685	93,685	93,685	93,685	93,685	93,685	93,685	93,685	93,685	93,685	93,685	93,685	1,124,219
Cookies	5.0%	60,202	60,202	60,202	60,202	60,202	60,202	60,202	60,202	60,202	60,202	60,202	60,202	722,424
Bread	5.0%	5,994	5,994	5,994	5,994	5,994	5,994	5,994	5,994	5,994	5,994	5,994	5,994	71,933
Rolls	5.0%	11,697	11,697	11,697	11,697	11,697	11,697	11,697	11,697	11,697	11,697	11,697	11,697	140,370
Catering	5.0%	4,923	4,923	4,923	4,923	4,923	4,923	4,923	4,923	4,923	4,923	4,923	4,923	59,081
Gluten Free Products	5.0%	2,149	2,149	2,149	2,149	2,149	2,149	2,149	2,149	2,149	2,149	2,149	2,149	25,792
Total Projected Retail Income		178,652	178,652	178,652	178,652	178,652	178,652	178,652	178,652	178,652	178,652	178,652	178,652	2,143,818
Total Actual		180,455	180,945	181,245	183,500	182,345	184,200	0	0	0	0	0	0	2,164,599
TOTAL PROJECTED INCOME		770,607	770,607	770,607	770,607	770,607	770,607	770,607	770,607	770,607	770,607	770,607	770,607	9,247,278
Total Actual Income		787,245	792,643	790,492	797,286	806,080	803,255	0	0	0	0	0	0	9,400,640

Microsoft® Excel™ screenshot. Copyright © 2018 Microsoft

Figure 13.4: Jim's Bakery Income Spreadsheet Example

The expense spreadsheet shown in Figure 13.5 also allows a higher fidelity in the model. It is particularly useful when doing budget planning. Since the rent for the retail space is likely to be a negotiation item in the Jim's Bakery deal, the rent for the retail facility can be changed to determine what the overall impact will be on the business. When looking at lease/buy decisions, the impact of variables such as depreciation can be factored into the decision.

EXPENSE	Year Jan	Year Feb	Year March	Year April	Year May	Year June	Year July	Year August	Year Sept.	Year Oct.	Year Nov.	Year Dec.	Year Totals
Admin Expenses													
Equip, Software and Trng	2,940	2,940	2,940	2,940	2,940	2,940	2,940	2,940	2,940	2,940	2,940	2,940	35,280
Dues & Subscriptions	4,961	4,961	4,961	4,961	4,961	4,961	4,961	4,961	4,961	4,961	4,961	4,961	59,535
New Oven	3,990	3,990	3,990	3,990	3,990	3,990	3,990	3,990	3,990	3,990	3,990	3,990	47,880
Interest Expense	10,500	10,500	10,500	10,500	10,500	10,500	10,500	10,500	10,500	10,500	10,500	10,500	126,000
Legal & Professional Exp.	1,654	1,654	1,654	1,654	1,654	1,654	1,654	1,654	1,654	1,654	1,654	1,654	19,845
Office Tel	2,100	2,100	2,100	2,100	2,100	2,100	2,100	2,100	2,100	2,100	2,100	2,100	25,200
Employee cell phone reimb	2,381	2,381	2,381	2,381	2,381	2,381	2,381	2,381	2,381	2,381	2,381	2,381	28,577
Travel	2,100	2,100	2,100	2,100	2,100	2,100	2,100	2,100	2,100	2,100	2,100	2,100	25,200
Meals and Entertainment	263	263	263	263	263	263	263	263	263	263	263	263	3,150
Rent -Retail	20,772	20,772	20,772	20,772	20,772	20,772	20,772	20,772	20,772	20,772	20,772	20,772	249,266
Pass through & Repairs	2,520	2,520	2,520	2,520	2,520	2,520	2,520	2,520	2,520	2,520	2,520	2,520	30,240
Utilities	1,323	1,323	1,323	1,323	1,323	1,323	1,323	1,323	1,323	1,323	1,323	1,323	15,876
Office Expenses	1,985	1,985	1,985	1,985	1,985	1,985	1,985	1,985	1,985	1,985	1,985	1,985	23,814
Bank Charges	1,260	1,260	1,260	1,260	1,260	1,260	1,260	1,260	1,260	1,260	1,260	1,260	15,120
Card Fees	5,565	5,565	5,565	5,565	5,565	5,565	5,565	5,565	5,565	5,565	5,565	5,565	66,780
Labor	67,675	67,675	67,675	67,675	67,675	67,675	67,675	67,675	67,675	67,675	67,675	67,675	812,095
Depreciation	57,694	57,694	57,694	57,694	57,694	57,694	57,694	57,694	57,694	57,694	57,694	57,694	692,332
Misc	2,625	2,625	2,625	2,625	2,625	2,625	2,625	2,625	2,625	2,625	2,625	2,625	31,500
Total Budget	192,308	192,308	192,308	192,308	192,308	192,308	192,308	192,308	192,308	192,308	192,308	192,308	2,307,690
Total Actual	189,787	189,337	190,588	190,843	190,947	190,900	0	0	0	0	0	0	2,296,247
Employee Overhead	44,925	44,925	44,925	44,925	44,925	44,925	44,925	44,925	44,925	44,925	44,925	44,925	539,104
Total Overhead Budget	44,925	44,925	44,925	44,925	44,925	44,925	44,925	44,925	44,925	44,925	44,925	44,925	539,104
Total Actual	43,425	44,421	43,674	43,287	44,110	43,332	0	0	0	0	0	0	531,801
TOTAL EXPENSE (less COGS)	520,872	520,872	520,872	520,872	520,872	520,872	520,872	520,872	520,872	520,872	520,872	520,872	6,250,469
TOTAL ACTUAL (less COGS)	501,299	501,585	500,193	503,777	502,686	502,067	0	0	0	0	0	0	6,136,842
Total Expense	680,859	680,859	680,859	680,859	680,859	680,859	680,859	680,859	680,859	680,859	680,859	680,859	8,170,306
Total Actual	661,038	657,970	659,579	663,020	659,141	661,975	0	0	0	0	0	0	8,047,876

Microsoft® Excel™ screenshot. Copyright © 2018 Microsoft

Figure 13.5: Jim's Bakery Expense Spreadsheet Example

Since the model now includes all the required data, it is possible to include factors such as the adjustments that will be used when establishing the current and projected value of the business. We will look more closely at this in the next chapter.

Chapter 14
Valuation

So here we are—this is the chapter you have been waiting for! Or maybe you just jumped ahead in the book, hoping to find a quick answer to your most important question. It's the question you are burning to have an answer to.

"What is my business worth?"

What you really want to know is: will you earn enough money from the sale of your business to make that retirement at the beach a reality? Or: will you make enough money from the sale of this business to fund the start of your next business. Or, maybe you're trying to find out if you'll make enough to help you get out from under a problem and pay off your bills. No matter what your circumstances are, you need to determine if you will be able to move on. Well, no matter why you're asking, here is my official answer:

"It depends!"

Now I understand that's probably not the answer you wanted. Try this one:

"The value of your business is whatever price you can convince a buyer to pay for it."

The problem is that most people are looking for a simple answer to a complex question. What you're looking for is a quick easy formula that provides an easy answer.

"I heard my business is worth two times revenue."

"I heard my business is worth ten times EBITDA."

Well, sure it is—if you can get someone to pay that much for it. We have already decided that some buyers—particularly strategic buyers—may be willing to pay more than others. Would you be willing to settle for a 2× multiple of revenue if you thought you could get 3×? Other buyers may not be interested at that price at all. How long do you want to wait for a buyer willing to pay a higher price? P.T. Barnum is famous for saying, "there's a sucker born every minute," so you never know. Maybe it's your lucky day. That buyer who is willing to pay an outlandishly high price might come along. It could happen!

DOI 10.1515/9781547400249-014

But instead of relying on luck, keep in mind that business buyers tend to do their homework and don't just buy on impulse at any price, so you might have a long, frustrating wait ahead of you. Before investing, business buyers want to know what a business is worth. There is no quick, simple method for determining the correct value to place on a business. But mistakes can cost a lot of money. There are in fact a number of methods for estimating the value of a business, but they rarely return the same results.

The problem is this: the best way to determine what your business is worth— its fair market value (FMV)—would be to receive offers from multiple buyers. Without that, any valuation or appraisal is merely an estimate of the value of your business. The problem with this, of course, is that you need to establish a price before speaking to buyers. It's "the chicken or the egg" problem. You need to determine an accurate estimate of the value of your business. Let's look at a couple of ways to get to this.

The best way to determine what your business is worth—its fair market value (FMV)—would be to receive offers from multiple buyers.

So, let's start here. What do YOU think your business is worth? Most business owners have a gut feeling for what they think the value of their business might be. Unfortunately, there are many things that can make the gut method go wrong quickly. There are just too many factors that come into the equation, and most small business owners have no experience determining the value of a business. It's too easy to make a mistake. Here is an example of a typical conversation with a small business owner:

> "I went to the industry conference last year, and I know as a fact that three of our competitors were being offered $5 million. That was easily two times revenue for them."

Now we need to ask some questions these folks might not have thought to ask.

> "Well, what state are they located in?"

> "Were they profitable?"

> "When was the last time they updated their equipment? Or were they still using old inefficient tooling or software?"

Maybe you need a gut check! Now you're getting defensive.

"I know one of them was doing very well and was making good money. He just finished modernizing his entire shop."

"He is a shrewd businessman, and I had trouble competing against him on a couple of contracts."

How do you know he didn't outsmart himself? Maybe he could have gotten $8 million instead of $5 million. That's a lot of money to leave on the table!

"I've already had an unsolicited offer for $5 million from a competitor."

That's great, but maybe the competitor is looking for a discount and was setting a low bar to see if you'd bite. Keep him in mind, though, in case you want to add him to your list of potential strategic buyers to approach later. Many owners make assumptions about the value of their business based on rumor and outdated information, but they may be making a costly mistake. Since this is an important deal for you, don't rely on your gut. Determining the value of your business is too important to make an uneducated decision.

Many owners make assumptions about the value of their business based on rumor and outdated information, but they may be making a costly mistake.

Financial Analysis and Certified Appraisers

There are in fact many techniques available for estimating the value of a business. Performing a true valuation (a business appraisal) is a complex task. Financial analysts have developed a number of models to help make accurate determinations. These techniques include market-based approaches, such as determining an FMV by looking at comparable sales; income-based approaches that rely on revenue and EBITDA multipliers; and more complex analytical methods like discounted cash flows and asset estimates. Often, the problem with these methods is determining which model to use! (It depends on the business circumstances.) But, at least this takes them beyond the gut feeling method!

You might think the financial analysis and the models used to assess the performance of your business would be the greatest determinant of business value. After all, isn't the bottom line the bottom line? If I invest $1 million in this business it will return $100,000 a year, but if I invest $1 million in another business it will return $200,000. Well, what happens if the business returning the $200,000 is a high-risk business? Is it worth the risk? Not if you are a strategic buyer looking for a business in a specific industry.

"Which business would be more valuable to YOU?" It depends.

"What price would you be willing to pay?" It depends.

Fair market value depends on the motivation of the buyer, and the best way for you to determine the fair market value for your business is to find multiple buyers.

Performing an accurate appraisal is a critical task at a time when you can't afford to make a mistake. Don't ask me—I'm not certified as an appraiser. Don't ask your cousin Jake. Don't "ask around." Have an appraisal performed by a certified business appraiser who can perform a comprehensive valuation of your business. The appraiser will give you an estimate of the fair market value of your business. But remember this, regardless of which method is used, it is still an educated estimate.

Get a professional valuation from a certified business appraiser to perform a comprehensive valuation of your business.

Value vs. Price

Now ask yourself this. Suppose you knew exactly, to the dime, what your business is worth—exactly what its fair market value is. Is that the price you would ask for it? Maybe you should list your business at a price that is a little higher than fair market value, knowing that a buyer will try to negotiate your price down. Why wouldn't you plus it up a little? What about the commission you are going to have to pay to your agent for the sale? Is your price going to try to cover all or part of that? The fair market value of your business and the price you ask for it are not the same thing. A buyer is trying to purchase the business at or below the fair market value. You—the seller—are trying to establish a price for your business.

For accounting purposes, the definition of fair market value was defined by the US Supreme Court as the following:

> "The fair market value is the price at which the property would change hands between a willing buyer and a willing seller, neither being under any compulsion to buy or to sell and both having reasonable knowledge of relevant facts."[1]

Does a strategic buyer have a compulsion to buy? We assume they do, and the reason we are looking for strategic buyers is that we expect them to pay more than

---

[1] *United States v. Cartwright*, 411 US 546 (1973).

a financial investor. Typically, strategic buyers will pay 10–15 percent higher than a financial buyer (an investor) because they have other compulsions (incentives) to buy your business.

The fair market value of your business and the price you ask for it are not the same thing.

You don't want to accept a price that is lower than the fair market value of your business, particularly if there is a chance to get a greater price from a strategic buyer. That would mean "leaving money on the table." You don't want to hold out for a much higher price and lose a potential offer at the fair market value, either. Your problem just got a little more complex. The appraisal you had done is an estimate that sets the bar for what you hope will be your minimum price. You will want to list your business above that.

Use Caution Applying Metrics

Let's go back to the real estate models we discussed in chapter 4 for a moment. In real estate, the model that is used to price a new property is a market approach. It looks at comparable homes that have recently sold in the area (referred to as "comps") to get the average price buyers paid for properties with similar characteristics. In this model, adjustments are made for minor differences between the properties to estimate the price for the new listing. If there are many comps in the area, a good estimate of a property's value can be established. There are differences, however, between the real estate market and the market for your business.

The residential real estate market is much larger than the market for a business. There may be thousands of comparable houses ("comps") in an area. By defining a common metric between the comps, such as price per square foot, it is possible to use that metric to estimate the price of a new home.

> "There were 150 homes between 5 and 10 years old with three bedrooms, a fireplace, and a pool that sold for an average $185/square foot, so this 2,300 square foot house with similar characteristics and age should be priced at $425,000."

By contrast, the local business market is much smaller. There may only be one business of that type in the area so there would be no valid comps to establish an average price for the business. A larger geographic area—maybe even nationally—might help to find comps for similar businesses, but it's difficult to find a simple metric as in real estate to estimate the price, because business pricing has far too many variables. We know, for example, that a business located on Main

Street would have a higher price than a similar business located on a back street on the outskirts of town, and we know that some towns are more affluent than others, which directly impacts the price of a business. Business prices cannot be established using a simple metric such as price per square foot.

There are many sources of business data containing information on industry trends and average industry sales (such as revenue and EBITDA multipliers) that can be used as guides. Because of the number of variables, there can be a wide variance in these multipliers. See the reference section at the end of this chapter. You must do your homework when using these databases and anticipate that the value of any multipliers you use will be subject to your negotiations with a buyer. You will be tempted to increase any multiplier, knowing that a small increase in the multiplier may result in a significantly higher valuation. The buyer on the other hand knows that even minor downward adjustments will result in significantly lowering the valuation. Any negotiations with a buyer over the correct value of a revenue multiplier or EBITDA multiplier is best handled by someone who can speak with authority on the subject. If your gut is telling you the EBITDA multiplier should be 11 instead of 7.5 and you have no solid backing for your position, you are likely to lose the negotiation and a good amount of money. This is a pure case of a little bit of knowledge being a dangerous thing. These negotiations are best done through an intermediary.

There are many sources of business data containing information on industry trends and average industry sales (such as revenue and EBITDA multipliers).

Now let's go back to our original car example for a moment. If you're planning to sell your car, you probably won't leave balding tires on it; you'll get it washed and have the oil and filter changed before asking a car dealer, "what's my car worth?" There is a *Blue Book* value[2] that can be looked up for a car, but the condition of the car remains a big variable. Better get out that bucket and sponge! Unfortunately, there is no *Blue Book* for a business. Everything you have been doing to position your business up until this point has been directed at optimizing your business to put it in the best possible condition. The goal is to maximize your return because you understand that the condition of a business is determined by more than soap and water. The financial, legal, and operations infrastructure positioning are all significant variables in determining the condition of your business. When you see industry trends, such as a multiplier expressed as two or three times ($2\times$–$3\times$)

---

2 *Kelly Blue Book* (www.kbb.com) is a pricing guide for new and used cars.

revenue, your goal in your positioning efforts is to put your business in the high end of that bracket.

Automation Can Help

There are software applications (apps) available that provide industry trends to generate a business valuation. These applications are very inexpensive (or even free). Don't be surprised when you get different answers from different applications, though. They may use different models or different data sources to determine fair market value, and they are genericized solutions (not specifically tailored to meet the unique circumstances of the business). You can use the results from these applications to help establish a general price for your business, but use them cautiously. When you use any of these software tools and databases try to honestly reflect the condition of your business.

If you just can't wait and need a reasonable estimate of the value of your business, I have found (and used) the ValuCast App from the Acquivest Financial Group.[3] It provides a reasonable answer—and it's free—so go ahead and try it.

Warning: Nothing in this chapter is intended to reduce, replace, or discourage you from hiring a qualified professional to advise you on the sale of your business.

No matter what method is used, no matter which financial analysis model is employed, the value you place on your business is an estimate, and, in the end, the price a buyer may be willing to pay is what eventually determines the true value of the business. The estimated fair market value of the business may not be the same thing. The true value of your business will be the price you eventually agree on.

How Can a Professional Appraiser Help You?

As you have seen, there are "a lot of moving parts" (many variables) to be considered for a business valuation and numerous ways to establish a price both the buyer and seller will eventually agree on. The most reliable way to establish a price for your business is to have a financial analysis performed by a certified appraiser who is trained to perform business appraisals. It should be a profes-

---

3 Acquivest Financial Group, www.acquivest.net/.

sional who has the experience to interpret the environmental factors and published industry data (including comparable current industry sales). The professional should also be able to realistically determine industry average revenue and earnings multipliers and will factor in the condition of your business and its geographic location. The financial analysis they perform should factor the cash, real estate, and other tangible and intangible assets of your business along with its revenues, earnings, and cash flows.

The most reliable way to establish a price for your business is to have a financial analysis performed by a certified appraiser who is trained to perform business appraisals.

Performing an independent valuation of your business makes tremendous sense. The cost for these services alone are generally modest—particularly when compared to the cost of an error that results in underpricing your business and not getting the full potential return or overpricing and not selling. If this is a once-in-a-lifetime deal or your retirement lifestyle depends on the price you sell your business for, hiring a professional is not a corner you want to cut. Even if you have a great outside accounting firm or CPA, they may not have the specific experience with the industry to do a valid appraisal. You will need to hire a specialist.

Many times, business owners simply take the recommendation from a business broker or investment banker (more about these services in chapter 16) to establish a price for their business. It's important to remember that these individuals work on commission and therefore may have a conflict when it comes to pricing your business. If they price high they get a higher commission, but if they price low they get their commission sooner. A banker or business broker can provide you with an "estimate of value" but only a certified appraiser can provide you with an actual "appraisal." If your banker or broker doesn't have a certified appraiser on staff, consider having an appraisal performed by an independent professional. This may put you in a better position to negotiate commission rates with your broker or banker later.

A business broker or investment banker may work on commission and therefore may have a conflict when it comes to pricing your business.

To be very clear: I am not recommending you avoid hiring a business broker or investment banker. Quite the opposite. I absolutely recommend you hire a broker or banker as your sales agent—*and* that you get an actual appraisal of your business performed by a certified appraiser.

Valuation References

Even though you are planning to reach out for professional help, you will need to know what questions to ask, and you will need to understand how to weigh their recommendations. There are many resources available to help you with this complex subject; if you want more information, it may be worth your time to check some of these references out before making this important decision. If you really want to dig into this subject, I recommend *Valuation: Measuring and Managing the Value of Companies*.[4]

There are also numerous web resources available, again many of them free or for a small subscription fee:

- ValuAdder is a great overall reference which I find handy because it provides links to a broad range of services (ValuAdder, "Small business valuation guide," www.valuadder.com/valuationguide/business-valuation-guide.html).
- International Business Brokers Association, www.ibba.org.
- AICPA (The American Institute of CPAs), "Forensics and Valuation Library," www.aicpa.org/interestareas/forensicandvaluation/resources/fvs-online-professional-library.html.
- US Census Bureau, www.census.gov. Note: Use the search term "small business."

Jim's Bakery Example

In the previous chapter I described a method for modeling a business and showed how this could be used to create credibility and trust with a buyer. That being true, the extension of the software model for a business to include an integrated valuation sheet makes this a great tool to use when explaining how you arrived at your valuation and how that supports your price. It allows the effect of changes to variables, like the effect of EBITDA adjustments and financial recasts, to be seen as changes in the valuation of the business.

The example valuation sheet for Jim's Bakery is shown in Figure 14.1. One of the conclusions you may jump to is: if I have this sheet, I won't need that professional. Wrong! I still highly recommend that you retain a business broker, an investment banker, or a certified business appraiser to assist you with this task.

---

4 Tom Copeland, Tim Koller, Marc Goedhart, and David Wessels, *Valuation: Measuring and Managing the Value of Companies*, 4th ed. (New York: John Wiley, 2005).

Determining the correct values for the variables, and adjusting the algorithms used in the model to match the recent sales in your industry and all the other variants discussed in this chapter, are still best done by a professional. Ask them to modify this sheet for you. The fact is, this sheet may turn out to be a much more useful tool for you than for your buyer. Play "what if?"—see the impact of your changes and make your decisions before ever speaking with a buyer.

Jim's Bakery Valuation Example	Year–2	Year–1	Year	Year+1	Year+2
Revenue Projected	$7,978,764	$8,670,060	$9,247,278	$10,209,744	$11,384,388
Expenses Projected	$7,271,724	$7,650,552	$8,047,876	$8,578,822	$9,007,763
Net Income Projected	$707,040	$1,019,508	$1,352,764	$1,630,923	$2,376,625
Adjustments	$957,084	$987,084	$1,067,598	$1,120,978	$1,177,027
EBITDA	$1,664,124	$2,006,592	$2,420,362	$2,751,901	$3,553,652
Revenue Multiple	2.00	2.00	2.00	2.00	2.00
Revenue Based Valuation	$15,957,528	$17,340,120	$18,494,557	$20,419,489	$22,768,776
EBITDA Multiple	12.00	12.00	12.00	12.00	12.00
EBITDA Based Valuation	$8,484,480	$12,234,096	$16,233,169	$19,571,073	$28,519,503

Microsoft® Excel™ screenshot. Copyright © 2018 Microsoft
Figure 14.1: Jim's Bakery Valuation Spreadsheet Example

The example valuation spreadsheet is linked to, and is driven from, the summary spreadsheet. It shows a current range of valuation from $16,233,169 to $18,801,280. The fact that these values are as of June for the current year (based on the model) and are likely to finish higher (certainly by the time the deal might close in January) if the current sales performance continues is a valid negotiating point with the buyer. The price for Jim's Bakery should be negotiated higher than the valuation numbers, but remember—it's a negotiation and the motivation when setting a price is also a variable.

As an additional note: The financial information contained in this chart is at the correct level to include under the financial section of your "Book," as shown in the example provided in Appendix B. By including the entire table, you will introduce the valuation into your negotiations and establish your expectations prior to the buyer submitting an offer.

Chapter 15
Partners, Vendors, and Other People Who Care

You may think that events, such as the sale of your business, are *your* life decisions to make, but what you will soon find out is that there are many other people who care and will have an impact on the sale of your business—"care" meaning they believe they have a vested interest in what happens to your business, not "care" as in they are concerned with your future well-being.

While you were growing your business, you were also building a network of people you worked with, interacted with, and relied on. They were your financial partners, vendors (suppliers), key employees, and customers, who all interacted and supported your business in many ways. They are the network of people your business has depended on. Some have been very loyal supporters; some are business acquaintances; and some you barely know but have developed a mutual business arrangement with for your benefit or theirs. As you move toward your sale, some of them may wish you well, but others may also see this as an opportunity for themselves, even when the opportunity they see may be detrimental to you.

While you were growing your business, you were also building a network of people you worked with, interacted with, and relied on.

Maybe it's just human nature or the way some people do business, but anticipate a line of people asking,

> "What about me?"

> "What's in the deal for me?"

Most of these people weren't there when you started your business, or when you took big risks, or certainly not when you were putting your house on the line and asked to give personal guarantees to creditors to grow your business, but they're going to be there now. A client once told me,

> "I can feel their hands in my pocket and the deal isn't even done."

Keep in mind, most of these people will no longer be doing business with you—although they may hope to stay in the casita at your beach house on occasion—once you move on from your business. You may have very little leverage or influence on them in the future. Breaking the network ties you developed over years

DOI 10.1515/9781547400249-015

can be difficult. It is best not to make any assumptions about the way those same people, even the loyal ones, will react to the news of your leaving.

Cleaning up the Ownership of Your Business

Does any part of the following scenario sound familiar? When you started your business, you were operating on a shoestring. You found a person with excellent skills to help you get your start-up going but you just couldn't afford that person's salary. To entice them to help you, you offered them part of the business if they would take a lower initial salary and come work for you. Ten percent, 15 percent, 25 five percent, or even 50 percent of the business—start-ups generally don't have much value, so the promise you made to hire that key employee didn't have much value at the time either. Maybe not back then in any case.

They helped you get going . . . chief engineer, sales manager, chef, jack-/jill-of-all-trades. You made a promise, and they kept their part by accepting a lower salary, putting in extra hours, or doing whatever it took to get your business going. Now you're ready to sell, and your business valuation today is $10 million. Now that promise has value attached to it. Your promise to your loyal key employee is now worth $1 million, $1.5 million, $2.5 million, or even $5 million. They were good at what they did and helped you get you to where you are, but let's face it—are their engineering, sales, cooking, or whatever skills they brought to the table worth that much? Far too many small businesses fall into this trap.

Far too many small businesses fall into this trap. The owner is far too generous and thinks about today's needs instead of tomorrow's value.

When you were starting your small businesses, you were overly generous and thought about today's needs instead of tomorrow's value. It's the only coin you had to trade. And to make it worse, your original promise was never formalized. It was just your word.

If making the promise was unavoidable to start your business, then plan on keeping that promise, even if it was verbal or documented only in an email or letter. You placed a value on it when you offered it. You just didn't know what that value was. Keep your word. This is not the time to test whether your employee knows a good attorney and it's not the time to create an obstacle that could get in the way of your closing.

"Yes, your honor, as this email confirms he offered me 10 percent of the business if I came to work for him, which I have done loyally for the last thirty years."

Let's complicate this scenario a little bit more. In your second year of business you needed growth capital and reached out to an angel investor who put in $1 million for 25 percent of the business. The good news is that you did formalize that relationship. But did you explain to your loyal key employee that their ownership was being diluted when you brought this new investor in?

In small businesses, the importance of key employees (whom you made a shareholder when you offered that person part of your business) tends to diminish as other employees are hired and as time goes by. They are no longer asked to play a role in strategic decisions, but their expectations and your promise don't diminish. You can bet that, when they hear that the business is being sold, they will not forget or hesitate to mention that initial promise. One of the greatest issues businesses face is the ownership promises they made as a start-up but failed to treat as valid afterward.

One of the greatest issues businesses face is the ownership promises they made as a startup but failed to treat as valid afterward.

And then there is your former spouse. It was a nasty divorce and your ex had a great lawyer that has a court decree giving her or him ownership of half of everything you owned. That was four years ago, when your ex accepted 50 percent of the stock in the business. You were glad they didn't want the cash back then, and your spouse knew that there was nothing to be gained by pushing the issue at that time. But today they will no doubt call their lawyer and ask what price you are getting for the business—and they won't care whether or not you can afford your new life at the beach with your new wife.

Maybe it's not a spouse but an ex-partner you had a falling out with. The partner walked out and left you so busy trying to run things by yourself that you never quite had the time to get with your attorney to legally dissolve the partnership. When you go into a partnership, it is almost the same as getting married— except without the family or the love! Now your ex-business partner, who didn't put in any of the work, not only wants his name off the Small Business Administration (SBA) loan, he wants part of the sale.

Your buyer will require that the ownership of the business be squeaky clean. They don't want unknown ownership claims to muddy the water after the sale. To keep these things from becoming obstacles to closing you will need to negotiate with these people in advance. It takes time to negotiate and settle ownership issues, particularly once a dollar sign has been attached to those shares. The cleanup may require its own negotiations and closings before you ever talk to a buyer. The best time to clean up the ownership of your business is prior to entering the sales process. There is nothing to be gained and a lot to be lost by delaying. If there is anything that could cloud your ownership, you need to get an attorney involved as soon as possible. These negotiations are often best held between third parties, but you will need your negotiation skills to be at their best. The other parties have everything to gain, and it will cost you. The closer you get to closing, the more difficult these negotiations will become. Take care of these issues before you decide to sell. Begin it today.

To keep these things from becoming obstacles to closing you will need to negotiate them in advance.

Prior Investors

Maybe you had some "family and friends" who invested in the business when you started or bought your business, or maybe you reached out to an angel investor at some point for growth capital. Maybe you even did a funding round with a private equity group or borrowed money from the bank. These are formal relationships that will need to be dispositioned at the closing. They must all be negotiated and payouts agreed to in writing in advance so that checks can be written and closing documents can be prepared.

If these were equity partners who bought shares in the business, you are going to have to review the terms of that purchase, have your CPA calculate the current equity value of their shares, and prepare to meet with them to explain your plan. If you have been regularly notifying them about your strategic plans, the sale won't be a surprise to them. Partners are often a good source of support when you are building a transition team or when you need someone to act as an independent operations assessor while you are preparing to sell your business.

> "I could use someone to assess the sales team and recommend improvements that might add value."

Because they are already vested and may have something to gain (or want to cut their losses), they are more likely to be enthusiastic about the sale than someone with nothing to gain. They may even turn out to be a potential buyer. Be careful what kind of deal they may try to talk you into! If the business has lost money since they invested, they may not be as enthusiastic about the sale, and you may have to stick to your guns with your decision to sell at this time.

Because they are already vested and may have something to gain (or want to cut their losses), they are more likely to be enthusiastic about the sale than someone with nothing to gain. They may even turn out to be a potential buyer.

Outstanding Debt

Special attention must be paid to any funds that were provided to the business as debt. You must carefully review the terms of those notes. Potential buyers will expect you to retire all outstanding debt. You will clearly want to end any note where you provided a personal guarantee. For some lenders this will be a straightforward transaction — *"here is your payoff"* —but with others there may be room for negotiation. In all cases you will want to establish a position with the lender and be prepared to pay off the note either before or on the closing date.

The exception to this may be the small operational accounts with vendors, primarily used in the normal course of doing business, such as advances on inventory and supplies. This type of rotating account should have been written against the business account (not your personal account) and should be transferred as part of the negotiation between the vendor and your new buyer. The buyer will likely wish to retain these accounts. If you gave a personal guarantee, you will need to be sure to change that and have your name removed. You need to make sure the buyer is aware that these accounts exist, so the buyer is prepared to have the conversation with the lender (or vendor). This is not the time to surprise your buyer.

Any existing capital equipment leases must be dealt with in the same manner; however, with these types of leases, early termination is generally not an option and not to anyone's benefit. Buyouts are possible but don't make sense unless it is late in the lease term. You will need to point these leases out to the buyer and maintain a position that they are, and will remain, part of the deal; they have already been factored in your balance sheet and income statements (which presumably they have).

Vendors and Critical Suppliers

Most people assume they can make a simple introduction of their critical vendors to the new owners, maybe over lunch, and it will be in the interest of the vendors and the new buyers to start a new relationship where yours is leaving off—particularly if the buyer plans to continue operating the business. Unfortunately, it doesn't always work out quite that way. If the new buyer is dependent on the same supplier, the supplier may see this as an opportunity to raise their prices. This has become a common practice in some industries.

> "We would be happy to continue as your supplier once you buy the business but we will have to raise our prices."

> "But I have had a contract in place with them for years and didn't miss a single payment."

You may even have paid in advance because you knew how important the supplier was to you as a critical part of your product or service. If the new buyer is planning to use different suppliers, then your current supplier may try to hold the new buyer to the terms of the existing agreement you already have in place. It is easy for these relationships to get off the rails. In either case, the supplier is creating an obstacle to your sale.

If the new buyer is dependent on the same supplier, the supplier may see this as an opportunity to raise their prices.

Whether your business is a manufacturer, buying critical components from a vendor; a software developer embedding third-party components into your application; or a florist depending on the supplier for expedited cut flower deliveries—all businesses depend on their relationship with vendors and critical suppliers to some extent. Most businesses could be brought to a standstill with the loss of a critical supplier. What is the risk to your business if a critical supplier stopped delivering?

Now look at your agreement with the supplier—the critical supplier you were in a hurry to sign with way back when you were dependent on them to release your product. Many small businesses are so glad to get an agreement in place with a critical supplier they sign the agreement without paying attention to all those little details—why bother having an attorney review it? Does this sound familiar? Many vendor agreements include a term that requires notification if your business is being sold or going through a major management change, which makes your sale cause for terminating the agreement. Well there's no risk there, right? After all, this has been a lucrative contract for the vendor. Why would they ever consider terminating their agreement with your business whether you're there or not?

Here is why they want to terminate a lucrative agreement and pretend to walk away from it: to make it more lucrative. You negotiated an agreement with them two or three years ago and got a great rate. They were happy to get that rate at the time. You weren't as dependent on them in the beginning and had another vendor you could have chosen, but because they offered you the best rates, you went ahead and designed your product around theirs. Maybe you made long-term commitments with your customers knowing you had a secure agreement with that critical supplier. It would be hard to change now, maybe impossible—and they know it.

Now that you are selling your business, and they have a contract with a termination clause just for that event, they may want to renegotiate the price of their product for what it lists for today—not at that two- or three-year-old price they negotiated with you in the past.

Many vendor agreements include a term that requires notification if your business is being sold or going through a major management change, which makes your sale cause for terminating the agreement.

The problem is, when a supplier raises their rates, and the buyer doesn't want to start off as the new owner by raising their prices, it cuts into the business's profitability. Your buyer will notice this and reflect it in the EBITDA value. They will immediately recalculate to justify lowering their offer. This is a difficult problem to resolve. It helps if you renegotiate your vendor agreement before the sale and insist on dropping that termination term. They may guess what you're up to but be willing to accept a small, guaranteed increase now instead of risking being dropped later. This will test your negotiating skills!

Remove Any Blurred Lines

Small business owners generally operate as members of their community and often make informal agreements with individuals and other businesses for mutually beneficial products or services. The barter method is generally alive and well with small businesses.

"I will provide you with computer support, and you will repair my truck."

"I'll provide fresh flowers for your store, and you will provide me with good cuts of meat."

These agreements do not always include a product swap or trading of something with tangible value. Sometimes they trade shared or common service the business has with another party, such as their landlord:

"Yes, you can park your truck in the driveway at our building across the street. No one parks there at night."

These are just a few examples of how the lines between one small business and another can become blurred. You might be a great guy. and the other party may have known you for years. and you might have done lots of mutual favors for one another. but the world as you and the other business knew it is about to change. Maybe you even agreed to hire your cousin Jake away from the other business a few years ago to keep them from having to fire him! The point is, small business owners tend to be integrated into their community—which is a good thing! —and they reach out and rely on that community often for many reasons. The problem occurs when you are selling your business is that those blurred lines may not be available to the new owner.

> "Of course, we would be glad to support your computers. Our rate is $45 per hour."

> "Sure, you can park your truck in the parking lot across the street—for $200 a month."

Without the existing relationship, the blurred lines become bright lines, and your buyer's expenses may go up. Your buyer may also see a blurred-line relationship where you are providing the service and no longer agree to provide it.

> "No, we have our own mechanic."

> "You will have to start paying for computer support."

Make sure you identify any blurred relationships you may have, give your friends notice as soon as possible, and either end the relationships or formalize them before you speak with a buyer. Your goal is to turn all blurred lines into formalized, bright-line relationships; if they are significant and could become a negotiated adjustment to your EBITDA calculation, try to end them. You want to remove any blurred lines and make all interfaces with your business bright-line, formal relationships.

Chapter 16
Who Are the Deal Makers?

Many of us grew up watching *Sesame Street* on TV and singing one of their songs with the lyrics, "Who are the people in your neighborhood?"[1] We just didn't realize they were giving us career guidance! There will be professionals on both sides of the deal that you will want to be familiar with. When you're selling your business, it's important to understand the roles these different people play and how they can assist you with your sale. Small business owners hesitate to reach out for professional help because they don't want to incur the fees these professionals will charge, but these professionals make their living putting deals together, getting them closed, and earning their keep. The work they do and the services they provide are closely aligned with your needs, so this may not be the time for you to think about cutting corners.

Finding Professional Help

Of course, some people do put a "For Sale by Owner" sign in the front window, hope for the best, and try to sell their business on their own. Obviously, this is not the recommended approach! You have industry contacts and acquaintances who clearly like your business—at least try to get more than one offer! If you are a "go it alone" type of business owner—*"I don't see the benefit of paying someone else"*—then you are accepting the risk and ready to put in the effort needed to make a sale. Some people have the experience and are equipped to take on this task. I certainly hope the information contained in the previous chapters helps you achieve your goal.

Maybe this is all new to you, but you decided to go ahead and sell the business to your cousin Jake, or you have taken the offer from one of your former competitors. The draw to get to the beach as soon as possible can be strong! Occasionally sellers are heard saying,

> "I didn't need a broker to sell my business. I cut a deal to sell my business with someone I already knew in the business (a competitor, a vendor, a relative)."

Keep this in mind: What these sellers don't realize is that, by trying to save on the brokerage commission, they risk undervaluing their business and may leave

---

1 "The People in Your Neighborhood," written by Jeff Moss; performed on *Sesame Street*, produced by Children's Television Workshop (CTW), Curious Pictures, and Sesame Workshop.

DOI 10.1515/9781547400249-016

money on the table. They also risk exposing their business to a strategic buyer that may have been using this as an opportunity to see how the competition works, never intending to close the deal. The fees professionals charge are often negotiable. It's a highly competitive industry so it pays to shop around. Be sure to look closely at the different services they provide. Now that you understand the sales process, be sure their services align with those you will need. Before you take a risk by deciding to cut them out, at least take the time to find out what the cost will be.

Sometimes, penny-wise owners even outsmart themselves, but the principal rarely benefits when there is no intermediary in a negotiation. That doesn't mean that you shouldn't look for a buyer who is already working in your industry. Finding someone already in the industry is a good thing. Putting someone between you and them in the negotiation is a better thing.

The principal rarely benefits when there is no intermediary in a negotiation.

By employing professional help, you are employing someone experienced with the business sales process because it is their full-time job—they know the game. You are employing someone who will act as an intermediary to help negotiate the deal for you. While you may only sell a business once or twice in your life, they are familiar with the complex sales process.

An experienced professional may already have a contact list of people who are buying similar businesses, particularly if they specialize in an industry, and they may be able to quickly advise you about how difficult or easy the sale of your business may be and what buyers in your industry are most interested in.

"I already have a list of investors looking for SaaS software development businesses."

You will need to decide who is best to act as your sales agent and intermediary for the sale. In general, you need to consider hiring either a business broker or an investment banker.

Business Brokers

A "business broker" is a licensed professional who works with business owners to assist in the sale of their business. Licensing requirements for business brokers vary from state to state. They are usually self-employed sales agents who work through a brokerage and are paid a commission that is a percentage of the sale. They are success oriented because they are on commission. Business brokers often specialize in certain industries (restaurants, retail, technology, etc.), so it is important to ask questions about previous sales and commissions.

"What industries have you sold into before?"

"How much (in dollars) have you sold over the last three years?"

In general, a business broker can help in determining a fair price for the business, ensuring the business's finances and financial records are in order, preparing marketing materials, negotiating a price, going through escrow, and closing the sale. Business brokers not only manage these steps, but also ensure confidentiality by requiring interested buyers to agree not to disclose the details of the potential business sale. Business brokers work to put a deal together and act as intermediaries for the sale.

Investment Bankers

Investment bankers also act as intermediaries in the sale of a business. The role of an investment banker however is often misunderstood. The primary role of investment bankers is that of a financial advisor to the capital markets. They help corporations raise funds for many reasons, such as for capital expansion projects, and they assist corporations with mergers and acquisitions—which is what draws them into the business sales process. They perform these functions by providing financial advice and by acting as fund raisers. They can provide the same services as a business broker and additionally are licensed to handle many more activities, including private stock offerings, placements, and equity financing; they are also licensed to underwrite deals (manage stock sales and transfers). Investment bankers therefore are licensed to provide a much wider range of services than a business broker and must be FINRA certified.[2]

Investment bankers are often involved in situations where larger corporations are merging (rolling up) many smaller businesses. For this reason, it is important to understand what role they are playing in your deal. Are they supporting the buyer or the seller?

---

2 In the United States, the Financial Industry Regulatory Authority, Inc. (**FINRA**) is a private corporation that acts as a self-regulatory organization (SRO). www.finra.org

You need to approach the fees charged by a professional intermediary with an understanding of your anticipated asking price in mind. It's easy to justify their fee if they recommend a higher sale price.

Types of Buyers and Investors

Deal makers are on both the sellers' and the buyers' side of the deal so it's important to know who may be sitting next to your buyer on the other side of the deal table. We talked in chapter 5 about some of the general categories of buyers you will look for. Some buyers may be individuals who have just moved to town or have saved for years and are ready to go out on their own. One of your employees or a group of them may even be ready to step up to buy your business. Buyers generally don't come on their own. They bring partners and financial backers along. Let's take just a moment to understand who some of the specific types of buyers or backers for those people might be.

Banks

A bank is not going to buy your business, but your buyer is likely to go to a bank for funding. This will be a loan just like the mortgage on your house. In the United States, business loans are often guaranteed by the Small Business Administration (SBA)[3] which will put some bureaucratic hurdles in front of your buyer that may take some time to work through. The SBA and the banks put stringent requirements on the business and the individual. To qualify for a loan, it takes the buyer some time (and it will take your patience) to complete the application process. You will be afforded a more complete exit, especially for smaller deals, and following the closing you will be off to the beach.

> "I was able to get an SBA guarantee, so I didn't need to get the seller to accept an earn-out to make the deal."

Venture Capital Companies

A venture capitalist (VC) is a person who provides equity financing to businesses with high growth potential. The money that a venture capitalist invests in the

---

3 US Small Business Administration website, www.sba.gov.

business is called venture capital. Venture capital firms are generally formed by a group of investors who leverage a money fund to increase their overall buying power. They are business investors whose goal is to acquire a portfolio of businesses with high potential, with the intention of reselling the business in three to five years at a high profit.

Because they plan to leverage your business, they are likely to offer a lower price than a strategic buyer, who intends to hold and grow it. They are more likely to offer you an upside on their eventual sale (paying later rather than sooner) or to offer to purchase only part of your business (51 percent).

> "I agreed to sell half my business now and collect the other half in three years at the increased value when they sell."

Depending on your personal situation and how well you have done positioning your business, a VC might make a lot of sense for you. This is especially true if you wish to remain with the business and manage it for another owner. Anticipate a conversation about the amount of money that will be paid to you in cash, and how much if any you will reinvest into the business (such as to pay down debt). This is also a great place to use the software model described in chapter 13 to play "what if?" and to see what the impact would be if the investor were to put additional capital into the business. How would those funds grow over two to three years, and what would that value be to you at that time?

If a VC company is attracted to your business, it is an indication they see a true upside in its value. VC companies often specialize in industries, so it is possible they know of some event that is expected to increase the value of businesses working in your industry. If this is the case, they may be buying several similar or complementary businesses, hoping to roll them up together with the expectation that the larger business will become worth more than the smaller ones they bought.

Angels

An angel is an investor with the personal resources to purchase your business. Generally, they are interested in buying it as an investment and have no immediate interest in operating it. They may want you to continue to operate the business or they may be backing someone else who is interested in ownership and who will operate the business for them. Finding an angel investor is a great way for a former employee to purchase your business.

Beware of Sharks

There is a popular television show called *Shark Tank*[4] that has created some confusion among small businesses (and start-ups). People love *Shark Tank* and can imagine themselves taking their newest business start-up idea on the show to sell the idea to their panel. The show has in fact provided a great amount of opportunity for would-be entrepreneurs. The confusion is usually with the show's name. I have spoken with people looking to buy a business whose comment is,

> "I am looking for a shark to help me get going."

In selling or buying a business a "shark" is someone who will "eat your lunch and then eat you so they can steal your business." You don't want to look for sharks—you want to look to avoid them. A shark is someone who offers you a bad deal by undervaluing your business, by offering you bad terms for your deal, or by finding other ways to cheat you. *Shark Tank* may be a catchy TV name but what you want is a buyer who is an "angel," not a shark!

---

4 *Shark Tank* (MGM Television, Mark Burnett Productions, Sony Pictures; broadcast by ABC).

Chapter 17
Loose Ends and New Beginnings

Moving on is an exciting prospect—turning to a new chapter in your life. A new beginning is about new opportunities and new chances to excel. Maybe you're the person who'll be driving the big sport-fishing boat out to sea for a day on the water or maybe you'll be the guy sitting on the pier soaking up the rays with a pole in your hand. Maybe you are now going to work for the new owner or preparing to take on a new entrepreneurial venture. In any event, plan to relax and enjoy life a bit and move into your next adventure doing what you know how to do best: by making a plan and executing it well. It's time. You worked hard. You truly earned it.

Selling a business is a life-changing event. You have been busy, first positioning and preparing your business for the sale, and then working through the sales process itself. It was no doubt stressful and may not have left time to consider the future. Before you make those life changes, however, take time to think about your transition to that new life.

"I was so eager to move on with my life that I just never thought about those things."

Transition Planning

Transition planning should be started before you make the change. You can't negotiate terms after the sale is closed. When you're planning your transition, keep this in mind—whether you are planning to stay on in some manner or planning to fully exit your business after the sale, expect to delay the start of that beach vacation while you support the transition of the business over to the new owner. Of course, this doesn't always happen. Sometimes the new owner wants you to make your personal exit immediately upon closing, but others will want you to stick around. If you are remaining with the business in some capacity for the long-term or for the short-term, you will need to reach an understanding prior to closing of how that will work—and you will want to have a clear understanding of your postclosing role. Planning your exit includes planning how you will transition out of the business.

> "I thought after closing on my business I would say goodbye, hold a party, and be done, but the buyer included my support for six months as a term of the sale."

If you remain with your business after the sale as an employee, you will need to be willing to give up control and start taking direction. If you think it's good

DOI 10.1515/9781547400249-017

news that, as an employee, you can now take your weekends off and let someone else worry about the business, think again—that's not generally how these things work. You will need to pay close attention to the employment contract you are offered, including any lock-up periods, if you are dependent on your salary for your livelihood. If, after negotiation, your compensation package isn't quite what you anticipated, consider asking for a performance bonus. After all, the buyer has performance expectations and will count on you to help them achieve their goals.

Future Insurance Needs

Two key items you will surely want to include in your negotiations are medical insurance and life insurance. In your previous life these were probably covered by your business. Health insurance is expensive when you're buying a private policy and no longer qualify for that group plan. The same goes for life insurance, especially as you get older. As part of the negotiation consider adding terms that include a paid life insurance policy, continuing payment of your future health insurance premiums, and conversion of your current life insurance. Most business policies won't allow a nonemployee to remain on the group policy so don't make any assumptions about the cost of your health-care premiums. You will need to pay for a private health policy. Try to negotiate those payments into your exit terms.

Two key items you will surely want to include in your negotiations are life insurance and medical insurance.

When you owned your business, you were an officer of that business and probably had liability insurance as an officer of the company. Check with your insurance agent to find out what the limits of that policy will be following your exit. New owners are often tempted to say, *"that was something that happened before we got here."* Find out what kind of tail that insurance includes, if it can be extended, and who will make the future payments if necessary. Don't assume the new owner will continue the policy if that isn't a written term in your deal. When you owned the business as a sole proprietor you may not have had an active board of directors. The new owners may have investors that are insisting on a board and have invited you to be on that board. What an honor! Maybe you agreed to retain part of the business following a partial buyout, and your membership isn't as much an honor as a term you asked for so you could keep an eye on your investment. No matter what the reason, you are now on the board of a business someone else is operating on a daily basis. Before you accept that board seat, or any other board seat, you need to limit any potential liability you might have for their decisions by making sure they carry directors and officers (D&O) liability insurance.

Buyers Change Hats, and You May Too

When a business owner who has operated his business for many years finally sells it and moves on, he often morphs into something else. After cashing out, this former business owner is sitting on a pile of cash and decides to invest some of those funds. He doesn't want to go back to work (the beach life appeals to him) but he decides he is going to put money into three or four other businesses. He morphs into an investor. He then decides to sell one or more of those businesses and transforms back into a seller. He changes hats—at one time he is a seller and at another he is a buyer. This may also be where you are headed, and it may be exactly where your buyer is now.

Taxes

When you sell your business, you will be liable for the taxes on your earnings from the sale. If you haven't planned for it in advance, your tax burden could significantly reduce your return from the sale. What you retain from the sale is the price your business nets minus your tax burden. You cannot wait for the sale to close before you begin to develop and implement a tax strategy. The amount of taxes you will need to pay are as large a determinant on what you will retain from the sale as is the price. You can incur a much higher tax burden by simply neglecting to make a few easy decisions before the sale. Get your CPA and tax attorney involved in looking at this issue early, prior to even listing your business for sale.

You will need to work with your CPA and tax attorney to develop a tax strategy, and you will need to understand that strategy before you accept any offers. This will help you with the down select of buyers by enabling you to do a true comparison of what you will retain following the sale and after taxes. For instance, taxes might be reduced through a multiyear strategy that limits your current year tax liability.

There are several things to consider as you develop a tax strategy. Receiving the entire purchase price at closing gives you security that you will be paid (new owners don't always survive long enough to make time payments) but a lump-sum payment will give you the greatest tax exposure. You may be more comfortable with the single payment, but it is worth the time and comparison to consider what your risk may be and whether it makes sense to accept delayed payments.

This is an area where you and your buyer may well disagree. Tangible assets are capital assets and subject to capital gains taxes. Your goal will be to include as many assets as possible, but negotiating this with the buyer won't be easy—capital assets are depreciable, and tax deductions for capital assets are amortized over a much longer period of time, which likely works against their plan.

The tax codes also allow for the establishment of different types of trusts and annuities that potentially could be used as tools to support deferred payments and to minimize your tax burden. These programs tend to change as the tax laws evolve so be sure to ask your tax attorney for advice on which one may fit your situation as you plan to move on and transition to your next life adventure.

Asset vs. Equity Sales

Deciding whether a business sale should be an asset sale or a stock sale can cause some contention between you and your buyer because the parties in the deal have different goals. Make sure you discuss your plan with your transition team before you are ready to speak with any buyers. Generally, buyers prefer asset sales, whereas sellers prefer stock sales. An asset sale is a purchase of the individual assets of the business, whereas a stock sale is the purchase of the owner's share of the business. While there are many considerations when negotiating the type of transaction, tax implications and potential liabilities are the primary concerns for both parties. Agreeing to which path to take may be your greatest deal-killing issue when selling a business, so if you are hard over and not willing to accept an asset deal make sure that is understood early on. Many owners end up surrendering on this point to get a deal done, but it is important you make an informed decision and understand what you are surrendering.

While there are many considerations when negotiating the type of transaction, tax implications and potential liabilities are the primary concerns for both parties.

In an asset sale, the owner retains possession of the business and the buyer purchases the individual assets of the company—such as equipment, fixtures, machinery, licenses, goodwill, intellectual property, and inventory. Asset sales generally do not include cash (bank accounts) and the owner will retain any debt unless specifically negotiated away in the deal.

In an equity sale, which is a stock sale, the buyer purchases the owner's stock, giving them ownership in the business. The assets along with any liabilities are acquired in a stock sale. The buyer will ask that any of the businesses assets or liabilities they do not want to include in the sale be negotiated or paid off prior to the sale.

For the owner, asset sales result in higher taxes because fixed assets can be subject to higher tax rates. For the buyer, there may be tax advantages because they can gain an improved tax depreciation advantage. This lowers their initial tax burden and improves the company's cash flow. Buyers also prefer asset sales because they help avoid inheriting potential liabilities caused by the prior owner including product liability and warranty issues, contract disputes, and employee lawsuits.

Lock-outs

After buying your business, the new owner doesn't want to find out they bought you out of problems and funded your next business as their new competition. The terms of your purchase agreement will likely include a "lock-out" clause that keeps you from working in a similar business for a set period of time (three to five years). During this time, you will be restricted from starting a competing business or working for an existing competitor. If you're headed to the beach this won't have much impact; but if you're selling your business to get out from under a bad business and will need a new job next week, this could have a big impact on your future. Be sure you fully understand the impact of any lock-out terms in your purchase agreement.

Be sure you fully understand the impact of any lock-out terms in your purchase agreement.

The new owner will also want to restrict you from hiring your former employees. Part of the reason for buying your business is because of its existing, already trained, and functioning staff. Unless there are employment agreements in place for your former employees, they are free to go to work for someone else—but not for you. You may need to explain this to a loyal former employee at some point after the sale. If the business you just sold developed software for the restaurant industry, and you are starting a new business developing software for the automobile industry, you may be in violation of your industry lock-out. If you plan to hire your lead software engineer from your old business, you may be violating a nonpirating term. If the buyer terminates your former lead engineer, you may still need to get an agreement to hire them into your new business. Be sure to review the terms of your agreement carefully and seek legal advice if you're not sure.

Taking the High Road

After selling your business you are going to hear a lot of things "via the rumor mill," or "through the grapevine," or even "over the bamboo telegraph." People will make comments about the new owners:

> "Oh, you wouldn't believe how terrible it is working there now."

> "We're still supplying them but we're about to cut them off because they don't pay us as quickly as you did in the past."

> "We fixed them—we won't let them park their truck in our place now that they are charging us for IT services."

Sometimes it is the new owner who starts to make comments about your former employees or vendors or the way things are running in their new business.

> "I don't know why you didn't fire that guy Jake years ago."

> "It took us a while to retrain your former employees to dress nicely—in our business, Friday is the only casual day. Boy, they were used to getting away with a lot!"

Your reply to all these comments should be a smile. Don't respond and don't comment. Take the high road. Don't take sides.

Become a Consultant

After selling your business you get a call from the buyer:

> "Jim, can you help us with something?"

They may be looking for advice on how an old product design works; it could be to use your established relationship to help solve a problem with a vendor; or it could be to come in and calm down your former employees who are resisting their new management. Of course, you'll help—you're a good guy and want to see the new owner succeed.

> "Jim came in and helped us and saved us a bundle with that vendor."

The problem occurs when they call again next week—and the week after that. You're a good guy but suddenly you find "call Jim" has become the new owner's hot line for support. It can become abusive before you realize it. There may be genuine cases where calling you makes sense and where you can save time and money advising the new owner, but you need to put a price on your time so it doesn't become abusive. It needs to cost more than a dime for them to engage your services. Resolve these problems by putting a financial value on your time and consider formalizing the relationship with a support contract; just don't be surprised when the answer becomes, *"no, we can't afford that yet."*

Appendix A
Example Marketing Handout

A marketing handout will need to be created to support the sale of the business. The example that follows was created for the sale of Jim's Bakery. The handout is a marketing document sometimes referred to as a "slick." It should be limited to a single page and printed on high-quality semi-glossy paper. Optionally it could also be created to be produced using a trifold format.

It can be freely handed out to anyone who express an interest in purchasing this type of business without the use of an NDA. Some discretion should still be used when you distribute it by only handing it to someone who is likely to be a qualified buyer. The handout provides a general description without specifically identifying the business. The goal is to notify people about the potential opportunity and provide enough information to motivate qualified buyers to request further information. In most sales, this document will be created by your sales agent. Contact information for the licensed sales agent that is handling the sale, along with the name and address of their business, must be clearly shown. Your agent will hand these out when needed, but you will also need to have some available.

DOI 10.1515/9781547400249-018

Unique Opportunity to Buy a Growing Food Services Business

 We know you will enjoy the aroma of the fresh baked bread coming from the ovens of this unique bakery. This business offers the best of small town friendliness in a well-established retail store along with a large-scale commercial bakery that combines the quality of homemade baked goods with regional distribution facilities to supply its growing list of commercial customers. Our client is offering this unique opportunity to purchase his well-established bakery business. When you realize what an outstanding opportunity we are offering you will begin to say, "That smells like money to me!" After 35 years growing an exceptional brand and financially strong business, the founder is preparing to retire and move to the beach.

This business includes two highly profitable operating divisions (commercial and retail) along with their highly valued brand, two properties on long-term leases, relatively new and well-maintained equipment and a highly experienced, professional staff. Annual revenues are approximately $10 million.

Commercial product sales are based on a recurring revenue model with customers signed to long-term contracts with a demonstrable retention rate above ninety percent. This business is expected to sell in excess of $20 million. Serious potential buyers can request further information by contacting:

For Information Contact:
Contact Name
Contact Brokerage Name
Contact Brokerage Address
Email
Phone Number

Appendix B
Example "Book"

The document that follows is an example of a typical Book used in the sale of a small business. The Book is fictitious, as is Jim's Bakery.

THIS IS NOT AN OFFERING. ANY SIMILARITY BETWEEN THIS EXAMPLE AND ANY REAL ENTITY THAT EITHER CURRENTLY EXISTS OR THAT MAY PREVIOUSLY HAVE EXISTED IS PURELY A COINCIDENCE.

The disclaimers and notices provided in the example are not given as legal advice and should not be used in your actual Book. Seek advice from an attorney on the actual disclaimers you should include with your Book. These statements have been included strictly as examples of the types of statements that you should consider including in your Book **after receiving advice from a qualified attorney**. You are not authorized to copy or use these statements.

Note how the content for the sections of this Book were generated as the work products of the earlier positioning activities. This is the reason, writing your Book, is one of the last activities you will perform in preparing to sell your business rather than one of the first activities, which seems to be the natural reaction of many small business owners.

DOI 10.1515/9781547400249-019

Jim's Bakery, Inc

Preparation Date

Book #_____

Assigned to: _____

Contact:
Contact Name
Email
Phone Number
Web Site URL

Jim's Bakery, Inc

Proprietary Rights Notice

This material contains financial projections and other forward-looking information based on assumptions that may be uncertain and beyond the control of Jim's Bakery. This is not an offering document for the sale of any securities. It is a discussion of interest in a possible transaction.

Overview

Welcome to Jim's Bakery (Jim's). We know you will enjoy the aroma of the freshly baked bread coming from our ovens. Jim's Bakery combines the best of small town friendliness in our well-established retail store, along with a large-scale commercial bakery that combines the quality of homemade baked goods with regional distribution facilities to supply our growing list of commercial customers. After 35 years of growing an exceptional brand and financially strong business, the founder of Jim's Bakery is selling his business and preparing to retire and move to the beach. When you realize what an outstanding opportunity we are offering you will say, "The aroma of that bread smells like money to me!"

The Jim's Bakery brand has a long-established reputation for good food and quality service that has lasted for over three decades. The business benefits from a loyal following of retail customers who return time after time to purchase personalized cakes and other specialty baked items. For years, Jim's has been the "must stop" place for special occasions and holiday celebrations. Going to "Jim's" has become the family tradition for enjoyable family events such as birthdays, graduations, and other happy occasions. Jim's loyal retail customers will continue to return as long as the quality remains.

Fifteen years ago, due to a growing demand for more products than the retail bakery alone could provide, Jim's Bakery expanded its operations by adding a commercial bakery that supplies the same quality Jim's breads along with other bakery items to restaurants and other outlets regionally. Jim's customers love finding Jim's Bakery breads and rolls in stores and restaurants throughout the region because they know Jim's is a brand they can count on for quality and consistency. Jim's Bakery takes great care to protect their brand and maintains their reputation for fresh-baked products. You cannot buy "day-old bread" from Jim's. We require our commercial customers to remove any unsold product within 24 hours of delivery.

Today, Jim's Bakery operates two facilities—their original retail bakery where they produce cakes and specialty items and their commercial bakery that supports their "Bread as a Service" (BaaS) product line. The commercial bakery and the administrative offices for the business, which are located above the commercial bakery, are in a leased facility. The founder's office is located in the back of the retail store, which Jim owns. Jim likes to walk into the front of the store where he can greet people, as a way to remain close to his customers. This is not just nostalgia. Jim realizes that many of his commercial customers also started as retail customers.

After 35 years in business, Jim is ready to sell the business and retire to St. Thomas in the U.S. Virgin Islands. He is looking for a buyer who will retain his current talented and well-trained employees and continue to grow the business while maintaining its reputation for exceptional service and quality products. All rights to the Jim's Bakery brand and recipes, which have been used and improved upon for 35 years, are included in the sale.

In a recent article by the *State Gazette*, Jim's Bakery was listed as one of the top places to work and shop in the region. The chairman of the state economic development council was quoted as saying: "Jim's Bakery has been identified as one of the top 50 small businesses in the state and seems to be ready to grow beyond its local roots."

Come and visit Jim's. Sit and have a cup of coffee and smell the aroma coming from our ovens. It is truly the aroma of opportunity.

Market

Jim's Bakery sells into two distinct markets (retail and commercial), so care must be used to distinguish between these markets when considering the impact of future sales. Jim's Bakery operates two divisions—the retail division, which was Jim's original store and sells to local customers in his home town; and the commercial division, which sells to businesses on a regional basis.

Retail Bakery Market

Jim's retail bakery is located in Jim's home town where it was founded. There used to be five retail bakeries in town but over time the number has dropped to three, including Jim's. According to a study completed by the local businessmen's association the population of the town last year was just under 50,000 residents. With an average age of 33, the town is largely comprised of young families, many of which are employed in the nearby city and commute approximately 20 miles to work. According to the local real estate board, the community where Jim's Bakery is located is growing by 400 families a month; this is creating a small building boom which is evident in the number of building permits being issued for new construction. Many of the current residents grew up going to Jim's Bakery, making Jim's customers multigenerational.

Within Jim's retail store they advertise their catering services for specialty events to single customers for holiday parties and weddings, and to commercial customers for business events and conferences. They give away free cookies to the children and samples of their other specialty items to adult customers to entice them to try new items.

> *"Have you tried our new mini-cannolis?"* invariably ends with *"Wow, those are good. I'll take a box."* Jim's retail marketing is "old school," but his retail customers will stand in line for a free sample.

As the boundaries of the town continued to expand, Jim's Bakery's ads have been targeted at turning Jim's into a destination location and attracting families who otherwise would shop on the outskirts of town into their store in the village. With the growth of the town, the village is seeing a bit of a renaissance, and residents are looking for places to hang out "downtown." There may be some additional growth potential for a buyer interested in adding curbside seating service. Customers who have grown up in families who frequented Jim's Bakery also have moved to nearby towns to start their own families. This may create opportunities to open additional Jim's Bakery retail stores in other towns within the region.

Jim occasionally advertises holiday specials but as a general practice the retail bakery doesn't discount their retail prices. Because the average projected income for families in Jim's home town are growing rapidly as new families move in, the increase in retail sales have been constant and are anticipated to remain constant at 10 percent per year.

Commercial Bakery Market

Jim's Bakery is in a region that encompasses most of the central part of the state. According to the most recent census the city has a population of just over 250,000 residents. Aside from the city, the region includes twenty towns with an average population of 16,000 residents, adding an additional 320,000 residents to the region and making the total population for the region just over 570,000 residents. The region is thriving economically with an additional 2,000 families a month moving into the region. The Small Business Administration's regional office states that there are 50,000 small businesses in the region, 10,000 of which are in the food services industry in some manner.

The latest impact studies for the region indicate a growing demand for retail services. Overall the regional growth projections are very favorable for continued growth across the entire retail sector and includes a prediction for 3.5 percent growth across the region in food services. The state business registration website indicates there are thirty-eight retail bakeries and four commercial bakeries in the region. The Jim's Bakery commercial bakery is the smallest of the four commercial bakeries by volume in the region. This creates tremendous opportunity for continued commercial growth for a new buyer, but penetration of the commercial market will depend on the execution of a strong strategic business model.

Jim's Bakery is leveraging the reputation of their retail business to draw commercial clients into long-term commercial relationships. Jim's commercial clients include restaurants, schools, nursing homes, and health-care facilities. The combination of a BaaS commercial business model and the regional recognition of the Jim's Bakery brand make continued penetration of the commercial market a real potential opportunity that easily supports our growth commercial projections.

Jim's commercial bakery uses a combination of inside and outside sales people. The inside sales team primarily takes long-term sales telephone orders and refers one-time sales to the retail bakery.

Competition

Jim's Bakery doesn't stand alone as either the only retail bakery in town or as the only commercial bakery in the region. But while it doesn't stand alone, Jim's certainly stands out.

Jim's is the longest operating retail bakery in town. During Jim's thirty-five years of operation, two other bakeries have opened and failed while Jim's has survived. The other retail bakery currently operating in town (Winnie's Baked Goods) has been in operation for over a decade. Jim's retail bakery is located directly in the village while Winnie's Bakery is located on the outskirts of town. This gives Jim's retail bakery a natural advantage in attracting passing customers and people visiting the "downtown" shopping and restaurant district. The growth in population in town provides a more than ample customer base to support both bakeries.

Competitive Matrix

	Competitor 1	Competitor 2	Competitor 3	Your Business
Feature1	X			X
Feature 2	X	X		X
Feature 3	X		X	X
Feature 4		X	X	X
Feature 5		X	X	X

As shown in the competitive matrix, the competitive strengths Jim's Bakery has over its retail and commercial competitors is its ability to offer a full range of services.

There are three commercial bakeries operating in the region. Jim's is the newest and the fastest growing. As shown in the matrix, the combination of a retail and commercial divisions has allowed Jim's to offer a greater selection of products than the competition (according to the products and services listed on the competitions' public websites). Due to the dependability of its service, which is an important discriminator for commercial customers, Jim's Bread as a Service (BaaS) product line has been favorably received by commercial customers across the region and has accounted for our fast penetration of the commercial market.

 Jim's initial investment into the large commercial ovens both enabled Jim's to offer this service and created a barrier to entry that has kept the competition from offering similar services.

Business Model

The Jim's Bakery business model takes advantage of its well-established reputation for quality baked goods and exceptional service. Jim's brand stands for great food and an enjoyable experience. By offering samples that draw retail customers into our store (the top of the sales funnel), we can introduce them to our products and services in a friendly, enjoyable environment.

Our sales strategy is best seen as an inverted pyramid or funnel where a high number of low-value retail customers enter at the top of the pyramid and a lower number of high-value commercial clients are driven down the pyramid to become committed long-term commercial clients. The goal is to capture commercial clients with less expensive products and services that meet their needs and then to migrate them down the pyramid toward higher value products and services. This approach makes tremendous sense when applied to a recurring revenue model. Clients can (and do) enter at any level but we take advantage of the nature of our products and services to attract a targeted commercial audience. Some customers never progress beyond the basic product while others become long-term commercial BaaS clients.

We draw customers into the pyramid by first inviting them to sample our bakery products for "free," enticing potential customers to purchase products and converting them into paying customers for our retail products. We invite retail customers to leave their business cards to win free prizes for their office. The goal is to drive down the sales funnel by identifying potential commercial customers over time. We know that everyone will not transition to the bottom, but we believe that even large commercial clients are likely to first become familiar with Jim's Bakery as retail customers at the top of our sales pyramid. This approach allows us to cast a wide marketing net by first making customers aware of our products and then making them aware of the services we provide.

Lower Value, Easy Entry Sales
Many Retail Customers

Free Samples

Basic Retail Product Sales

Specialty Retail Products
and Catering

One-Off Commercial
Orders

Bread as a Service
(BaaS)
Contracts

Higher Value, Long-Term Commercial Contracts
Fewer Client Sales

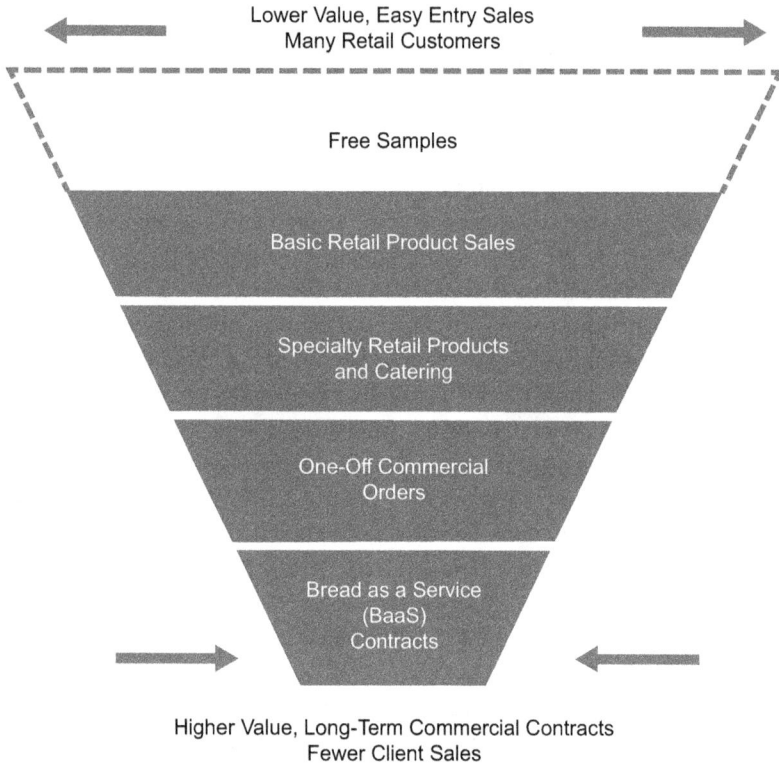

Jim's Bakery business model

The growth of Jim's Bakery may appear to its customers to have occurred organically, but in fact, it has occurred by following a deliberate and strategic business model that has succeeded according to a repeatable and predictable business plan.

Product Descriptions

Whether it is a once-in-a-lifetime wedding cake or a continuing daily delivery of fresh breads and rolls delivered to a regional franchise chain, Jim's offers the quality products customers want. But don't just take our word for it—ask Jeff and Pam Brown. We catered their wedding and provided the three-tiered wedding cake Pam had always dreamed of. We also supply the fresh bread and dinner rolls served daily at Bob and Carol Seidel's family restaurant as well as the freshly baked sub rolls for the five Nancy's Subs' franchises. Ask anyone about the amazing taste of Jim's baked goods. And while you're asking, ask the Mid-State Regional Hospital about the Jim's baked goods they serve every day to over a hundred patients and to their staff in their cafeteria.

Jim's Retail Product Lines:

- Cakes: Customized birthday cakes made to order for walk-in and telephone customers. High margin product.
- Cookies: Sold in batches and handed out to children of all ages as loss leader samples in the retail store. Profitable stable product line with recurring sales.
- Bread: Baked fresh daily in five varieties. Aroma from baking attracts people from throughout the downtown area. Bread sales are constant but waste (left-over products) must be controlled.
- Rolls: Sold as a necessary staple of the business, but not a profitable line.
- Gluten-free products: These products are custom-made and must be ordered in advance. Gluten-free products also represent a growing commercial bakery product line.

Jim's Commercial Product Lines:

- Bread as a Service (BaaS): High recurring sales to contracted commercial accounts including restaurants, schools, and industry cafeterias.
- Rolls: High-volume sales as expanded BaaS product offering for sandwich preparation.

Jim's sales team offers the Bread as a Service program to meet the long-term needs of its commercial clients. Under this program, customers are charged a fixed monthly fee for the delivery of baked goods on an agreed-upon periodic schedule (daily, weekly, or monthly programs are available). By using Jim's BaaS program these customers know they can count on the Jim's Bakery reputation for quality, dependability, and exceptional service on a continuing basis. It relieves them of the daily chore of placing bakery orders for products they use every day.

Sales Performance and Projections

Over the past five years the sales growth of Jim's Bakery has averaged 5 percent in the retail division and over 10 percent growth in the commercial division. Because of its established track record of performance, we are comfortable extending these growth rates and continuing this rate in our future projections. The exception to the 10 percent rate is our BaaS program, which has been regularly growing at over 15 percent annually.

Future sales projections are based on sound strategies and a strong proven business model. The approach to financial management used at Jim's means our sales projections are well-thought-out in advance. The result has been predictable sales performance that has exceeded projections year after year.

Our sales team is divided between the commercial and retail divisions. In commercial, we use a combination of inside and outside sales; in retail, our sales team are sales clerks working in the store. Our sales team is well trained and focus on customer satisfaction. Our retail sales clerks understand that they are the front line in identifying potential commercial customers and forwarding these contacts over to the commercial division. Commissions for all sales team members are paid on a team basis depending on the person's seniority and length of service.

The $9.4 million shown in the Sales/Revenue Performance chart is a midyear projection which we are already on track to exceed.

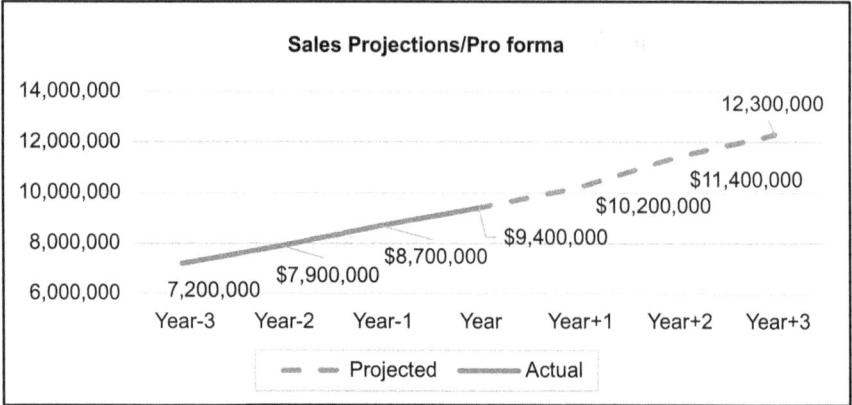

The Jim's Bakery BaaS program is very "sticky" with a customer retention rate of over 98 percent. Customers sign an annual agreement which is automatically renewed at the end of the contract period. Because of this our sales pro forma uses annualized values (customers do not need to be resigned each year). This allows us to focus our marketing efforts on identifying and signing new customers instead of marketing to our existing customer base. As our BaaS program continues to gain traction, we are seeing an increase in our sales curves. We believe the projections provided here are conservative and, assuming our performance continues as it historically has, we are likely to exceed the projections for year+1 and year+2.

Operational Description

Jim's Bakery has two operational divisions (commercial and retail). Each division is equipped to support its unique market niche. Common functions, including administration and finance, operate as umbrella functions supporting both divisions. This structure gives Jim's a competitive advantage because it can lower the costs allocated to the operating divisions, thus helping both to keep their prices low. The organization chart that follows depicts the operating structure of Jim's Bakery.

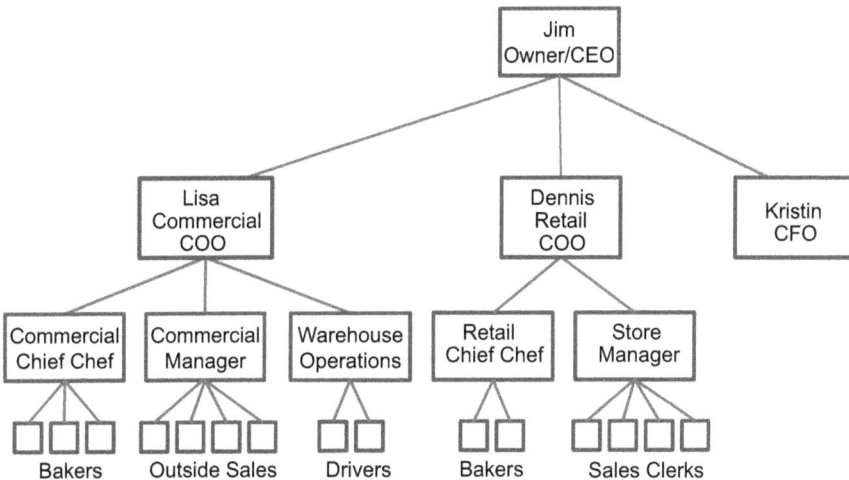

All management team members exceed industry norms for education and experience. Detailed descriptions of all employee functions along with mission statements for key management positions (with the biographies of key team members) will be provided prior to due diligence.

Each of the divisions is in its own facility; however, there is a high degree of cooperation between them. Customers are systemically shared and passed from one division to the other. For instance, the retail division actively attempts to identify potential commercial customers. The commercial division provides the bread and rolls that are sold from the retail store, allowing the retail bakery to concentrate on the creation of their specialty products.

Catering has been a breakout service that is growing in both the retail and commercial divisions. The original Jim's retail bakery operated strictly as a takeout store. Today it has seating for forty-five people and takes advantage of the growing attraction of customers who want to shop and eat in the village. Commercial catering on the other hand is a delivery party service originally provided in response to a special customer request, but which has seen strong growth as customers sought the Jim's Bakery brand for their events.

As a food manufacturer, Jim's Bakery seeks to be overcompliant with public health standards and regulations. A strict maintenance and cleaning policy has been implemented across both divisions. Procedures for daily, weekly, monthly, and annual maintenance were written and are implemented by an employee committee, giving all employees a say in how these functions are performed. This gives all employees a sense of pride in their workplace and a feeling they are contributing toward the success of the business.

Number of Employees: 24
Facilities:
- Commercial bakery (leased facility)
- Retail store (real estate owned personally by Jim; negotiable in sale)

Financial Summary

Jim's Bakery has followed a rigorous financial management approach throughout its history. In the revenue vs. expense chart that follows, the performance curves reflect a consistent level of financial management and expense control resulting in a growing record of earnings.

Performance

Jim's Bakery is ahead of its projected earnings for the current year and expects to exceed its financial goals. This year's earnings will exceed $1.4 million and result in an EBITDA after adjustments of over $2.4 million (and an annual EBITDA of over $2.7 million next year and $3.5 million the following year). Detailed financials will be available during due diligence, as will an independent third-party audit recently performed by the XYZ accounting firm.

One of the reasons for the outstanding financial performance of Jim's Bakery is the software model they have created for the business. This allows Jim's to examine the impact of strategic decisions in advance of executing them. The model allows our staff to play "what if" before making financial commitments. A copy of our financial model will be provided in advance of closing to give the new owner the ability to explore the financial potential of the business in detail.

Valuation

The outstanding of performance of Jim's Bakery makes this an exceptional opportunity for either a financial investor or a strategic buyer. The valuation chart that follows uses value multipliers representative of recent sales in the food services industry.

Jim's Bakery Valuation Example	Year−2	Year−1	Year	Year+1	Year+2
Revenue Projected	$7,978,764	$8,670,060	$9,247,278	$10,209,744	$11,384,388
Expenses Projected	$7,271,724	$7,650,552	$8,047,876	$8,578,822	$9,007,763
Net Income Projected	$707,040	$1,019,508	$1,352,764	$1,630,923	$2,376,625
Adjustments	$957,084	$987,084	$1,067,598	$1,120,978	$1,177,027
EBITDA	$1,664,124	$2,006,592	$2,420,362	$2,751,901	$3,553,652
Revenue Multiple	2.00	2.00	2.00	2.00	2.00
Revenue Based Valuation	$15,957,528	$17,340,120	$18,494,557	$20,419,489	$22,768,776
EBITDA Multiple	12.00	12.00	12.00	12.00	12.00
EBITDA Based Valuation	$8,484,480	$12,234,096	$16,233,169	$19,571,073	$28,519,503

Because the BaaS program is a large component of the Jim's Bakery revenue model, we anticipate all potential buyers will consider projected values when making their offers.

Index

DOI 10.1515/9781547400249-020

www.ingramcontent.com/pod-product-compliance
Lightning Source LLC
Chambersburg PA
CBHW060249220326
41598CB00027B/4037